HOMOPHOBIA IN THE HALLWAYS

Heterosexism and Transphobia in Canadian Catholic Schools

Section 15 of the *Canadian Charter of Rights and Freedoms* ensures equality regarding sexual orientation and gender identity in Canada. Despite this, gay, lesbian, and gender-nonconforming teachers in publicly funded Catholic schools in Ontario and Alberta have been fired for living lives that Church leaders claim run contrary to Catholic doctrine about non-heterosexuality, while requests from students to establish Gay/Straight Alliances have been denied.

In *Homophobia in the Hallways*, Tonya D. Callaghan interrogates institutionalized homophobia and transphobia in the publicly funded Catholic school systems of Ontario and Alberta. Featuring twenty interviews with students and teachers who have faced overt discrimination in Catholic schools, the book blends theoretical inquiry and real-world case study, making Callaghan's study a unique insight into religiously inspired heterosexism and genderism. She uncovers the causes and effects of the long-standing disconnect between Canadian Catholic schools and the *Charter* by comparing the treatment of and attitudes towards lesbian, gay, bisexual, transgender, and queer teachers and students in these publicly funded systems.

TONYA D. CALLAGHAN is an assistant professor in the Werkland School of Education at the University of Calgary.

Homophobia in the Hallways

Heterosexism and Transphobia in Canadian Catholic Schools

TONYA D. CALLAGHAN

UNIVERSITY OF TORONTO PRESS
Toronto Buffalo London

© University of Toronto Press 2018
Toronto Buffalo London
utorontopress.com
Printed in Canada

ISBN 978-1-4875-0345-1 (cloth)
ISBN 978-1-4875-2267-4 (paper)

Printed on acid-free, 100% post-consumer recycled
paper with vegetable-based inks.

Library and Archives Canada Cataloguing in Publication

Callaghan, Tonya D., 1968–, author
Homophobia in the hallways : heterosexism and transphobia in
Canadian Catholic schools / Tonya D. Callaghan.

Includes bibliographical references and index.
ISBN 978-1-4875-0345-1 (hardcover).   ISBN 978-1-4875-2267-4 (softcover)

1. Homophobia in schools – Canada – Case studies.   2. Heterosexism in
schools – Canada – Case studies.   3. Discrimination in education – Canada –
Case studies.   4. School environment – Canada – Case studies.   5. Catholic
schools – Canada.   6. Transphobia – Canada.   7. Homophobia – Religious
aspects – Catholic Church.   8. Heterosexism – Religious aspects.   I. Title.

LC212.83.C3C35 2018   371.826′640971   C2017-907274-9

This book has been published with the help of a grant from the Federation
for the Humanities and Social Sciences, through the Awards to Scholarly
Publications Program, using funds provided by the Social Sciences and
Humanities Research Council of Canada.

University of Toronto Press acknowledges the financial assistance to its
publishing program of the Canada Council for the Arts and the Ontario
Arts Council, an agency of the Government of Ontario.

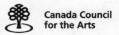

ONTARIO ARTS COUNCIL
CONSEIL DES ARTS DE L'ONTARIO
an Ontario government agency
un organisme du gouvernement de l'Ontario

Funded by the   Financé par le
Government   gouvernement
of Canada   du Canada

*To Lee Iskander and other secondary
school student leaders like her*

Contents

Acknowledgments

In undertaking this study, I spent several years reading theory, analysing news media accounts, and struggling through reams and reams of homophobic documents from the Catholic church and Catholic schools. Without suitable guides throughout this process, I doubt I ever would have made my way.

My gratitude is due to the following exemplary scholars who in various ways helped me navigate the often treacherous terrain of academic study: Dr Kathy Bickmore, Dr Kari Dehli, Dr Tara Goldstein, Dr Didi Khayatt, Dr Tatiana Gounko, Dr Raymond Morrow, Dr André Grace, Dr Owen Percy, Dr Jonny Flieger, Dr Robyn Read, Dr Michael Tavel Clarke, Dr Pamela McCallum, Dr Jeanne Perreault, Dr Louis Cabri, Frau Doktor Professor Nicole Markotić, and Frau Doktor Professor Carolin Kreber. I would like to thank my editor, Rosemary Nixon, and UTP acquisitions editor for social sciences Douglas Hildebrand, who were enthusiastic about the topic from the start and encouraged me throughout the book's long journey to completion. I would also like to acknowledge that this research was supported by the Social Sciences and Humanities Research Council of Canada.

It is unlikely this study would have been completed without the unconditional support of many friends and family. No scholar could imagine greater allies.

Finally, I owe countless thanks and more to my partner, Dr Suzette R. V. Mayr, a talented novelist with the keenest powers of observation and critical thinking I have ever come across and without whom this book surely would not have been possible.

HOMOPHOBIA IN THE HALLWAYS

Introduction

In 2004, after suffering several months of bullying because of his sexual orientation, a promising drama student in the Canadian Catholic high school where I was teaching committed suicide. As a lesbian forced to keep my sexuality a secret while at my job, I experienced a combination of grief and rage I had never felt before. It was not the first time I had encountered homophobia in schools where I had taught, but it was the first time I had been so intimately exposed to the most terrible results of homophobia. I recalled at the time that at every Catholic school I had taught in, I regularly heard homophobic jokes or comments from students and, during conversations at lunch or during meetings in the staff room, colleagues belittling or dismissing sexual minority breakthroughs, such as the legalization of same-sex marriage. I have enjoyed a varied teaching career spanning more than 15 years, working in institutions ranging from international schools in Europe to a small K–12 school in rural Alberta, and it was in the Catholic schools that I witnessed the most systemic homophobia. From my own experiences as a student and a teacher in these schools and after being confronted by this student's death, I concluded that Canadian Catholic schools are particularly ripe for homophobia.

Disheartened by how our school had so clearly failed this student, I met with my principal to discuss the duty required of all members of the Alberta Teachers' Association (ATA) to create a safe and caring school environment for all students. I was told that the Catholic school district does not necessarily adhere to every guideline of the ATA. Furthermore, I was told that our board was developing its own "Catholic response" to sensitive issues, such as sexual orientation, in Catholic schools. The subtext of this "Catholic response" does not bode well for lesbian, gay, bisexual, transgender, and queer (lgbtq)[1] people because this usually means maintaining close ties to punitive Catholic doctrine. Our publicly funded school failed this boy because he did seek counselling at the school but clearly did not receive enough help. This gay student's tragic death moved me to take action regarding the Catholic school system's sanctioned and institutionalized homophobia by engaging in research about it. I resigned from my teaching position to pursue graduate studies and write about the ways some publicly funded Catholic school districts in Canada ignore their legal, professional, and ethical responsibilities to protect *all* students and to maintain a safe, caring, and inclusive learning environment.

This book uncovers the stories of lgbtq students and teachers in some publicly funded Alberta and Ontario Catholic schools[2] through interviews with 20 participants and through media accounts. It also examines two little-known but influential Alberta and Ontario Catholic curriculum and policy documents regarding sexual and gender minorities. The study uses various critical theories to gain insights into the experiences of lgbtq people in Catholic schools and hypothesize about the potential for change. The purpose of this study is to gain a better understanding of religiously inspired oppression against vulnerable gender and sexual minority groups in publicly funded Canadian Catholic schools. My goal

---

1 Researchers who examine sexual and gender diversity generally use the initialism LGBTQ in uppercase because members of this population often use the words that compose the acronym to describe themselves (Baird, 2007). I use lowercase because it is less jarring to read and is less likely to linguistically set up the population as an obvious Other. In North America, the lgbtq population is also referred to as *non-heterosexuals*, *gender and sexual minorities*, and *gender and sexually diverse persons*. These terms are often more appropriate as a label for those who have immigrated to North America from countries that do not recognize lgbtq identities.

2 In Canada Catholic schools have a long and somewhat complicated history going back to Britain's victory over France for the colonies of North America in the early eighteenth century. The two main faith groups at the time were Catholics and Protestants. As a concession to the minority faith group in any given community, a separate school system was established to ensure that Catholic families could send their children to Catholic schools if living in a predominantly Protestant area and vice versa. Publicly funded separate schools currently have constitutional status in Alberta, Saskatchewan, and Ontario. These separate schools are operated by civil authorities and are accountable to provincial governments rather than to church authorities. Religious bodies do not have a constitutional or legal interest in separate schools and, as such, Canadian Catholic separate schools are not private or parochial schools as is common in other countries. See McGowan's (2013) *A Short History of Catholic Schools in Ontario.*

in undertaking this study is to engage in a form of radical democratic politics that examines the state of sexual diversity in Canadian Catholic schools from a specific vantage point and invites dialogue and debate – an important step in making such schools more accepting of sex and gender differences.

The specific perspective I am highlighting here is that of sexual and gender diverse individuals who have experienced the homophobic and transphobic policies and curriculum of Canadian Catholic schools. I am certainly not the only one who has noticed these injustices. Students with a keen eye for fairness have also tried to draw attention to the problem. I am going to start with a story from the students.

Student Activism

On a cold day in March 2011, an inconspicuous, unremarkable group of students at St Joseph's Catholic Secondary School in Mississauga, Ontario, did something remarkable, something that, in their school – indeed in Catholic schools across Canada at the time – was unthinkable. They requested permission to establish a club, a Gay/Straight Alliance (GSA) club in their school. To the unenlightened eye, their action appeared small, routine even. It was a logical request for an in-school club whose focus would be to make the school a safe space for lgbtq students and their straight allies by raising awareness about, and so hopefully reducing, school-based homophobia. It was not even an original idea; GSAs had originated in the United States almost 25 years before. Unbeknown to these students, they would soon be taking on a significant battle for Canadian lgbtq rights. Their actions set off a series of events that would reverberate across the country.

The students quickly learned that St Joseph's school was not ready for such a club. A maelstrom ensued. The students, led by 16-year-old Leanne Iskander, encountered strong opposition first from their principal and then from administrators at the district level. By June, they remained in a standoff. The students vowed to continue their fight in the next school term.

The establishment of a GSA in a secular Canadian public school barely seems an issue worth noting, judging by the lack of media stories about such attempts. There is, in fact, no formal mechanism in place to ban GSA clubs in non-religious public schools. Starting a GSA club in a secular public school has often, though not always, proved no more controversial than setting up an anti-racism or debate club. Students who join a GSA in a non-religious school have the right to broadcast their club meeting schedule over the school's public address system, actively solicit other students for their club using posters and other means, meet on school property, and name their club a GSA without any concern over the use of the word *gay*. Note that publicly funded separate Catholic schools are accountable to civil, not church, authorities. Religious bodies do not have a constitutional or legal interest in separate schools, and, as such, Canadian Catholic separate schools are not private or parochial schools as many are in other countries.

In Canadian Catholic schools, such as St Joseph Secondary School in Mississauga, however – a publicly funded school, I must emphasize – Leanne Iskander and friends' request to establish such a club was rejected outright more than once and caused serious alarm, not only for the administrators of St Joseph's but also for its school district, the Ontario bishops, and the Ontario provincial government.

The increasingly public battle between this particular group of students in St Joseph's Catholic Secondary School and their Catholic school administrators is significant because it represents the growing discontent between publicly funded Canadian Catholic schools and Canadian society at large. In Canada, same-sex legal rights have been steadily advancing – in 2005 Canada became the fourth country in the world to legalize marriage equality nationwide (Rayside, 2008) – and Canadian gay Pride parades regularly attract millions of tourist dollars. In the publicly funded Canadian Catholic school system, however, advances in same-sex legal rights have been virtually non-existent. When trying to determine how to manage the existence of lgbtq people (students, teachers, aids, and support staff included) in Canadian Catholic schools, Catholic education leaders turn to Catholic doctrine rather than to their legal authority – Canadian human rights law. Catholic doctrine describes "homosexual acts" as "acts of grave depravity" that are "intrinsically disordered" and count among the list of "sins gravely contrary to chastity" (cited in Ontario Conference of Catholic Bishops [OCCB], 2004a, p. 53). Needless to say, relying on Catholic doctrine as a guide for curricular and policy decisions makes Canadian Catholic schools hotbeds for homophobia.

Homophobia

Homophobia is most commonly defined as an irrational hatred and fear of non-heterosexuals, specifically lgbtq individuals. The term *homophobia* was first used among American psychologists in the late 1960s and early

1970s to describe a fear held by heterosexuals that others might perceive them to be homosexual (Herek, 2004). Although psychologists were the first to use the term, it is not listed as a bona fide phobia in the American Psychiatric Association's *Diagnostic and Statistical Manual of Mental Disorders*. It is therefore more of a cultural than clinical term. As an illustration of this cultural usage, in his foreword to a book devoted to teaching about sexual diversity, Archbishop Emeritus Desmond Tutu referred to homophobia as a "crime against humanity" comparable to apartheid (van Dijk & van Driel, 2007, p. vii). As my interviews with lgbtq students and teachers reveal, within Catholic schools, lgbtq students are treated as though they have a disease that must be "cured," and lgbtq teachers who are not adept at hiding their sexual orientations are sometimes fired from their jobs or, at best, harassed – all *in spite of* the *Canadian Charter of Rights and Freedoms* (1982), which has an equality rights provision that protects against discrimination having to do with personal characteristics, including sexual orientation.

The banning of a GSA at St Joseph Secondary School in Mississauga, Ontario, is just one of many incidents of homophobic discrimination that have occurred in Canadian Catholic schools, many of which actively ignore the legal and professional responsibilities mandated by the state to protect all students and to maintain a safe, caring, and inclusive environment for everyone, including non-heterosexuals. This book records the efforts of young queer activists who have refused to stay silent in the face of religiously inspired homophobia in their Catholic schools and, instead, chose to take their stories to the media. In doing so, the Ontario student agitators gained powerful allies and eventually influenced the passing of Bill 13, the *Accepting Schools Act*, in June 2012. This Act attempts to reduce school-based homophobic bullying by mandating that all Ontario schools – including publicly funded, faith-based schools – must allow students to establish GSA support groups. Bill 13 includes a notable provision that requires schools to allow students to use the word *gay* in the name of their GSA (Bill 13, 2012). This provision was necessary because, as this book describes in detail, Catholic education leaders have been resistant to GSAs and especially to the use of the word *gay* and celebratory symbols, such as the rainbow Pride flag, because they are considered too affirming of non-heterosexuality. Similarly, two years later in Alberta, student activism regarding inconsistencies in the ability to establish GSAs in the province's schools led to the passing of Bill 10, *An Act to Amend the Alberta Bill of Rights to Protect Our Children* (Bill 10, 2014). Like Bill 13 in Ontario, Alberta's Bill 10 also had to specify that students should be allowed to start a GSA in any Alberta school, including religious schools, and that students should be allowed to use the word *gay* or *queer* in the name of their GSAs (Bill 10, 2014). Not surprisingly, Catholic education leaders and clergy members were not supportive of these bills and directed Catholic school administrators to find creative ways around them.

What are the causes of this lingering disconnect between publicly funded Canadian Catholic schools and the larger Canadian society? And what are the effects of this discrimination on current and former Alberta and Ontario lgbtq Catholic schoolteachers and former Alberta and Ontario lgbtq Catholic students? Because most of the Catholic leadership in preparing curricular and policy documents on the topic of homosexuality has come from the Ontario Conference of Catholic Bishops (OCCB) and from the Alberta Catholic Bishops (ACB) (ACB, 2001; OCCB, 2004a), many Catholic education leaders in Canada regard Ontario and Alberta as models and authorities when it comes to devising directives on how to manage sexual minority groups in Canadian Catholic schools.

At the core of this book are the 20 interviews with lgbtq teachers and former students from Alberta and Ontario Catholic schools. To contextualize the interviews and reveal the extent of the influence of Catholic doctrine on these students and teachers, I have included media accounts that report on explicit acts of homophobia in Canadian Catholic schools and two influential and much-consulted Catholic curriculum and policy documents that may be unfamiliar to many people outside the Catholic school system.

I learned about the experiences of the 20 participants through semi-structured one-hour interviews with them, and I have presented their stories for this book in the form of life-narrative vignettes. All participants identify as either lesbian, gay, bisexual, transgender, or queer (lgbtq), except for one Alberta teacher who identifies as a "straight ally." The interview questions derive from overarching questions that direct the study with a view to uncovering how power operates in Canadian Catholic schools.

News media

Canadians would not have known about St Joseph's ban on GSAs and Leanne Iskander would not have made any progress with establishing her GSA had it not been for the diligent reporting of the Canadian news media. Nor would Canadians have any knowledge of ground-breaking lgbtq-rights cases, such as Marc Hall's fight to take his boyfriend to his Ontario Catholic high school prom (Oziewicz, 2002) or Delwin Vriend's legal battle to have sexual orientation included as a prohibited ground for discrimination in Alberta human rights legislation after he believed he was fired from his teaching position at King's College in Edmonton for being gay (Pratt, 2008). The outrage and activism that resulted from these cases were largely due to the media bringing them to the attention of the Canadian public. This suggests a crucial link between media reports and their potential to influence changes to Canadian law and highlights an earlier disengagement with Canadian law that is meant to protect against discrimination based on sexual orientation and gender identity.

This nexus is further explored by communications scholar Dane Claussen (2002) in a book that he edited called *Sex, Religion, Media*. Drawing upon the 19 essays he collected for his book, Claussen uncovers North American journalists' abysmal record in competently reporting on news stories that combine the treacherous topics of religion and sexuality. Claussen (2002, p. 280) concludes that while journalists are not altogether avoiding stories involving the intersections of faith and sexuality, they tend to overtly deny, or even outright dishonestly portray, the nuanced views of human sexuality held by various religious organizations. Claussen's observation may account for the lack of media coverage concerning earlier attempts to set up GSAs in Canadian Catholic schools, but the amount of media coverage Iskander received in 2011 suggests the trend is changing. Note that the Canadian media have not taken a uniformly critical view of homophobia in Canadian culture and institutions. Although the media cannot be portrayed as heroes in the struggle against homophobia in Canadian Catholic schools, they nevertheless play an important role in disseminating stories about religiously inspired homophobic discrimination. A newspaper article can become the topic of dinner conversation, which can, in turn, become the beginning of a protest movement. Iskander is not the first schoolgirl who attempted to establish a GSA in a Canadian Catholic school (Callaghan, 2007a), but hers is the first story of this kind to be covered in the Canadian media – in spite of traditional journalistic resistance to stories that simultaneously examine religion and sexuality.

The media can play a major role in heightening awareness of this little-known problem in Canadian schools, whether reporting in large, established media outlets such as *The Globe and Mail*, the Canadian Broadcasting Corporation (CBC), or smaller outlets such as *Xtra! Canada's Gay and Lesbian News.* Iskander's quest for her club was reported in national media outlets, including *The Globe and Mail,* and reached international news outlets, such as the British *Pink News* and the American *The Advocate,* the latter of which reported on Iskander's "controversial" (in Catholic circles) move to establish a club where she and her friends could be freely lgbtq and use gay Pride symbols like rainbows to promote their club, just as students can do in non-Catholic public schools (Baluja & Hammer, 2011; Garcia, 2011; Geen, 2011). *Xtra!,* despite being a comparatively small weekly newspaper with lower circulation numbers, has been key in breaking significant lgbtq news-related stories long before the larger outlets do.[3] *Xtra!* reporter Andrea Houston, for example, diligently covered the Leanne Iskander story weeks before the story hit more mainstream, and traditionally more heteronormative, Canadian publications, such as *The Globe and Mail.*

Although media coverage of such stories may unwittingly reproduce heteronormative views of sexuality and gender, the fact that such stories are now being covered at all suggests an important turning point that we can only trust will lead to greater discussion of the disturbing problem of homophobia in Canadian Catholic schools. The media's role is vital, for Catholic doctrine is at the root of the religiously inspired homophobia occurring in Canadian Catholic schools. Catholic doctrine regarding lgbtq people, who are referred to in Catholic parlance as "persons with same-sex attraction" (OCCB, 2003, p. 3), can be distilled into the colloquial Christian expression "love the sinner; hate the sin." This irreconcilable concept underlies curricular and policy decisions regarding sexual diversity and the existence of sexual minorities in Canadian Catholic schools. Hence my examination of the two primary documents from Alberta and Ontario written by Catholic bishops and education leaders to clarify for Catholic educators the official Catholic doctrine on non-heterosexuality. The 2004 Ontario text is titled *Pastoral Guidelines to Assist Students of Same-Sex Orientation* and the 2007 Alberta text is titled *Towards an Inclusive Community.*

This combination of participant interviews, media accounts, and Catholic documents reveals the powerful negative effects of Catholic school

---

3 *Xtra!* was founded in 1984, and published biweekly print editions in Ottawa, Vancouver, and Toronto from 1993 to 2015. In 2015, it switched to an online-only publication at DailyXtra.com. Because this study focuses on media coverage from 2000 through 2011, references are to the print publication. *Xtra* continues to be an important source of lgbtq-related news and opinion.

policies regarding "persons with same-sex attraction" on the very people for whom such policies were designed. Policies are not always followed in practice, however, and there fortunately have been instances of resistance to the religiously inspired homophobia waged by church hierarchy. This leads to the question: How does power operate in Canadian Catholic schools then – from the top down solely, or can power rise up from the bottom as well? The first part of this question resonates with Marxist theories of the state's role in oppressing people, which have largely focused on a hierarchical one-way direction of power. The question about the possibility of power operating from the bottom up evokes a Foucaultian analysis that attempts to move theorizing about power beyond the notion of power as repression of the powerless by the powerful to an exploration of how power operates between, among, and within people and institutions, including the role individuals can play in affirming or resisting repressive, top-down power. Religiously inspired homophobia involves multiple forms of power – certainly the coercive, regulatory, and repressive kind of power but also, paradoxically, the productive elements of power born out of oppressive measures.

To illuminate aspects of the empirical data that might begin to partially explain the phenomenon of "holy homophobia" in Canadian Catholic schools, consider the critical theories of Gramsci (1971), Althusser (1970/2008), Foucault (1975/1995), and Giroux (2001) – all of whom have formulated theories regarding the function and mechanics of repressive power within cultural institutions. Each theorist's concepts about ideology, hegemony, and disciplinary surveillance are premised on different, and, in some ways, incompatible assumptions. Althusser, for example, is particularly problematic not only because of his questionable politics but also because of his non-poststructuralist concept of there being a truth. Althusser's theory of the ideological state apparatus refers to institutions, such as churches, schools, media, family, law, and unions, which are formally outside state control but nevertheless manage to transmit the values of the state to help maintain order in society. Although Althusser's theory of the ideological state apparatus is at times uncomfortably abstract for an empirical study, and although the theory also suffers from many flaws, it is nevertheless useful in exploring how the Vatican functions in relation to Catholic schools. One way of mitigating the flaws of Althusser's overall theory of the ideological state apparatus is by supplementing it with Foucaultian micro-analyses of power; that is, the effects of two key institutions, the church and the school, on students and teachers and the role that these people play in affirming or resisting those effects. Gramsci's *Prison Notebooks* of 1929–35, which were edited and translated from Italian into English in 1971, explore such topics as education, intellectuals, and hegemony and in this way represent an important conceptual bridge between Althusser and Foucault. Although Gramsci, Althusser, Foucault, and Giroux belong to fundamentally different theoretical traditions, it is not impossible to imagine a basis for their convergence. Indeed, many scholars have worked out how some of these theorists do converge, especially in terms of the ways different theories can fill in the lacunae or omissions in each other's concepts; this issue is taken up in more detail in Chapter 5, Theorizing the Data.

Goals and Questions

My desire is that educational stakeholders become aware of the contradictions that underpin their educational policies and practices, and hopefully become inspired to change them in the interests of freeing members of sexual minority groups from heterosexist oppression. This emancipatory goal is not new – second-generation Frankfurt School critical theorist Jürgen Habermas espoused a critical social theory comprising an emancipatory cognitive interest in an attempt to account for the origin of meanings, values, and practices in social life (Habermas, 1971). Henry Giroux, one of the leading theorists of resistance in education, also aligned with the Frankfurt School ideologies in his studies that explored how educational policy and practice serve the interests of dominant groups but simultaneously make room for the possibility of emancipation through human agency and resistance (Gibson, 1986).

To uncover the information and understanding required to accomplish these research goals, *Homophobia in the Hallways* is designed using a multi-method qualitative inquiry framework that helps to answer the following questions:

1. How does power operate within and across Alberta and Ontario Catholic schools?
2. How do Catholic documents portray teachers and students as subjects?
3. What effects do Catholic documents have on the experiences of lgbtq individuals in Alberta and Ontario Catholic schools?
4. Is resistance possible in an educational context so dominated by the repressive force of religiously inspired homophobia?

Guided by several theorists, this book will consider the day-to-day practices of Alberta and Ontario Catholic schools regarding sexual minority groups and the particular participants' perspectives of those practices. Let's begin with the bishops.

Context of the Problem

Catholic bishops in the Canadian provinces of Alberta and Ontario who are involved in preparing curricular and educational policy documents on the topic of "persons with same-sex attractions" recognize that sexual minority groups "are often the victims of verbal, physical and more subtle forms of abuse [and that] suicide rates among homosexual students are higher than those of their heterosexual peers" (OCCB, 2003, p. 3). Still, these bishops see no inherent contradiction in writing curricula and educational policy that teach the homophobic Catholic doctrine that requires lgbtq individuals to be chaste and celibate for the rest of their lives (ACB, 2001). The dissemination of this type of discriminatory curriculum is incongruous in a country such as Canada, which is considered one of the most socially progressive countries in the world, in large part because of its *Canadian Charter of Rights and Freedoms* (1982) and the leadership it has shown in protecting basic human rights. Nevertheless, it is important to note that some lay Catholics who teach in Catholic schools are authentically grappling with the tensions presented by Catholic curriculum and educational policy that is out of step with Canadian law. These teachers find creative ways to stay loyal to their faith while still doing their best to ensure the safety and well-being of vulnerable sexual and gender minority youth in their care.

The importance of having a federal anti-discrimination policy in the Canadian *Charter* is evidenced by the frequent and consistent legal victories lgbtq complainants have attained against discrimination on the basis of sexual orientation and gender identity. Section 15 of the *Charter*, known as the equality rights provision, has been the chief tool for the advancement of same-sex legal rights in Canada since the *Charter* became law in 1982. Legal demands for same-sex equality have been on the rise since 1995 when sexual orientation was "read in" to the *Charter* as a prohibited ground of discrimination and came to be understood as analogous to the types of discrimination originally listed in Section 15, such as race or age (Hurley, 2005). Many non-heterosexual Canadians – adults and youth alike – are becoming increasingly aware of their *Charter* rights and expect them to be respected in all government-funded institutions, including Catholic schools.

Yet with this steady advancement of same-sex legal rights in Canada has also come conservative Catholic resistance. Conservative resistance or backlash to progressive advances for lgbtq rights is not confined solely to conservative Catholicism. Part of the reason religiously inspired homophobia is so pervasive in the Catholic Church and, by extension, in Catholic schools can be attributed to the high level of ambivalence about sexual diversity in Canadian society more generally. Homophobia and heterosexism also continue to be formidable forces in Canadian publicly funded secular schools. The difference in publicly funded Canadian Catholic schools is that homophobic discrimination is actively institutionalized through the use of Catholic doctrine. Highly publicized human rights cases involving discrimination on the basis of sexual orientation – such as the 2002 Marc Hall case involving the right to take a same-sex date to the high school prom – sparked a response on the part of bishops, primarily in Alberta and Ontario, who began writing local catechisms for Catholic school districts to "be clear about the authentic teaching of the Church on sexual morality and in particular in the area of homosexuality" (OCCB, 2003, p. 1). The local catechisms, also known as pastoral guidelines, are essentially curriculum and policy documents written and designed by local bishops to direct Catholic schools on issues of morality (Callaghan, 2007b). Of the three Canadian provinces that continue to publicly fund their Catholic schools (Ontario, Saskatchewan, and Alberta), Ontario and Alberta are the two powerhouses for Catholic schooling in Canada because of the larger populations of these two provinces, their bishops who have written copiously on the subject, and the long-standing historical connection with Catholicism and early Upper Canada (now known as Ontario). Alberta and Ontario are therefore ideal for a comparative analysis; Saskatchewan was not one of the units of analysis.

In addition to reiterating the official Catholic doctrine on non-heterosexuality, local catechisms for Catholic school districts admonish teachers in their schools who do not enforce the doctrine. "It is not sound or acceptable practice," the authors of one catechism write, "for Catholic schools to teach that certain behaviour is contrary to Catholic teaching, but then to take no action when it is exhibited openly in a school context" (OCCB, 2003, p. 1). The OCCB calls upon teachers to use stricter measures for enforcing Catholic doctrine related to homosexuality, while at the same time professing that "students experiencing same-sex attraction should be treated with sensitivity and compassion" (p. 3). On the topic of harassment against students "with same-sex attractions," the Ontario bishops declare that teachers, counsellors, administrators, and chaplains should "ensure that all members of the school community are aware that the Church teaches that abusive behaviour toward any person, for any reason, is unacceptable" (p. 3). Contradictory and confusing treatment of sexual and gender minority groups makes Catholic schools in Canada particularly vulnerable to homophobia and other forms of discrimination on the basis of sexual orientation or gender identity. Catholic education leaders, such as superintendents and principals, often turn to area bishops for guidance on how to manage controversial issues associated with gender and sexual diversity in schools that clash with Canadian common law and Catholic canonical law. The direction they usually get is to adhere closely to Catholic doctrine. However, as this book will elucidate, the struggle over the establishment of GSAs in Catholic schools has revealed that some Catholic principals are siding with provincial legislation on the matter. This offers great hope for change. These tensions can be read as opportunities for reform and subversion in an era of growing acceptance of gender and sexual diversity among mainstream lay Catholics.

Before the rise of same-sex legal rights in Canada in the mid-1990s, there was no push on the part of Catholic bishops to disseminate homophobic Catholic doctrine in Canadian Catholic schools (Callaghan, 2007b). At the beginning of the twenty-first century, however, new local catechisms or pastoral guidelines on the topic of "persons with same-sex attraction" began to appear, such as those from the ACB (2001) and the OCCB (2004a). The appearance of these new pastoral guidelines following the highly publicized advancements of same-sex legal rights in Canada suggests a Catholic backlash to Canadian equality rights laws for sexual minority groups. This backlash is observable in some publicly funded Canadian Catholic schools, which exist as small pockets of human rights violations while simultaneously receiving full public funding from provincial governments.

This anomaly raises the question: Shouldn't educational institutions in receipt of public funding respect the *Canadian Charter of Rights and Freedoms* (1982)? The religious freedom that is guaranteed by Section 2 of the *Charter* should not be interpreted as the freedom to deny basic human rights to specific groups in the name of that very religious freedom. Section 2 of the *Charter* lists the fundamental freedoms that apply to everyone in Canada, regardless of citizenship status. According to

Section 2, "everyone has the following fundamental freedoms: (a) freedom of conscience and religion; (b) freedom of thought, belief, opinion and expression, including freedom of the press and other media of
communication; (c) freedom of peaceful assembly; and (d) freedom of
association" (*Charter*, 1982).

Section 2 is often at the crux of the argument advanced by faith-based
institutions seeking to exempt themselves from respecting certain forms
of equality outlined in Section 15 because of its perceived conflicts with
religious beliefs. Section 15, the equality rights provision of the *Charter*,
states that "every individual is equal before and under the law and has
the right to the equal protection and equal benefit of the law without
discrimination and, in particular, without discrimination based on race,
national or ethnic origin, colour, religion, sex, age or mental or physical
disability." A solution to this problem may lie in Section 1 of the *Charter*,
which is a limiting clause that has the capacity to legally restrict *Charter*
rights and freedoms if the expression of one right calls for the suppression of other rights. Under the heading "Guarantee of Rights and Freedoms," Section 1 states: "The Canadian Charter of Rights and Freedoms
guarantees the rights and freedoms set out in it subject only to such
reasonable limits prescribed by law as can be demonstrably justified in a
free and democratic society."

Although the law may not be a sufficient means for securing and maintaining rights, the mounting of legal challenges has been an effective
beginning in the struggle against homophobic discrimination in Canadian institutions. Advances in same-sex legal rights have been extremely
beneficial for lgbtq Canadians who look to them when facing religiously
inspired discrimination in publicly funded institutions, such as Canadian
Catholic schools. Although there are limitations to rights-based arguments, they are nevertheless a worthwhile starting point.

Not only have advances in same-sex legal rights in Canada confirmed
equality rights for lesbian and gay Canadians, but they have also caught
the attention of teachers' associations across Canada, which have started
to develop policies that protect the rights of lgbtq teachers and students
(Grace, 2005). These inclusive and diversity-friendly policies are also
reflected in other education governance documents, such as provincial
school acts and teachers' codes of professional conduct, which have
been updated to reflect changes in provincial human rights codes and
the *Charter* in terms of protecting against discrimination on the basis of
sexual orientation or gender identity (Canadian Teachers' Federation,
2002). Keep in mind, however, that official policies are often far removed
from *enacted* policies and *experienced* practices in the schools.

The power of such progressive policies to protect vulnerable sexual minorities is significantly weakened by the fact that Catholic school districts often deftly sidestep them, claiming that they are contrary to Catholicity (Callaghan, 2007a). Homophobic catechisms affirming the Catholic teaching that "homosexual inclination" is "objectively disordered" and "homosexual practices" are "sins gravely contrary to chastity" (Canadian Conference of Catholic Bishops [CCCB], 1997b, para. 2358 and 2396) are clearly in violation of equality provisions outlined by government, in school acts, and in teachers' codes of professional conduct across the country.

The further travesty is that Canadian Catholic education leaders' conservative reaction to advances in same-sex legal rights has gone virtually unnoticed in educational and social justice circles in Canada. Catholic doublespeak (Callaghan, 2007a) contained in local catechisms or pastoral guidelines enables homophobia in Canadian Catholic schools, but it also interestingly makes space for certain slants of light in the form of dissention to find expression as well. The rationale behind continued public funding for these privileged faith-based schools has been called into question. In describing these schools as "privileged," I am referring to the United Nations Human Rights Committee rulings in 1999 and 2005 declaring Canada to be in violation of Article 26 of the International Covenant on Civil and Political Rights because it provides public funding only to Catholic schools and not to other faith-based schools (Civil Rights in Public Education, 2005). They are privileged in that they preferentially receive full public funding while other faith-based schools do not.

Not only do Canadian Catholic schools receive preferential funding from the state, but they also enjoy the benefits of Canadian legal precedent, which has historically granted denominational schools the privilege of exercising the rights of the religious group over the individual rights of teachers (Covert, 1993). The right to be free from discrimination on the basis of sexual orientation or gender identity, guaranteed by Section 15 of the *Charter* and reflected in subsequent educational governance documents, as noted earlier remains in jeopardy in Canadian Catholic schools.

Of all the Catholic doctrine that could be enforced in these schools, it seems the doctrine related to non-heterosexuality was the most popular in the era of conservative Catholic leadership under the direction of Pope Benedict XVI, who took a keen interest in the topic. When he was known as Cardinal Joseph Ratzinger, for example, Pope Benedict XVI was responsible for a Vatican encyclical that condemned the homosexual orientation as "an intrinsic moral evil" and "an objective disorder"

(Vatican Congregation for the Doctrine of the Faith, 1986, item 3). The *Catechism of the Catholic Church*, which teaches that "homosexual acts are intrinsically disordered" (CCCB, 1997b, para. 2357), has been used to regularly intimidate, harass, and dismiss lgbtq individuals in Canadian Catholic schools who are open about their sexuality, sexual expression, and gender identity (Callaghan, 2007b).

Until the 1999 and 2005 United Nations rulings became well circu-lated, few called into question the public funding of separate school sys-tems in Canada. Questions about historical funding models for Cana-dian Catholic schools led to questions about the operation of these schools under Catholic doctrine, particularly when the adherence to Catholic canonical law clashes with adherence to Canadian common law. The Canadian public noticed that publicly funded Catholic schools in Canada use their denominational school rights, guaranteed by Sec-tion 29 of the *Charter*, to ensure their students and teachers adhere to contentious Catholic doctrine regarding sexual minorities, even if this infringes on the human rights guaranteed by other sections of the *Charter*. Few noticed, however, that while Canadian Catholic schools are working hard to justify their existence and differentiate themselves from the secular public schools, including by preparing contradictory curricula and educational policies that, drawing upon Catholic doc-trine, proclaim that "homosexual persons are called to chastity," they are simultaneously refusing to acknowledge that this chastity require-ment constitutes a "sign of unjust discrimination in their regard [that] should be avoided" (CCCB, 1997b, para. 2359 and 2358). The problem is the Catholic doctrine is contradictory and confusing, making it dif-ficult to notice and contest. Of course, ensuring that more members of the Canadian public are made aware of the homophobic discrimina-tion occurring in Canadian Catholic schools does not guarantee that Catholic education leaders would take action to redress this problem. Nevertheless, a heightened awareness about this discrimination – in the form of the United Nation's public admonishment of Canada for preferential funding of Catholic schools, an increase in news media coverage of homophobic incidents in Canadian Catholic schools, and studies such as this one – is a good place to start.

Homophobia in Educational Contexts

Members of religious groups who oppose homosexual behaviour on moral grounds have objected to the term *homophobia* because it suggests their opposition is fear-based rather than legitimately tied to sacred religious texts and grounded in what many religious people regard as a socially accepted prejudice (O'Donohue & Caselles, 1993). Despite objections to the term *homophobia* and its questionable semantic accuracy, its early use in the 1970s cemented it as the most common way to describe prejudice and discrimination directed towards lgbtq people.

In institutions of higher learning, homophobia is often studied in conjunction with other forms of discrimination, such as racism, sexism, and classism. Anti-homophobia education and activism address the myriad forms of homophobia, including institutionalized homophobia and interpersonal homophobia. Attempts to reduce homophobia in public schools are expressed as anti-discrimination provisions in various levels of legislation and through popular movements, but these are invariably met with counter resistance campaigns from certain religious groups.

Institutionalized homophobia

Some scholars reject the notion that homophobia is an irrational fear of non-heterosexuals because of its pervasive presence in influential institutions, such as the military, education, and justice systems (Herek, 2000). These scholars argue that to understand homophobia as an irrational fear is to associate it with a personal anxiety disorder, such as social phobia, rather than to see it as a cultural phenomenon that has found systemic expression in societal institutions. Institutionalized homophobia is used to describe discrimination against lgbtq people that has its roots in social and cultural relations associated with societal institutions, such as religion, education, media, and government.

In the military, for example, many governments around the world have historically engaged in a form of institutionalized homophobia by banning homosexuals from serving in the armed forces (Levy, 2007). This kind of discrimination started to fall away, however, because of social change (throughout the Western world) occurring in the 1960s, which sparked what was then known as the Gay Liberation Movement in North America, Western Europe, Australia, and New Zealand (Carter, 2004). Gender and sexually diverse activists staged public campaigns and demonstrations that ultimately increased social acceptance of sexual and gender minorities and led to several advances in same-sex legal rights. Aware that their policies banning homosexuals from serving in the military were not in keeping with the social values of the times, most Western armed forces removed their homophobic policies in the 1970s, 1980s, and 1990s (Segal, Gade, & Johnson, 1993).

In educational institutions, such as public schools, institutionalized homophobia is expressed in the absence of references to, or support for, sexual and gender diversity. Schools often lack educational policies written specifically to protect students, teachers, and others working within school systems from discrimination on the basis of sexual orientation or gender identity (Goldstein, Collins, & Halder, 2008). Similarly, it is rare to find mainstream curricular materials that mention non-heterosexuals and even more unlikely to find any that present lgbtq people positively by referring to their historical and cultural contributions (Bickmore, 2002). Curriculum theorists refer to this kind of omission as a null curriculum – a marked absence that shows what is actively *not* taught is just as important and revealing about a culture as what *is* overtly taught (Flinders, Noddings, & Thornton, 1986). The meagre presence of queer-positive curricula in public schools shows that decisions about what should be taught in schools are made by people in power whose perspective reflects that of the dominant culture. The heteronormative orientation of school curricula, policies, and practices is not only about denying rights to sexual minority groups but also about centring and privileging heterosexuality as the norm.

Interpersonal homophobia

Homophobia in schools is physically or verbally expressed in the form of discriminatory bullying and harassment of those who either openly identify as lgbtq or who are perceived by others to be lgbtq. Homophobic bullying reinforces social hierarchies that exist outside the school in the dominant culture, thereby maintaining a balance of power that privileges the heterosexual majority. Homophobic bullying ranges from homophobic epithets, lewd gestures, sexualized teasing, malicious gossip about an individual's sexual orientation or gender identity (both in the school environment and on the Internet), threats of violence, actual violence, and various forms of physical aggression, including hazing and stalking (Rivers, 2011).

The prevalence of homophobic bullying in schools was the impetus behind the establishment of specialized schools where lgbtq students could receive their education in a safe and caring environment. An early example is Harvey Milk High School, named after the first openly gay politician elected to public office in the United States, who was assassinated in 1978 ("First Public Gay High School," 2003). Established in 1985 with the help of private donations, Harvey Milk High School now operates under the auspices of the New York City Department of

Education. In 1995 the Toronto District School Board established the Triangle Program, another example of an alternative school for lgbtq students, in Toronto, Ontario.

Homophobic harassment also exists in less violent forms and can target lgbtq adults in the school as well (Kissen, 1996). In my research for this book, I collected media reports of homophobia occurring in Canadian Catholic schools that filled six file folders. While collecting this data, I discovered reports on homophobic incidents occurring in Catholic schools in other parts of the world, which I filed in six separate folders labelled with the country of origin: Australia, British Isles, Malta, Poland, Spain, and United States of America. Based on my study of these data, I would posit that Western media outlets are reporting more frequently than their non-Western counterparts on cases of homophobic harassment in schools throughout the late twentieth and early twenty-first centuries.

School boards from the above-noted countries, including Canada, have caught widespread media attention for the following types of homophobic incidents: firing lgbtq teachers for publicly disclosing their sexual orientation or gender identity; firing lesbian and gay teachers because they married their same-sex partners; firing lesbian and gay teachers because they wanted to have children with their same-sex partners; censoring curricular material that discussed homophobia or presented sexual minority groups in a positive manner; attempting to prohibit gay and lesbian students from attending their high school proms with their same-sex dates; barring students from appearing in gender variant clothing for official school photographs or functions, such as the prom dance; and denying students the right to establish GSAs.

The use of the media and legal remedies to reduce homophobia in schools

Western media coverage of the noted types of news stories has served to heighten awareness of homophobia occurring not only in North American but in Australian and European primary, secondary, and postsecondary schools. This attention has ignited public debate in those countries and continues to contribute to the development of further legal protection against discrimination on the basis of sexual orientation or gender identity, which directly affects public schools.

In Canada, for example, educational institutions available to the public are considered public services and are therefore required to uphold Section 15, the equality rights provision, of the *Canadian Charter of Rights and Freedoms* (1982), which protects against discrimination on the basis of sexual orientation and gender identity. Similarly, Canadian public educational institutions, whether they are privately or publicly funded, are also legally bound to observe all anti-discrimination clauses in provincial human rights acts. In Ontario, the Ministry of Education launched its *Equity and Inclusive Education Strategy* in 2009, which provides direction for all schools in Ontario on how to reduce discrimination, such as homophobia (Ontario Ministry of Education, 2009a).

Likewise, the United Kingdom's *Equality Act* of 2006 and subsequent Sexual Orientation Regulations of 2007 provide similar directives for schools to begin actively reducing homophobia, as do Australia's various federal and state anti-discrimination laws (Australian Human Rights Commission, 2007; UK Legislation, 2007).

Popular action to combat homophobia in schools

In addition to legislative efforts, there are also grassroots initiatives to reduce homophobia in schools. US educators are well-known for being the first to organize GSAs for public schools. Another US initiative was the formation of the Gay, Lesbian and Straight Education Network (GLSEN). Founded in 1990 as a small support group for gay and lesbian teachers in Massachusetts, GLSEN quickly expanded into a national organization that strives to ensure schools are safe spaces for all students by calling attention to homophobia and devising ways to eradicate it (Gay, Lesbian and Straight Education Network [GLSEN], 2011a). Accordingly, GLSEN sponsors the National Day of Silence, a student-led action in which students take a daylong vow of silence in the month of April to symbolize the silencing of lgbtq students and their allies in the face of the ever-present threat of homophobic bullying and harassment in schools (GLSEN, 2011b). Canada hosts a similar event called the National Day Against Homophobia, coinciding with the International Day Against Homophobia held on 17 May, the day the World Health Organization removed homosexuality from its list of mental disorders in 1990 (Fondation Émergence, 2011).

During 2010 a dramatic rise in the suicide rates of gay youths in North America prompted US human rights activists to launch an Internet campaign titled It Gets Better, urging suicidal queer youth to find ways to carry on until they can leave high school (Savage, 2010). Discouraged by the apparent inability of educators to ensure schools are safe spaces for all students, It Gets Better dismisses almost all school systems as inadequate and focuses instead on a future, safer time, away from school-based homophobic harassment.

Opposition to anti-homophobia action in schools

Opposition to anti-homophobia legislation, education, and activism has been both overt, in the form of public protests, and stealthy, in the form of acts of omission and resistance to progressive reforms. Stemming primarily from certain religious groups and leaders of various faith-based schools, the opposition is based on a belief that homosexual acts and gender variant expression are immoral behaviours, or possibly illnesses, which can be stopped or cured by sheer will or prayer. Catholic schools in Alberta and Ontario are prime examples, having frequently disregarded anti-homophobia legislation affecting school policies and curriculum. My research into the problem of religiously inspired homophobia in Catholic schools has also uncovered media reports describing other Catholic schools seeking exemptions from the Sexual Orientation Regulations in the United Kingdom and the anti-discrimination laws in Australia.

Focus on the Family (FOTF), a US evangelical Christian organization, collaborated with Alliance Defence Fund (ADF), another US Christian non-profit organization, to oppose GLSEN's National Day of Silence by encouraging Christian parents to keep their children home from school that day. In addition, FOTF and ADF mounted a counter protest, originally called the Day of Truth and now known as the Day of Dialogue, in which student participants pass out cards to students in their schools inviting them to an open discussion about homosexuality and informing them that other unspecified alternatives to acting on homosexual desires are possible (Focus on the Family [FOTF], 2010).

The intersections between religion, sexuality, and gender expression are not without controversy, given that they are typically considered to be highly private matters that are also complexly related to social life. These convergences are at the forefront of a new frontier in anti-homophobia education.

1

Critical Theory for Emancipation

Homophobia in Schools

Twentieth-century educational research demonstrates that heterosexism and homophobia reinforce specific forms of power and privilege that define and regulate an atmosphere of "compulsory heterosexuality" (Rich, 1986, p. 23) in public schooling (Britzman, 1995; Griffin, 1992; Harbeck, 1992; Khayatt, 1998; Pinar, 1998). This atmosphere of compulsory heterosexuality often forces teachers, students, and support staff to be closeted about their non-heterosexual identity. Nevertheless, studies from the same period show some lgbtq individuals in US public schools are choosing to be open about their sexuality and that some of these public schools are accepting and even welcoming their openness (Kissen, 1996; Smith, 1994; Woog, 1995).

This openness towards the existence of sexual minorities in public schools does not mean that heterosexism and homophobia are declining in these milieux. On the contrary, many twenty-first century studies continue to reveal oppression and discrimination towards sexual minorities in school settings (Chesir-Teran & Hughes, 2009; Goldstein, 2006; Meyer & Stader, 2009). One observation that has implications for this book is that those educators who are "coming out of the closet" (i.e., being open about their lgbtq status) in their professional lives are doing so most freely and fully in non-religious schools, as indicated in the Introduction. Faith-based schools are usually not safe spaces to address the needs of sexual minority groups, and those who have tried have often experienced negative repercussions (Callaghan, 2007b; Ferfolja, 2005; Grace & Wells, 2005; Litton, 2001; Love, 1997; Maher, 2003; Maher & Sever, 2007). Religious faith is increasingly cited as a legitimate rationale for institutionalized discrimination against non-heterosexuals and gender nonconformists (Baird, 2007).

In the case of Catholic schools, safe spaces for lgbtq individuals are difficult to achieve because contradictory Catholic doctrine forms the basis of curricular and policy decisions. The fear of experiencing doctrinal disciplining for acting on their sexuality forces many sexually active lgbtq individuals into a type of Foucaultian self-surveillance known as the Panopticon (Foucault, 1975/1995) during their time in Catholic schools. These individuals do not know when they are being observed or by whom, so they check their behaviour constantly to avoid reprisals from school leaders. The few studies on the experiences of non-heterosexuals in Catholic schools are predominantly American or Australian and may not apply to Catholic schools in Canada, where the political and cultural climate is somewhat different. With this in mind, I chose to write a book that examines policy and curriculum documents related to sexual minority groups and includes interviews with lgbtq-identified individuals associated with Catholic schools in Canada to determine the effect of such policy and curricula on their lives.

Canadian curricular attempts to redress homophobia in schools

Several curriculum guides and resources have been developed in Canada to assist teachers who want to redress the homophobia and heterosexism they witness in their classrooms and schools. Some of these supplementary curricular materials are designed to directly correspond with goals and outcomes related to diversity and inclusivity outlined in official Canadian provincial curricula. For the most part these are additional curricular resources – teachers may or may not turn to them for assistance in designing their courses, units, or lesson plans. One exception is the Ontario health and physical education curriculum, colloquially known as *sex ed*, which was revised in 2015 to include topics such as gender identity, sexual orientation, homophobia, and gender-based violence (Ontario Ministry of Education, 2015). Even though the educational policy and governance documents referred to earlier clearly outline teachers' legal and professional obligation to remedy homophobic prejudice that abounds in schools, the problem of teacher workload intensification (Apple & Jungck, 1993) suggests that even teachers who want to may be too overwhelmed to adequately attend to the matter. A great disparity thus exists between "curriculum-as-planned" and "curriculum-in-use" (Werner, 1991, p. 114).

The likelihood of teachers actually consulting these secondary curricular sources diminishes even further in Catholic schools because teachers in these schools may experience reprimands for consulting teaching materials that have not been officially approved by their local Catholic school board (Callaghan, 2007b). And Catholic school boards generally do not approve of supplementary curricular materials that present the "homosexual condition" (Vatican Congregation for the Doctrine of the Faith, 1986, item 3) in a positive light because they are deemed to be contrary to "Catholicity," therefore having no place in a Catholic school. Michael Bayly, the author of a supplementary curricular guidebook titled *Creating Safe Environments for LGBT Students: A Catholic Schools Perspective*, concedes that implementing the ideas in his book may not be possible in many dioceses or communities because of a Catholic backlash against safe school initiatives that gained momentum under the conservative leadership of Pope Benedict XVI (Bayly, 2007, p. 6). Many see great hope in Pope Francis's welcoming tone towards gender and sexually diverse people, but tone alone will not change the genderism and homophobia that is occurring in Catholic schools – Catholic doctrine on homosexuality needs to change. Although a concern for the dignity of all people is a cornerstone of Catholic social teaching, this study shows that sexual and gender minority teachers and students continue to be educationally marginalized and dispossessed in Canadian Catholic schools. As Catholic education leaders around the world struggle with how to respond to non-heterosexual people in their schools, they tend to abandon the tradition of Catholic social teaching and turn instead for guidance to the formidable Catholic canonical law on the topic of homosexuality, which has not changed with the new pope. In so doing, they also disregard secular human rights legislation in their jurisdictions. Pope Francis's (2016) long-awaited encyclical on marriage and family issues, *The Joy of Love*, reaffirms the Roman Catholic Church's opposition to same-sex relationships, declaring these can never be considered the equal of heterosexual marriage. Catholic education leaders tend to opt for insulating students from learning about particular human rights violations, which is untenable given that the best protection against human rights abuses is human rights education and, as critical pedagogue Kathy Bickmore (1999) makes clear, homophobic violence can be alleviated only by expanding rather than restricting the knowledge and experiences made available to students.

Canadian Catholic schools and sexual diversity

Although publicly funded Canadian Catholic schools are mandated to deliver the provincially approved curriculum, they consistently opt out of the human sexuality component of the physical education or life management curriculum because of perceived conflicts with religious doctrine (Callaghan, 2007a). Canadian Catholic school boards develop their own guidelines for teaching human sexuality, which is taught in a family life unit comprising approximately 20% of a course simply called Religion, where the Catholic heteronormative version of human sexuality can be safely presented within the confines of Catholic doctrine. For example, in 2006 the OCCB revamped its family life education program called Fully Alive for grades 1 through 8 and currently uses two resources for the high school levels called Turning Points for grades 9 and 10 and Reaching Out for grades 11 and 12 (Durocher, 2007; OCCB, 2006). The development of the human sexuality curriculum for the Religion classes taught in Canadian Catholic schools relies heavily upon the *Catechism of the Catholic Church* (CCCB, 1997b), which teaches that sexuality is solely for procreative purposes between male and female spouses (para. 2361), that any type of contraception other than the rhythm method is "intrinsically evil" (para. 2370), and that "homosexual acts are intrinsically disordered" (para. 2357). It is clear from these examples that students in Catholic schools receive ideologically laden misinformation about sexuality.

This homophobic doctrine informs curriculum and policy in Catholic schools but there are ways that this message is subverted. For example, some lgbtq teachers in Canadian Catholic schools are able to be "out" to varying degrees at work (i.e., open about their non-heterosexuality) and are able to include their same-sex partner in their employee benefits packages, and some lgbtq students have taken same-sex dates to their high school events without issue. This suggests that Catholic doctrine related to non-heterosexuality, which informs the development of Catholic school policies and curricula, is not always adhered to in Canadian Catholic schools. As Michel Foucault (1982, p. 225) observes, "it would not be possible for power relations to exist without points of insubordination," and clearly some lgbtq individuals have found ways to resist and subvert the religiously inspired homophobia that pervades Canadian Catholic schools.

Foucault describes this as the "micro-physics of power" (1975/1995, p. 139) or the very minute operations of power that can occur from the bottom up or among and between different constituents within a school. I am as interested in charting any resistance to doctrinal disciplining as I am with describing disciplinary control itself. The task of describing how oppressive power operates in the Catholic schools of this study is facilitated by the application of three key critical theories to the empirical data collected for this study: Antonio Gramsci's (1971) notion of hegemony, Louis Althusser's (1970/2008) concept of the ideological state apparatus, and Foucault's (1975/1995) theory of disciplinary surveillance, referred to in more detail in a later chapter.

Critical theory

Broadly considered, the critical theory tradition includes the contributions of what is known as the Frankfurt School, Marxist and post-Marxist thought, semiotics and discourse analysis, structuralism and poststructuralism, postmodernism and postcolonialism, critiques of ideology, psychoanalysis, feminism, queer theory, and deconstruction (Simons, 2004. p. 1). Scholars conduct critical analyses throughout all disciplines and interdisciplinary studies within the humanities and the social sciences. Critical sociology specifically scrutinizes social forces that reduce human potential, restrict individual freedom, and reinforce social domination (Buechler, 2008, p. 26). If social rituals, traditions, and institutions can be regarded as products of human reason – as opposed to divine law or natural order – then there is great hope for change, because it is possible to imagine that human reason can also cause them to be constructed and deconstructed in a manner that would be beneficial to all humanity. This is the hope that I see with critical theory. As Karl Marx suggests, the goal is not to simply understand the world but to change it (Rasmussen, 1996, p. 11).

If Marx compels workers to revolt against the chains of economic exploitation, then the Frankfurt School for Social Research invites individuals to see the interconnectedness of other oppressive chains that act as powerful forces of social control (How, 2003). In showing how domination and exploitation limit human potential, the Frankfurt School hoped to encourage progressive social change. The Institute for Social Research, founded in Frankfurt in 1923, is often associated with critical theory (Jay, 1996; Rasmussen, 1996). Critical theory is both general and specific (Rasmussen, 1996) and does not form a unified system of thought among all its advocates (Held, 1980). The theorists associated with the Frankfurt School were generally accepting of Marx's social class analysis, but following the events of the early twentieth century, many were dubious that the workers of the world would unite against their capitalist oppressors and become the revolutionary agents of change.

The theorists associated with the Frankfurt School recognized that Marx's emphasis on labour and economic exploitation was an important point of analysis, but they also saw that the various configurations of capitalism control people in myriad ways. Frankfurt School thinkers turned their attention to critically building on Marx's analysis, broadening the scope from exploitation at the material base of society to other multiple dimensions of domination. Their focus was therefore on the superstructure of society – the Marxist notion of the political, cultural, and ideological realms of social consciousness – that today we may loosely describe in terms of concepts such as hegemony or discourse (Marshall, 1998). Antonio Gramsci's (1971) theorization of hegemony – cultural domination through consent – is regarded by critical theorists as equally important as the Marxist concept of the material base in maintaining an unjust society. The critical theorists of the Frankfurt School adopted Marx's critical spirit and attempted to extend Marxism into a critical social theory focused on analysing various forms of social domination with a view to transforming society into a more egalitarian state. In that sense, critical theory has emancipatory aspirations.

Critical pedagogy, conscientization, and critical methodologies

Critical theory in education has also been referred to in educational literature as critical pedagogy. Critical pedagogy aims to emancipate the oppressed and mobilize people through a common and accessible understanding of critique to end various forms of human suffering (Kanpol, 1994, p. 27). Its chief theorist is Paulo Freire (1921–97), a Brazilian educator who united the ideas of liberation theology and critical theory of the Frankfurt School to form a critical pedagogy designed to relieve parts of poverty-stricken Brazil through social justice education and political activism (Kincheloe, 2007, p. 12). Freire's pivotal text *Pedagogy of the Oppressed* (1967/1970) incorporated education into the insights on social forces advanced by the Frankfurt School; it brought critical pedagogy to an international audience and is regarded as one of the most important and influential books published on liberation pedagogy (Darder, Baltodano, & Torres, 2003; Giroux, 1983; Kincheloe, 2008; Torres, 1998).

The Freirean notion of conscientization – critical consciousness-raising – has influenced educational research and practice, most notably in the forms of participatory action research and popular education (Torres, 1995). Critical pedagogy calls upon educational researchers to enter into relations of cooperation, mutuality, and reciprocity with research participants, giving rise to educational methodologies such as critical ethnography, which contests the so-called "objectivity" of mainstream ethnographic research (Lather, 1986; McLaren & Giarelli, 1995). In contrast to the supposed "disinterestedness" of the positivist, quantitative researcher, research informed by the methodology of critical pedagogy welcomes the decided "interestedness" of the researcher whose goal is often to produce knowledge that will inform action towards positive social change (Duncan-Andrade & Morrell, 2008; Kincheloe & McLaren, 1998). Critical methodology is informed by the enriching, empowering, and emancipatory epistemologies of critical theory, liberation pedagogy, critical race, and poststructural feminism (Lather, 2007).

Critical pedagogue Joe Kincheloe (2007, p. 11) observed that one of the greatest failures of critical pedagogy is its inability to engage Indigenous scholars. Denzin, Lincoln, and Tuhiwai Smith (2008, pp. ix – xi) respond to this profound absence by declaring a new "decade of critical, Indigenous inquiry" premised on the belief that Indigenous scholars can show critical pedagogues how to learn from the local while striving for social change, social justice, and authentic democracy. These authors believe that the common emancipatory goals of critical and Indigenous methodologists create an opportunity for both to come together and work to liberate the oppressed of all kinds, including lgbtq individuals (p. x).

Whether working from poststructuralist, postcolonial, feminist, deconstructionist, or queer epistemologies, anti-oppressive researchers espouse a critical perspective that sees oppression as a social dynamic that privileges certain ways of being while marginalizing others (Kumashiro, 2000; Kumashiro & Ngo, 2007). Anti-oppressive educational research exposes how racism, sexism, classism, ableism, heterosexism, and other forms of oppression operate in schools and proposes ways to redress discrimination and domination in school settings. There is a healthy scepticism at the base of anti-oppressive research. As Brown and Strega (2005) contend, critical, emancipatory, and anti-oppressive approaches to research seek to "trouble" (p. 7) the connections between what constitutes knowledge and who is entitled to participate in knowledge production. They stress that research from the margins is not "research on the marginalized but research by, for, and with them/us" (p. 7).

Validity Issues

Validity addresses questions readers of the research may bring to either the design of the research project or its findings, such as: "How do I know your interpretations or the results of your study are valid?" or "Since the entire investigation was conducted by one researcher, why should I believe you?" Requiring that the findings of this study will (or must) be valid depends on a belief in unalienable fact or absolute truth and certainty. Here, "fact" refers to a description of objects and events that is not simply an account of what the researcher sees, hears, smells, touches, or tastes but is also a *claim* that what the researcher *perceived* through his or her senses is in some way real, precise, or unambiguous. "Truth," here, is understood in the sense that the findings are believed to accurately represent the phenomena under study, and "certain" refers to an acceptance that the findings are supported by adequate evidence. "Certainty" also suggests that there are no reasonable grounds from which to doubt the findings of the study and that the evidence offered as the basis of the claims made by the study is stronger than any other evidence that may be offered for competing claims (Schwandt, 2007).

As a qualitative researcher committed to critical theories, I must admit that I am somewhat suspicious of the validity criterion. For me, critical scholarly work is about engaging in close and explicit evaluation or judgment of knowledge claims, which involves a process of thinking critically and placing all familiar "truths" and established "facts" under close scrutiny. Indeed, truth itself is a highly contested notion and is the subject of many philosophical debates among both supporters and detractors of qualitative research. For Michel Foucault, one of the chief theorists championed by feminist, poststructuralist, and queer theorists, truth is not an abstract entity as many Western philosophers contend. Rather, he claims "truth is of the world, it is produced there by virtue of multiple constraints" (Foucault, 1979, p. 46). For Foucault, truth is produced and reproduced in the power and knowledge system of domination that characterizes the self and society.

For example, in *Two Lectures,* an address by Michel Foucault collected in a series of essays called *Power/Knowledge* (1980/1972), Foucault points out that institutions are increasingly vulnerable to criticism. He observes, "a certain fragility has been discovered in the very bedrock of existence … [especially that that is] most familiar, most solid and most intimately related to our bodies and to our everyday behaviour" (p. 80). Here, Foucault is drawing our attention to abstract institutional processes that seem to conspire together to establish one way of seeing as fact or knowledge while simultaneously discrediting other ways of seeing that are equally valid. Foucault's compound phrase "power/knowledge" underscores that whenever knowledge is produced, there is also an attendant claim to power. Offering some important examples that illustrate this point, Mills (2003) notes that there are many books about women but few about men; many books about Black people but few about whites; and many studies of homosexuality but very few about heterosexuality. The institutionalized disproportion in power relations between women and men, Blacks and whites, and homosexuals and heterosexuals has produced more studies on those at the margins of society who hold less power, though this is changing.

Foucault's (1981, p. 56) concept of "the will to truth," a series of exclusionary practices meant to determine distinctions between statements so they can be understood as either true or false, is important for exposing the power of the Catholic doctrine in claiming the only truth on the topic of non-heterosexuality. Canadian Catholic school systems have their own "regimes of truth," which actively restrict the circulation of any affirming truths about sexual diversity in the schools. I want to deconstruct the Catholic "regime of truth" that casts homosexuality as "an objective disorder" by replacing this message with one that is more balanced and "true." However, a problem arises because, according to Foucault's schema, this new "truth" would also be as equally fictional and constructed as the original one. The new truth being offered would not be exempt from the workings of power/knowledge. Questions of which alternative and affirming version of sexual diversity should be put forth would arise in a complex contest between truth and politics, knowledge and power. Foucault (1980) argues that knowledge is always implicated in power and that the "will to truth" is an inseparable expression of power/knowledge. Note, however, that this concept of the "will to truth" does not mean that any truth is as plausible as any other or that pronouncements of truth claims are altogether arbitrary. The Foucaultian task is to trace how it is that some truths become authorized as *the* truth. Hence, the findings of this study would have to be subjected to a Foucaultian "will to truth" as well.

Since this study is largely informed by a critical world view, it is challenging to incorporate into it the notion that researchers can discover the truth about the world, or that there is some kind of solid truth to uncover in the world. If a kind of truth does exist, according to the theoretical paradigm that informs this study, it is arbitrary and any attempt at validity would be relative to a particular world view. To a certain extent, then, it is almost meaningless to muse about attempting to create a valid or true account of the world in one's research because no single interpretation or explanation can be judged as superior to any other (Lather, 1993). In the Foucaultian tradition, all we really have is an ongoing interchange of different interpretations and "wills to truth."

Regardless of the theories that may inform this study, it appears as though the dominant perspective regarding the notion of validity currently circulating the halls of Western academia is that of "fallibilism" – the belief that attempting to assess the validity of a claim is a useful and productive test of whether the claim accurately represents the social phenomenon it purports to represent (Schwandt, 2007). Fallibilists contend that there are good reasons for accepting an interpretation as more valid than another but are careful to underscore that interpretations are not infallible and are subject to change. Fallibilism does not claim that the world is unknowable; rather, it simply highlights that our knowledge of our world is never absolute and certain. One well-known fallibilist, educational theorist Martyn Hammersley (2007), asserts that scholars can assess the validity of an account by checking whether it is (1) plausible; (2) credible, considering the subject under investigation; and (3) believable, given the circumstances of the research and the characteristics of the researcher. If the plausibility, credibility, or believability are at all in question, then scholars can proceed to scrutinize the trustworthiness of the evidence offered in support of the claim. At a time when there is increased pressure in the academy to serve evidence-based policymaking and practice, there is a renewed challenge to qualitative inquiry, and the arguments Hammersley makes (2008) are becoming increasingly important.

With that in mind, I accept Maxwell's (2005) suggestion that the idea of an "objective truth" is not essential to a theory of validity that a researcher attempts to put in place as a way of establishing the credibility of his or her findings and distinguishing them from those accounts that are not so tenable. As Maxwell (2005) contends, researchers are not required to attain absolute truth for their study to be credible, compelling, and useful. "All we require," maintains Maxwell (2005), "is the possibility of *testing* these accounts against the world, giving the phenomena that we are trying to understand the chance to prove us wrong" (p. 106, emphasis in the original). An important aspect of validity is therefore the validity threat – or the ways in which I might be wrong in my interpretations.

This study is informed by critical theories, which are often at odds with the positivist presumptions of traditional sociological research, but it also attempts to adhere to acceptable standards of qualitative research design. Although these can be difficult tensions to navigate when negotiating issues of validity, Maxwell (2005, p. 105) soothes the matter by assuring qualitative researchers that "validity is a goal rather than a product; it is never something that can be proven or taken for granted. Validity is also relative." Collecting a variety of strong forms of evidence is one way of ruling out threats to a research study's validity.

Maxwell (2005) identifies two relatively common types of validity threats that surface in discussions of qualitative studies: (1) researcher bias and (2) "reflexivity" or "reactivity" – the effect the researcher can have on participants. Given the title of this book, it might be assumed that I had already concluded that Canadian Catholic schools exert power and domination over lgbtq individuals before conducting the study. While this is certainly an overwhelming finding from my previous study, in designing this study I was particularly keen to discover a more positive rival theory that revealed the various ways lgbtq individuals might use their personal agency to effectively resist the doctrinal disciplining instituted by the Vatican. I therefore actively searched for evidence, such as competing explanations and discrepant data, that would be able to challenge findings from my previous study. In this way, this study does not succumb to researcher bias or end up becoming some kind of self-fulfilling prophecy.

In terms of reactivity or reflexivity, Hammersley and Atkinson (1995) have already proven that eliminating the influence of the researcher on participants is impossible. However, as Maxwell (2005) points out, the goal in qualitative research is not to try to eliminate reactivity but to understand it and use it productively. When it came to working with the research participants, I proceeded under the belief that it was important at the outset to establish my credentials as a lesbian who has herself struggled with various Catholic school environments. I did this with a brief introduction of who I am and what the goals of my research project were. This hopefully put at ease participants who might have been accustomed to having to be secretive about their sexuality. A participant who knows she is speaking with someone who understands firsthand her predicament might be more willing to disclose details of her experience. I regard this as a positive consequence.

As Maxwell (2005) makes clear, "validity threats are made implausible by *evidence*, not methods; methods are only a way of getting evidence that can help you rule out these threats" (p. 105, emphasis in the original). Nevertheless, methods and procedures are essential to the process of ruling out validity threats and improving the credibility of the findings. Specifics about the methods of data collection and analysis are found at the beginning of each data chapter. I turn next to a discussion of ethical issues in Chapter 2, as this is the method of data collection that involved the participation of human subjects.

2
Participants: Domination and Resistance

Qualitative researchers Kvale and Brinkmann (2009) insist that good qualitative research requires the investigators who interview human subjects to be transparent about all their methodological procedures for readers to properly evaluate the quality, validity, and transferability of the interview findings. The authors outline seven stages of research interviewing, from the initial conceptualization of the interview project to the final report. One stage they overlook, however, is securing research participants.

Whenever I present on the methodological aspects of this study, conference delegates invariably ask: "Yes, but, how did you find people to interview?" Scholars pose this question because they are aware of the invisible nature of the lgbtq population in general and because they understand that the need for lgbtq individuals to be closeted about their sexuality or gender identity tends to be more pronounced in religious institutions, such as Catholic schools. This is slowly changing, however, as later chapters in this book reveal. Progressive provincial legislation in Ontario and Alberta regarding the establishment of GSAs in *all* schools, for example, make it easier for gender and sexually diverse people to be out in Catholic schools. Nevertheless, some conservative Catholic education leaders continue to find ways to resist such progressive changes in Canadian society, legislation and law, educational policy, and curriculum. In many ways, stepping into a Catholic school under conservative leadership is like entering into a time warp in which time seems to stop or even go backward. Because of this, the experiences of the participants in this study have a timeless quality. Religiously inspired homophobia does indeed hinder the process of finding suitable participants for such a study. I certainly had my difficulties. Below is a qualitative description of the steps, procedures, and decisions I took to secure participants.

Defining the Population

Sexual orientation is a complex construct involving identity, behaviour, and desire (Laumann, Gagnon, Michael, & Michaels, 1994). Educational researchers who examine sexual orientation in educational contexts generally use the acronym LGBTQ because this is the way many sexual minority groups now describe themselves (Baird, 2007). I prefer to use lowercase letters because the initialism is less jarring to read and is less likely, linguistically, to set up the population as an obvious Other.

Within the initialism lgbtq, the terms *lesbian* and *gay* refer to women and men whose main emotional and sexual bonds are with people of the same gender; the term *bisexual* refers to people who are sexually and emotionally attracted to both males and females (Parks, Hughes, & Werkmeister-Rozas, 2009). The term *transgender* or *trans* refers to people whose gender identity or gender expression does not match their assigned gender at birth. Trans people may or may not have had sex-reassignment therapy or surgery, and the term *trans* may also include transvestites (cross-dressers) and intersexuals (those born with a reproductive or sexual anatomy that does not seem to fit the typical definitions of female or male) (Baird, 2007). Gender is "performative" (Butler, 1999, p. 9) – it is something one does – how a person presents to others as a man, a woman, or as a trans person. The concept of *gender identity*, used occasionally throughout this book, refers to an individual's sense of self as a man, woman, or trans person; a person's gender identity may not be the same identity as his or her biological gender. The term *queer* has a rich history that I explored elsewhere (Callaghan, 2007b) and will therefore not go into here, but in contemporary usage, it is a term preferred by those who eschew rigid gender boundaries or sexual identities. For many, the fluidity of the term *queer* can be liberating. One female teacher participant in this study identifies as a *straight ally*, a colloquial expression for a heterosexual person who values sexual diversity, supports lgbtq rights and social movements, and is willing to challenge homophobia and heterosexism on personal and institutional levels.

Some Demographic Details of the Participants

Martin and Meezan (2009) point out that lgbtq populations are particularly vulnerable to exploitation and harm as a result of their participation in a research study because of their marginalized and devalued position in the greater community. For this reason, I do not offer any identifying details of the participants such as their names, the names of their schools, or the names of their cities or towns. Of the 20 participants, 10 are from Alberta and 10 are from Ontario. To protect the privacy of the participants, I indicate only that they live in a town or a city in either northern or southern Alberta or Ontario. There are four participants from northern Ontario (one town, three small cities) and six participants from southern Ontario (all mid-size to large cities). There are five participants from northern Alberta (two towns, two small cities, one large city) and five participants from southern Alberta (all mid-size to large cities).

All the 20 participants who took part in this study are over the age of 18. All have had some experience in a Catholic school in Alberta or Ontario, either as a current or former teacher or as a former student. Students' stories are gathered from 13 recently graduated young people who are over the age of 18. For this study, I define *young people* or *youth* as people between the ages of 18 and 24. The term *student* refers to the young people's role within their Catholic school before graduating. Although they are no longer students at the school, the stories they tell describe a time when they were, hence the term *student*. Likewise, the term *teacher* refers to the seven participants who are faculty members from different Catholic schools throughout Alberta and Ontario, including one teacher assistant, one substitute teacher, four teachers, and one principal.

An important determining factor in selecting a participant for this study had to do with his or her sexual orientation identity and its representativeness on the lgbtq spectrum. Because my pilot study drew primarily upon the experiences of white gay male teachers, I limit their inclusion in this study. Several young, gay, white males contacted me about taking part in the study, but I had to turn some away to ensure that lesbians, bisexuals, and transgender people could also participate. I also wanted to interview more students than teachers since my pilot study involved teachers only.

Of the 20 participants, there are three transgender people: two female-to-male (one a substitute teacher and the other a student) and one male-to-female student. There are eight lesbian participants (five students, two teachers, and one teacher assistant). There are eight gay participants (six students, one teacher, and one principal). One of the female participants is a teacher who no longer teaches in a Catholic school system and identifies as a "straight ally." No bisexuals expressed an interest in participating. Existing research shows "bisexuals display patterns that are unique" (Rodriguez Rust, 2009, p. 124) and do not necessarily identify as bisexual or identify with lgbtq issues, which could account for the difficulty in reaching this population.

In terms of race and ethnicity, the majority of participants identify as white or Caucasian of European origin (English, Irish, Scottish, German, Dutch, French, and Italian). Only five participants identify as non-white (three Southeast Asian, two Metis). Wheeler (2009) posits three reasons for the low representation of non-white participants in lgbtq studies: (1) there is a social stigma associated with lgbtq issues in non-white communities, (2) researchers have not gained the trust of non-white communities, and (3) researchers examining lgbtq topics consider sexual orientation identity to be more important than racial identity. I knew it was going to be difficult to find lgbtq Catholic participants in general, including those 18 to 24, so I did not want to further complicate recruitment by specifying a percentage of non-white participants. I did, however, ensure that anyone who identifies as non-white and contacted me with an interest in participating in my study was included in the project.

Another inclusion factor involved the willingness of participants to share details about the intersections between their sexuality and their Catholic school experience. This is significant given that lgbtq individuals are not always open about their sexuality, especially in faith-based communities where discrimination along moral lines is more prevalent than in secular settings. Having participants who are more comfortable with their sexuality and therefore more forthcoming with reflections on their experiences resulted not only in more robust stories but, more importantly, in less stress for the participants. I tested potential participants' willingness to divulge details about their experiences in a Catholic school with a few screening questions posed in e-mail or Facebook messages. All participants had a lot to say about being a gender or sexually diverse person in a repressive school setting.

In preparation for the interviews, I drafted questions in advance and used them to guide the conversations with case study participants (see the appendix for the interview questions). The in-depth qualitative interviews (Denzin & Lincoln, 2005; Maxwell, 2005; Merriam, 1998; Stake, 1995; Yin, 2009) explored how purposefully selected participants (Patton, 2002) perceived and experienced Catholic educational policies, curricula, and practice and how their perceptions fit with their knowledge of *Charter* advances for non-heterosexuals in Canada. That is, if participants' equality rights were being violated, it was important to determine how aware participants were of this violation. The interview questions focus upon educational policies and curricular issues pertaining to gender and sexual minorities in Canadian Catholic schools. The semi-structured interview questions flow from the research questions that direct the study and are crafted with a view towards uncovering how power operates in Canadian Catholic schools.

I invited research participants to answer questions to (1) develop a description of their personal experiences in Catholic schools, (2) discover their awareness of non-heterosexual related curriculum and policy currently being implemented in Catholic schools, and (3) assess their personal safety and general well-being in Catholic schools. Semi-structured questions helped guide the interviews without constricting the participants' responses. To ensure consistency, the interview questions were the same for each interview. Of course, room was also made for variation and flexibility to properly explore any issues that arose during an interview.

Of the 20 participants, 18 were interviewed over the telephone once for 45 minutes to an hour on average. The other two participants chose to have their interview with me in writing via e-mail and Facebook. All telephone interviews were digitally recorded and transcribed verbatim (Maxwell, 2005). The participants' experiences that I retell using the method of narrative inquiry (Chase, 2005; Clandinin & Connelly, 2000; Van Maanen, 1988) are the most illustrative and potentially illuminating. As Krathwohl and Smith (2005) make clear, "the key to qualitative sampling is choosing those cases from which one can learn the most" (p. 128).

Narrative inquiry is well suited as a linguistic form for expressing human lived experience (Ricoeur, 1986/1991). In this study, narrative inquiry is a powerful way of illustrating the effects of Catholic Church doctrine on Canadian lgbtq students and teachers.

The Narrative Inquiry Method of Analysis

In this book, I have chosen to focus on the pattern of how power operates on a day-to-day, personal basis in and around Canadian Catholic schools. To understand the pattern, I have also drawn on media accounts reporting on homophobia in Canadian Catholic schools and Catholic documents that instruct teachers and administrators in these schools on how to deal with lgbtq-related situations, students, and personnel.

Narrative vignettes are the tools life-narrative researchers use to transform educational practice and contribute to theory building (Chase, 2005; Clandinin & Connelly, 2000; Ellis & Bochner, 1996). From what I have witnessed in school settings and in education conferences, authentic transformation of oppressive educational policy and practice begins with sharing schooling experiences. Stories have an invitational quality that can help to establish empathy. Empathy opens up space for discussion and can lead to positive change. Some of the most effective anti-oppressive educational conferences I have attended involve personal testimonials, especially from members of marginalized groups whose experiences with oppressive educational contexts are not widely known.

One particularly transformative conference involved the use of dramatic skits designed following a theatre technique called Theatre of the Oppressed developed by Brazilian theatre director and intellectual Augusto Boal in the 1960s. Boal's (1974/1979) method involves enacting everyday challenges faced by ordinary people and acting out new, creative, and non-violent ways of confronting these challenges. Skits set in the homophobic environment of a Catholic school enabled audience members to learn to recognize homophobia and find ways to stop it (Callaghan, 2007c). Participants were able to take what they learned from the Theatre of the Oppressed techniques back to their school settings and begin their own practice of anti-homophobia education. Through sharing stories and acting out skits, conference attendees learned the theory that, like drama, our social reality is constructed and can be reconstructed (Conrad, 2005).

From my experiences with real-life enactments of Boal's Theatre of the Oppressed techniques to develop anti-homophobia activism in Canadian Catholic schools, I recognized that the basic building block of these powerfully transformative skits was the personal story. Stories have the power to invite readers to reflect on moral complexities in a much more transformative way than traditional forms of argument. Data on their own do not tell stories; it is the task of the narrative inquirer to draw meaningful stories out of the data and re-present them in a way that holds readers' interest. If a narrative inquirer can draw in readers with an interesting story, he or she has a better chance at engendering the empathy that is so necessary for social change.

Narrative inquirers analyse interview transcripts more holistically by reading them several times to get a sense of the most striking and important elements they must then re-presented in writing by using the brief form of the narrative vignette (Chase, 2005; Clandinin & Connelly, 2000). The narrative is a research text that represents the product of the analysis.

Sociologist and narrative inquirer Susan E. Chase (2005, p. 663) describes the process of analysis in narrative inquiry as follows: "When it comes to interpreting narratives heard during interviews, narrative researchers begin with narrators' voices and stories, thereby extending the narrator-listener relationship and the active work of listening into the interpretive process." Chase (2005, p. 663) underscores that the interpretive process of narrative inquiry is "a move away from a traditional theme-oriented method of analyzing qualitative material." It is therefore typical not to find themes in narrative analysis. Though the process of narrative analysis is not fully definable in terms of procedure, it is no less empirical than the process of coding. I chose narrative inquiry over the more traditional qualitative process of coding because I wanted readers to get a sense of the people in this study.

Mulholland and Wallace (2003) organize their quality criteria for qualitative research into three similar categories: (1) strength, (2) sharing, and (3) service. Strength refers to the requirement that research must be conducted in ways that provide evidence of thoroughness and integrity. Sharing refers to the presentation of the research in a way that enables the reader to experience vicariously the world of the participant and become convinced of the study's claims. Service refers to the usefulness of the study; that is, the ways in which the field of education is enhanced because the study was able to "expand perception and enlarge understanding" (Eisner, 1991, p. 114) of a particular aspect of educational practice.

In terms of secondary writing such as conference papers, journal articles, or book chapters that feature a retelling of participants' stories in the form of narrative vignettes, narrative researchers recognize that, as the research process moves from the field itself (interviews) to field texts (transcripts) and then to secondary texts (narrative vignettes), contact with the participants is reduced and the researcher becomes more concerned with weaving together a plausible and engaging account than with constant consultation with participants (Clandinin & Connelly, 1994; Polkinghorne, 1995; Wallace & Louden, 2000). Within the field of narrative inquiry, questions of ownership and voice are of prime importance and are situated within the postmodern debate about the nature of knowledge and truth, authority and power (Britzman, 1991; Brodkey, 1987; Lather, 1991). As Wallace and Louden (2000) point out, early examples of narrative inquiry stressed the importance of arriving at a shared meaning between researcher and research participant in some research texts, but their experiences as narrative inquirers have uncovered that shared meanings are possible only when there is close philosophical agreement between individuals.

I recognize that the participants' stories, which I constructed from the transcriptions of my interviews with them, may not be the stories that they would have told about themselves. The ethical decisions I made in terms of which details to stress and which to overlook are in keeping with the overarching theme of emancipatory research, which was communicated to the participants at the beginning of the study through a process of relational ethics. In retelling the participants' experiences in the following narrative vignettes, I sought details that pointed not only to examples of homophobia within the school setting but also to any possible resistance to this form of discrimination. Length limits were important in a qualitative study involving 20 participants, as the research problem needed to be revealed through the retelling of the participants' stories without being overwhelming.

The emancipatory paradigm directing this study is the guide I used to determine which details from the participants' interviews to include and which to discard. I sought asides and anecdotes participants told that described the problem of being non-heterosexual in a heterosexist and homophobic institution. I also sought descriptions of how participants coped with their situations, paying particular attention to acts of resistance and attempts at leadership. Since my previous study involved the experiences of lgbtq teachers in Catholic schools, I wanted to give more space to the experiences of the students in this study. I determined which details to stress and which to overlook by reading and rereading each transcript, searching for the most meaningful narratives that would be in keeping with the goals of this study. I excluded parts that involved descriptions of homophobia or transphobia that occurred outside the school setting, details about colleagues or peers, partners or families, and particulars having to do with legal action. These were excluded primarily because they are details that could potentially reveal the identity of the participant and secondarily because they took place outside the principal focus of this study – the Catholic school.

In each of the following narrative vignettes, all real names of participants are replaced by pseudonyms. During preliminary discussions with potential participants, I suggested they could choose their own pseudonyms. None did, so I selected Biblical names that had some resonance with the participants' actual names, suggested them to the participants, and invited them to choose other Biblical names, if they wanted. Each participant accepted the name I suggested. Details about the participants' home and workplaces are obscured by generalities. Participants' regular habits, such as their usual teaching assignment, volunteer commitments, or leisure activities, are changed so that they are less identifiable and the participants' confidentiality is better maintained.

Throughout the narratives, segments of text in quotation marks are verbatim quotations from participants in the telephone interview or in an e-mail or a Facebook message. Occasionally, I use quotation marks in the narrative vignettes to introduce a word that I am using as an ironic comment, as in use of the word "roommate" to describe a romantic partner, for example. I also use quotation marks to introduce an invented expression such as the "Positive Space" campaign. Detail in the context of the sentence will enable readers to discern if the text in quotation marks is from a participant or is being used to introduce an ironic comment or an invented expression.

The remainder of this chapter presents six teacher vignettes followed by 12 student vignettes. Further analysis of the narratives in terms of their meaning can be found in Chapter 5, which attempts to theoretically explain and develop a more abstract understanding of the phenomenon of religiously inspired homophobia in Canadian Catholic schools.

Narrative Vignettes

Teachers

MARK

Teaching since the mid-1990s, Mark is now a principal of a Catholic elementary school in Alberta. He wears his wedding band on his right hand. A gay man who loves to throw parties and entertain friends, he was thrilled with the invitation to host the staff beer and barbecue at his home – for a nanosecond. His new vice principal and secretary were standing before him, smiling and nodding while he quickly evaluated the situation and remembered that his partner, John, could not be part of the equation. *John will have to go away on a business trip,* he thought, and *I'll have to put away all of our wedding photos, make sure there's only one bathrobe hanging on the back of the bathroom door, get rid of all the shoes in the front entranceway. Basically, I'll have to de-gay the house. Do a major sweep.* He wondered if he could buy some more time from the vice principal and secretary by asking if he could get back to them the next day. Deciding they would be suspicious of this, he smiled his best fake smile and said: "Well, sure! I'd love to!"

Mark notes experiences vary among the dozens of other lgbtq colleagues he is aware of, whom he refers to as "terrorist cells" because of their tendency to isolate themselves from one another. Mark marvels at one teacher assistant he used to work with who he says is "genetically male" but presented as female every day at school. This teacher assistant wore his long hair in a ponytail, accessorized with earrings and bangles, and would occasionally "reach inside the shoulder of his shirt and pull up his bra strap." Mark observed that "the kids would call him 'Mr' and his first name," but not all parents and staff seemed to realize that the woman they were interacting with was biologically male.

This kind of acceptance and tolerance were not available to Mark, nor to one of Mark's gay friends who taught grade 1. According to Mark, this young teacher was "flamboyantly gay" and he unfortunately became a bit of a target by keeping his Pride sticker on his car and by revealing too many details about his personal life to colleagues. Everyone knew the grade 1 teacher was gay, and his principal used that knowledge to intimidate and blackmail him. Eventually, the teacher felt forced to resign. He got the last word, however, when he came back to the school to clean out his classroom wearing a t-shirt that said: "That's 'Mr Fag' to you!"

But back to Mark. As a leader in the school, Mark knows he is being closely watched and heavily scrutinized. Once, during a parent council meeting, a parent suggested that, as the principal, Mark should be the one to say grace at the graduation banquet. Another parent disagreed saying it was not appropriate because it was common knowledge that Mark was married to a man. When this was later recounted to Mark, he remembers thinking: *OK, is this going to be it? Is this going to be the hill that I die on?*

Mark describes himself as an excellent colleague who has out of necessity become a great listener and knows exactly when to block a line of conversation from getting too personal. He says: "You go back to something safer, or else you go: 'Wow! I've got to be on supervision!'" He is nervous, though, about a weekend leadership retreat he will have to attend later in the year that involves bunking in a room with another principal for two nights. To assuage his anxiety, he is already strategizing how he will pull off this 48-hour acting job. "I won't be the one closing down the bar," he says, "I'll plan my exits well." He already has his icebreaker games ready for the trip and he's doing everything he can to make sure this retreat won't be "the hill he dies on."

LUKE

Luke has been teaching English in a Catholic high school in Ontario since the mid-1990s. He is more relaxed now about the conflict between his homosexuality and his workplace than he was in his first few years of teaching. "My first year of teaching," Luke remembers, "I was completely naive." Like many beginning teachers who are lgbtq, Luke assumed there would be no problem with his sexuality at school, even at a Catholic school, because he was able to be out in every other sphere of his life. Plus he thought, *This is Canada, after all, right?* In his first year, Luke volunteered to help out with the school play, and on opening night he brought his partner, Anthony. From the moment they entered the school, Luke sensed he was going to have to hide their relationship.

He has not brought Anthony to any school function since because he is too worried people will realize they are partners and he will be fired for living outside of Catholicity. It is not that he is completely in the closet. He has been able to be out to some of his colleagues. His "nightmare scenario" is that one of his teacher friends may let something slip about his gayness when speaking with members of the administration. This is what he calls his "Oh, God. This is the day I'm going to be fired" nightmare. Luke knows this is a very real fear because of the Catholicity clause in teachers' employment contracts requiring them to uphold Catholic doctrine – a clause that has been successfully used in Alberta and Ontario to get rid of gay teachers who live with their partners.

Luke knows he can only control himself, not others. When he had to teach the homophobic human sexuality component of religion class, he knew he would not be able to do it, so he called in sick that day. Likewise, when the school chaplain wanted to engage the whole school in a public Catholic procession to the nearby church for the first of many school Catholic Masses (which involves getting students to carry Catholic banners and walk reverently to the church) Luke also called in sick. He feels guilty about this, though, because he sees himself as letting down the lgbtq students in the school who cannot so easily absent themselves from homophobic curriculum or activities because they do not have the benefit of knowing what is on the schedule.

To make up for this, Luke encourages student influences on curriculum. For example, during a unit about diverse marriage in the course Anthropology, Psychology and Sociology, some of his students asked to do a project on same-sex marriage and Luke did not object or give them the usual Catholic rationale as to why it would be offensive in a Catholic school. Instead, he let the students do their presentation in front of the class and he later put their poster about it up on the multi-use classroom wall.

Luke also spars with school administrators over their indoctrinating methods. One of his greatest outlets for expressing his sense of human rights activism was the student Amnesty International club. Bishops informed Catholic schools throughout Ontario that Amnesty International was at odds with the Vatican on the topic of abortion and therefore could no longer operate in Catholic schools. Luke strenuously protested the removal but to no avail. Similarly, during a recent provincial election in Ontario, the school chaplain sent out e-mails to all faculty urging them not to vote for the Green Party because they support abortion. Luke met with the principal to point out the blatant misuse of the chaplain's leadership role within the workplace to try to influence voting, but the principal disagreed with Luke and said she saw no problem with the chaplain's e-mail.

Luke is certain that his increasing boldness regarding the injustice he sees around him is making him a more authentic classroom teacher and, for him, that is what counts.

JOB

Job is a government-certified substitute teacher who taught for approximately a half year with a Catholic district in rural Alberta before getting fired in 2008 because he said he was transitioning from female to male. The process of transitioning is a very lengthy one, and Job identified as female for the majority of his time with the Catholic school board. Given the rhythms of the school year, Job decided it would be best to inform his school board of his medical condition in the summer so that the board would have some time to adjust to the change before his return to work in the fall.

Receiving no reaction, Job was back on the substitute list in September. Competent and reliable, Job is a substitute teacher in high demand. His first week of work was so packed with assignments, there were many he had to turn down. On the Friday of his first week, Job received an unusual call from the district deputy superintendent informing him that the district had taken the matter of his gender reassignment before the archbishop of the diocese. Together, they decided Job's decision to change his gender was incompatible with Church teachings, and so he would be relieved of his duties, effective immediately.

Job's request to have the notice of his termination in writing was met with surprise and resistance. When Job explained that Alberta Welfare Assistance would require some kind of proof as to why a fully qualified teacher was suddenly not working, the district deputy superintendent reluctantly produced a letter. "The teaching of the Catholic Church is that persons cannot change their gender," the letter states. "One's gender is considered what God created us to be." It elaborates further: "Since you made a personal choice to change your gender, which is contrary to Catholic teachings, we have had to remove you from the substitute teacher list. Your gender change is not aligned with the teachings of the

Church and would create confusion and complexity with students and parents" (personal communication, October 14, 2008).

The trouble is, as Job argued in his case that was heard by the Alberta Human Rights Tribunal, no Catholic doctrine exists on transgenderism or on gender reassignment. To complicate matters, as a substitute teacher, Job was never asked to sign a continuous contract containing a Catholicity clause. Even if he had signed such a contract, he could not be accused of behaving in a manner contrary to Catholicity because Catholic doctrine does not address transsexuality. Furthermore, Job was hired with the full knowledge that he ascribes to a Christian religion other than Catholicism. It is unreasonable for the Catholic school district to suddenly require that Job uphold purported Catholic doctrine when they hired him knowing he is not Catholic.

Existing beyond objections at the school level are those at the provincial level. The Alberta Teachers' Association's *Declaration of Rights and Responsibilities for Teachers* includes gender identity as a prohibited ground of discrimination for teachers. This professional standard reflects Alberta human rights legislation and the *Canadian Charter of Rights and Freedoms* (1982), both of which protect against discrimination on the basis of sexual orientation or gender identity. Publicly funded Catholic school districts in Alberta have a duty to uphold these common laws. As Job points out, "Catholic boards hire Alberta Teachers' Association teachers, so why should they get some special arrangement that exempts them from contentious parts of operational rules?" Recognizing the blatant discrimination levelled against Job, the ATA was supportive of pursuing his case before the Alberta Human Rights Tribunal. Nevertheless, the matter has devastated Job financially.

NAARAI

A teacher assistant in Catholic community schools in rural Alberta, Naarai's tasks mainly involve tutoring students individually or in small groups to help them master assignments and to reinforce concepts presented by the classroom teacher. Naarai loves working with young people. It is the adults in the building who cause her trouble.

Naarai's first job was in a Catholic high school in 2007. She found she could be herself around the 15- to 17-year-olds; she understood their humour, laughed easily and often around the teens, and established an enviable rapport with them. What she did not realize, though, was that her growing comfort with her work environment meant that she was not on guard for the workplace harassment she was about to encounter.

One of her co-workers started to gather, through conversational details and daily observations, that Naarai is a lesbian who lives with her female partner. During lunch breaks, Naarai's co-worker would expound at length on her disapproval of same-sex marriage and speak in other disparaging ways about homosexuality. Naarai noticed that her co-worker never brought these kinds of topics up around other staff members. Naarai started to get the feeling that her co-worker might somehow blackmail her at work, so she became more guarded about her personal life and called her union for advice. A union representative advised her that, in Canada, people cannot lose their jobs because of their sexual orientation. With this news, Naarai relaxed somewhat. However, when other job opportunities became available within the district, Naarai jumped at the opportunity to take a teacher assistant position at another school.

Not wanting to expend so much energy hiding her life from her colleagues, Naarai made a conscious decision to be open about her sexuality in her new job. She and her partner were contemplating starting a family and Naarai excitedly shared this journey with some of her co-workers. A bond developed between Naarai and her colleagues and they invited her out to the local pub, a regular Friday after school gathering for faculty. Not one for normally socializing with co-workers, Naarai reluctantly agreed. When her partner later came to collect her from the pub, various staff members managed to cajole her into visiting with them for a bit. It was not long before the principal of the school began to grill the couple about their plans to start a family. He claimed the Church would not approve of their constructed family, and they should therefore consider adoption.

On the way home, Naarai and her partner fumed about the audacity of this man telling them how to plan their family. In the months that followed that one-time pub visit, Naarai started to see a fertility specialist and had to book an afternoon off work for an appointment. The day before the appointment, her principal called her into his office and asked, "What is the nature of your medical condition?" Naarai told him it was none of his business, other than that it was female in nature. The principal stood over Naarai, crossed his arms, and said, "I know what is going on with you and your medical condition. I warned you that the Church does not approve of this." Naarai protested that she thought she would be safe, considering that a union representative told her she could not be fired for being a lesbian, the school is publicly funded, and it incorporates Indigenous teachings into its Catholic ethos. He icily responded: "Well, you are not safe and you assumed wrong."

Naarai contacted her union again and they arranged an out-of-court cash settlement in exchange for Naarai's quiet departure from the Catholic system. Nevertheless, Naarai remains devastated by the events.

NAOMI

Naomi and her partner of several years travelled together to a small, northern Ontario town in 2004 so that Naomi could take up her first teaching position in a Catholic elementary school on a contract to replace a teacher on maternity leave. People stared at them a lot and whispered to one another about them while doing so. They were so heavily monitored and scrutinized in the insular, traditional community that they regularly asked themselves: "Are we going to make it? Are we going to survive this?"

Naomi says the town's wrath was directed primarily at her, rather than at her partner, because she was the one who signed on to be a teacher with the Catholic board. Parents of the students she taught were constantly asking her if she was living in a one- or two-bedroom apartment with her "roommate." The suspicion grew so intense that, once when Naomi and her partner were out of town, one of the parents went up onto their back deck to try to get a look into the bedroom window, as Naomi's neighbour reported to her upon her return. When she returned to school the next morning, she heard her colleagues whispering about it in the staffroom.

The staffroom became a dangerous place for Naomi. She felt the teachers started to "gang up" on her, finding ways to interject into conversation the message that "homosexuality is a sin" while staring stonily at her. She says she can still feel the pain of those verbal jabs. She coped by avoiding the staffroom and her colleagues in general. On the brief occasions that Naomi would dash into the staffroom to grab her lunch from the fridge, one teacher colleague, whom Naomi initially read as a lesbian, would stop whatever she was doing to draw attention to Naomi. She would call out from the lounge chairs to Naomi across the room, saying something like: "Hey, Naomi! I think I saw you and your girlfriend at the hockey rink the other day." Usually, Naomi would just ignore her and retreat as quickly as possible.

Naomi learned the hard way that ignoring is the only way to handle tough topics in that district. Earlier in the year, a five-year-old student asked her if it was okay for two men to get married. Naomi said, "Yes, if two people love each other, then they can get married." When the boy's mother heard this, she came to the school the next day and threw a "huge

scene." Naomi's principal called her into his office and told her she was
wrong to say that to the young boy and that the best practice is to just
"ignore" such questions. One of the Catholic district superintendents said
it was board policy to not discuss homosexuality in the schools, and, if students raise the matter, teachers are just to ignore it. If students kept asking
about it, teachers are to tell them that such questions are inappropriate at
school and that disciplinary action would be taken if they persisted.

Naomi's mental state started to deteriorate. She experienced tremendous anxiety and panic attacks. She says, "I felt like people were watching me because they were! I just kept looking over my shoulder and I
started getting all of these physiological symptoms because of the stress."
She would wake up every day and think, *OK, is today the day that all of this
is going to blow up in my face?* The town's hostility increased to drive-by
shouts of "Dyke!" and "Get the hell out of this town!" and culminated in
two occasions in which three men tried to run her off the road while she
was driving. Naomi knew she could not report these attacks to the police
because one of the police officers was a parent of one of her students.

Through counselling in a nearby city, Naomi was able to finish out her
contract. She is now working as a supply teacher outside of the Catholic
system while pursuing graduate studies.

ANNA

Anna identifies as a "straight ally," or a heterosexual person who sym-
pathizes with non-heterosexuals and the social justice movement. Her
teaching career is wide and varied – an avid traveller, she goes where the
work is. In 2003 she landed in southern Alberta and took a temporary
position teaching art at a high school in the local Catholic school board.
Gregarious and charismatic, Anna was a hit with students. She would
always stop and chat with them in the hallways while on her way to class
and students were soon whispering to one another: "If you need to talk,
go check the art teacher. She likes kids and she will listen to you."

Eventually, a dozen or so students started hanging out in the art room
at lunchtime. It was a relaxed, non-structured space in which students
could easily chat with one another, eat their lunch, listen to music, and
draw pictures. Anna says her classroom attracted the "weirdos" and misfits
of the school, or in high school parlance, the "goths," the "emos," the
"hard rockers."

In the lunch club, Anna noticed a handful of lgbtq kids. They had many
questions for her about the contradiction in Catholic doctrine that tells
them it is okay that they are gay as long as they do not act on it. Anna did
her best to help them understand it, but she too was confounded by the

doctrine and felt she did not help much. The local teachers' convention was scheduled for the next week, and Anna made a point of attending workshops about lgbtq students and sexual diversity, even though information about the workshops was purposefully left out of the program for Catholic teachers. Armed with the excellent strategies from the workshops, Anna returned to her little lunch group and informed the lgbtq kids about all the resources available to them in the city. She stuck "Positive Space" and Pride flag stickers on the window of her classroom door.

Within hours of the stickers going up, the sensible-shoe-and-necktie-wearing female principal visited Anna and told her to take them down because they were "in conflict with Catholicity." Anna could not believe these words were coming from this principal, whom everyone in the school believed to be a lesbian. The principal then chastised Anna about her unauthorized lunch club, saying: "We cannot promote the gay lifestyle in a Catholic school. It's against the philosophy of the board and you can get fired for this." Despite the principal's obvious threat, Anna did not take the stickers down. The next morning, however, she found the custodial staff had removed them.

A short time later, tragedy struck. A grade 12 student hanged himself after suffering months of homophobic bullying at the school. The lunch club kids showed up in Anna's room crying and in obvious pain. Drawing on the resources she had gained from the recent lgbtq workshops she attended, Anna asked the students to write in their private journals, to draw their feelings out on paper, and to make a list of deescalating responses to homophobic bullying.

The principal called Anna to her office, ostensibly to discuss how her temporary position was being opened up to district-wide competition for a continuous contract. The principal told Anna she was out of the running because her forbidden lunch club ran contrary to Catholic doctrine, and her future with the board would end with the school year. Anna considered fighting her dismissal through legal channels but eventually chose to see being fired as a new opportunity. She is currently teaching and still strongly advocating for lgbtq youth in another part of the world.

Alberta students

JUDITH

All throughout Judith's kindergarten to grade 12 Catholic school experience, she identified as a straight male. Today, she identifies as a lesbian woman. Presenting as a straight male was a 24-hour acting job for Judith while she attended Catholic school in Southeast Asia and until she graduated from a high school in southern Alberta in 2006. She describes this time as extremely uncomfortable and energy consuming; it was when she had to "put on an acceptable face" for those around her, both at home and at school. Attending Catholic high school in southern Alberta was alienating for Judith, mostly because the gender divide was so strongly pronounced. As someone whose outward appearance was male, Judith was expected to use the male washrooms and locker rooms and take physical education class for boys. Deep inside, though, Judith felt abundantly female. She felt exceedingly out of place in these male-only spaces. According to Judith, the underlying message of the entire school system was "be straight and procreate." It was a confusing time for her; she felt isolated and alone.

One ray of light for Judith was the music teacher. His slim body, slight stature, and expressive hand gestures made him seem feminine to Judith. "He made me feel more comfortable," Judith says. "I recognized some similarities in me when I saw him." She was not at all surprised when she heard the rumour that he was gay. She often wondered if maybe she, too, was gay but she usually concluded that she just wanted to be a woman. It was a deeply confusing conclusion for Judith in her teenage years and many times she just did not know what she was feeling. If it was perplexing for her, she knew it would be exponentially so for her friends. She decided to just keep thoughts about her gender identity to herself.

It did not take long for Judith to discover just how wise this protective instinct was. In her first year at the high school, Judith made friends with another Southeast Asian boy. She was drawn to him because of his lithe movements, long hair, and flamboyant scarves. Even though they never discussed it, shortly after grade 11 midterms, Judith's friend suddenly started coming to school dressed as a female. At first it was just a bit of foundation, then eye makeup and some experimentation with crimping her hair. Finally, one day she arrived at school in high-heeled leather boots, stockings, a black suede skirt, a bra, and a V-neck sweater. The friends they had in common were completely shocked and acted as though they did not know her. When she showed up to first period social studies class, the macho Italian teacher called in the vice principal, and Judith's friend was quickly escorted from the school. She transferred to another Catholic high school within the system and managed to get her diploma by passing as female for her remaining years in high school.

Seeing what happened to her friend made Judith even more convinced that she had to keep acting as a male and not mention her confusion about her gender identity to anyone. Even though she longed to express herself in the brazen manner of her now absent friend, Judith dressed plainly with the objective of blending in with her male peers. She concentrated on her studies, paying particular attention to lessons on human hormones in biology class. Looking back on her high school experience, Judith does not know how she survived it. She wishes there was something in the curriculum about people like her so she would not have had to feel so detached and excluded.

JACOB

Today, Jacob identifies as a queer trans-guy. When he hit puberty while in Catholic school, he knew he liked girls. That is, as a girl who likes girls – a lesbian. He says his transition from female to male was a good fit for him because he went from being a tomboy in primary school, to a butch lesbian in secondary school, to being a man a few years after graduating from high school in 2007. He didn't have to make a conscious decision about coming out because he was so "visibly queer."

These days, Jacob gives back to the queer community by volunteering as a sexual health educator for queer youth groups. He does this primarily because he had such an abysmal experience with the family life programs in Catholic school. He recalls, "The best sex ed class I ever had involved a question and answer box in grade 7." The teacher he had at the time did her best to answer all the questions, including one that said, "How do gay men have sex?" Clearly uncomfortable, she managed to muster a respectful tone and this made 12-year-old Jacob trust her enough to come out to her as a lesbian.

Unfortunately for Jacob, his religion teacher told the principal – a man Jacob knew did not like him very much. "He pulled me into the office," Jacob remembers, "and told me he was going to bring my parents in so I could tell them, which was terrifying. Telling my parents was much scarier than telling random people at my school. So, that went badly." Convinced it was "just a phase," Jacob's parents reacted by sending him to reparative therapy in the hope that he could be counselled into becoming straight. Unbeknownst to his parents, however, for about a year before coming out as a lesbian, Jacob had been getting up at 1:00 in the morning to tune into *Queer as Folk*, the television series about a group of gay men. *Queer as Folk* taught Jacob that "there is nothing wrong with being gay and that you couldn't therapy someone out of being gay," so he was resistant to the reparative therapy.

Another solution his parents came up with was to ban Jacob from watching television, reading the newspaper, or going to the library. Nevertheless,

Jacob found ways to smuggle gay books and DVDs home from the local library. These library materials helped a lot, Jacob says, "because they gave me some idea of at least other people's stories and gave me a concept of what was and what wasn't OK." Seeing that the counselling was not working, Jacob's parents kept switching therapists, and after a while they were no longer as discriminate and inadvertently connected Jacob with a gay therapist. This counsellor told Jacob, "There's nothing wrong with you. Your parents are nuts!" Emboldened by this medical confirmation, at the age of 14 Jacob told his parents, "I'm done with this!"

Six months later, Jacob's parents kicked him out of the house. His staunchly Catholic grandparents were "spectacular" during this time but they did not live in the same municipality, so Jacob got his own place and learned the responsibilities of paying rent at the age of 16. He started working as a sexual health educator for a queer non-profit organization, joined a band, earned a spot on the junior girls' rugby team, and started dating girls. Jacob says he was no "85 lb girl," and was in "pretty good shape." There was no way he could hide his muscular, masculine energy. Everyone knew he was gay, "like, really, really gay." He exuded confidence and vitality.

That's why he felt ready to take on his grade 10 homophobic religion teacher who went on a rant about how she "didn't approve of the gay lifestyle and hoped none of her kids was gay." When Jacob told her he was a lesbian, she warned him to be careful because he was "going to get AIDS and die." The argument escalated to the point of Jacob walking out of class. As he was heading to the principal's office, he heard his name being called over the public address system to report to the counselling office. He demanded to see the principal, though, because he "knew there was no reason any student should have to put up with this crap." He and the principal worked out an arrangement that allowed him to take the rest of his required religion courses by correspondence.

Jacob is convinced that his tough demeanour spared him from encountering any physical violence in high school, but he was "terrified" by its ever-present threat anyway. He experienced a lot of verbal harassment, being called "dyke" and being subjected to obscene hand gestures and jokes about cunnilingus. He found "the faster you get up in their face and make it known that's inappropriate," the sooner the bullies backed down. Jacob employed street smarts in high school: he didn't set himself up to be in dangerous situations, he didn't drink alcohol, he didn't hang out with groups of people around whom he felt unsafe, and, most of all, he "didn't act like a victim."

Jacob knows that what worked for him may not work for other queer kids who are being harassed in school. He suggests people in this situation should find someone in authority they can trust and tell them about it. He stresses that queer kids suffering from bullying have to be "really, really smart" about who they approach for help in a Catholic school. Jacob and his friends tried to start a GSA, but every time they tried, the administration would find another reason to refuse them. Jacob feels GSAs are vital because it is the "kids who are going to save the kids" from homophobic bullying in Catholic schools. In Jacob's experience, Catholic school principals, counsellors, and teachers do not seem to have the capacity for change.

CALEB

Caleb saw being admitted to an Alberta university hospital at the beginning of the school year in 2008 as an amazing stroke of luck. Not only because he would be getting the help he needed for his self-harming issues but also because he could finally get a break from those who were tormenting him at his Catholic K–12 school.

Growing up in his small town in northern Alberta, Caleb quickly learned to hide the fact that he was gay. He tried to "butch it up" by wearing western-style clothes, complete with a cowboy hat and boots. His classmates assumed he was gay anyway, though, because of his jewellery and his soft-spoken manner. His peers would mutter "faggot" under their breath as they passed him in the school hallways on a daily basis, and he would get called "Brokeback Mountain" whenever he wore his cowboy hat to school. Caleb started dating one of his many female friends thinking this would throw his bullies off, but the taunts only got more vicious. The rumour "Caleb's gay! He's only dating that girl for a cover!" circulated around the school.

The harassment reached the point where Caleb became "horrified" to walk down the school halls. The teasing and name-calling pierced him so deeply that he became depressed and lost his "fighter instinct." He would cope by trying to make himself physically smaller. He thought, *They can call me whatever they want, but so long as I am this weight, so long as I look this way, it won't hurt me too bad.* Caleb went to see the school counsellor about his growing eating disorder, but she did not believe he had a problem because, the way she saw it, eating disorders only affected girls. Caleb knew he needed help, so he went back to the school counsellor again and said, "I think I might be gay." She responded by saying, "Well, you don't want to tell *that* to anyone in this town."

A few months later, the school principal brought some Catholic youth ministers into the school to speak to the students. All the boys in the school went into one room while all the girls went into another. The focus of their presentation was "homosexuality is a sin" and the teachings of the Catholic Church around homosexuality. Shortly after that, Caleb started cutting himself. His only reprieve was when he was sent to the hospital.

After his second month in treatment, Caleb started to trust the doctors and nurses enough to come out to them. He learned that the stress of having to hide his authentic self in such a homophobic school climate was part of what triggered his self-harming behaviours. Part of his year-long treatment involved visualizing his future life and building confidence. He kept these skills with him when he got out of treatment and moved in with a relative in a different small town in northern Alberta.

He enrolled in a new Catholic school and started volunteering with an on-site daycare program and also as an assistant in a junior high classroom. It did not take long for Caleb to come out to a few trusted adults. Their acceptance of his difference was a welcome and unexpected surprise. Similarly, Caleb received no harassment from the student body. He attributes this to a major shift in his own attitude. He had found his "fighter instinct" again and started off his new school year believing "This is who I am and I am not going to change it, even if you don't like me."

As a volunteer, Caleb shared the power of positive thinking and creative visualization with younger students who seemed lost. He knows from his own hard experiences that it does get better. He also knows that he needed a lot of help in visualizing a better life because he is certain he probably would not have survived on his own. He plans to continue helping young people by becoming a teacher.

SIMON

Simon attended Catholic schools in northern Alberta from kindergarten until he graduated in 2010. He cannot remember when he first realized he was gay, but he definitely remembers his first boyfriend in junior high who was about three years his senior. He could not resist telling his best girlfriend about him at the beginning of grade 9. She came from a conservative, staunch Catholic family, and Simon was worried about how she would react. To his tremendous relief, she was very accepting. Emboldened by this, Simon told a couple more of his close friends with whom he had been going to school since kindergarten. When they both responded positively, Simon relaxed and returned to his usual fun-filled junior high antics.

At Simon's junior high, the assistant principal also functioned as the school counsellor. He was a highly respected and well-liked teacher and counsellor. Simon got to know him pretty well during his first two years at the junior high school, mostly by telling him jokes. One day, when the assistant principal was on supervision duty, Simon approached him to ask him for advice about how to come out to his parents. The assistant principal asked Simon if he would prefer to have this discussion behind closed doors in his office and Simon said yes. They scheduled an appointment for after school that day.

After Simon arrived in the counselling office, the assistant principal closed the door and said, "Actually, Simon, I'm glad you came to me today to ask about this because I've been meaning to speak to you about your behaviour lately. You see, Simon, I've been getting some comments from parents. They're telling me that they don't like their children being around you. Some staff members have also mentioned to me that your behaviour has to be reined in." Shocked, Simon responded, "Are you serious?" The assistant principal assured Simon that he was and said, "I'm afraid something might have to be done if this continues. You see, we don't recognize the homosexual lifestyle in the Catholic school system," and then he started laughing with nervousness. Simon did not know how to respond, so he returned to the original question about coming out to his parents. The assistant principal composed himself enough to remark offhandedly, "Well, I just say go full out and tell them." Simon thanked him and left.

All the way home, Simon thought about what the counsellor had just said to him. *Why would some parents not want me around their kids?* he wondered. He also could not imagine what behaviour of his was any different than usual. He felt terribly valueless, like he was "not worth the time to be on the planet." He called his boyfriend, who immediately came over, sat him down and said, "OK, here's what you have to do. You have to tell your parents about it. I'll be here for you." With that, he left and Simon went upstairs to tell his parents that he was gay.

His parents broke down in tears, experiencing shock and disbelief. Then, when Simon told them about how he was treated by the school counsellor that day, they became incensed. "We love you and support you no matter what happens," they assured him. Simon remembers the day he came out to his parents as one of the most positive days of his life. The next morning, Simon's mother came with him into the school, and together the two of them went to the assistant principal's office. Simon's mother lowered her voice to an even, flat tone, "You ever do that again," she said, "I'll have a lawsuit so far up your ass, you won't be able to find it!"

Simon is glad he had this experience in junior high because it prepared him for "the world of high school where some people were so cruel." He was called "fag" a lot and was subjected to cyberbullying, but it did not bother him as much as it could have because he knew his parents loved him and he had some supportive friends. He knows, too, that not all teachers are like his junior high counsellor. He says three of his Catholic schoolteachers were accepting of sexual diversity and willing to talk about it. He noticed a significant change, though, when Bill 44 came into effect in 2009 requiring all schools in Alberta to notify parents in writing in advance of addressing the topics of religion, human sexuality, and sexual orientation in the classroom. Those three open-minded teachers Simon appreciated and respected started to say, "Sorry, I can't discuss that here," whenever students would ask why the Catholic Church is so opposed to homosexuality.

Simon was disappointed by this, but he made up for the gaps in his education by attending queer youth groups and camps and learning about lgbtq history such as the Stonewall Riots and famous lgbtq people such as Harvey Milk. He also used the Internet to explore human rights and social justice issues and closely followed media accounts of lgbtq youths who were discriminated against by their schools. Simon made several attempts to start up a GSA in his school, but each was "shot down." Nevertheless, he did manage to be a mentor to younger gay youth in the school who approached him about being gay and coming out. His hope is that GSAs will finally be allowed in Catholic schools so that this important mentoring can continue consistently.

MARY

Mary attended publicly funded Catholic schools in southern Alberta from kindergarten until her graduation in 2007. She started to realize she liked girls in junior high. In grade 8, Mary was lucky enough to find herself in the same English language arts class with a group of her friends. In one unit, the teacher was trying to underscore the importance of empathy in appreciating literature. She asked the students to take part in a weeklong project, which involved creatively imagining themselves as a member of a subordinate group, such as a person of colour, a differently abled individual, or someone belonging to a religious minority.

Mary and her friends approached their language arts teacher to inquire about the possibility of exploring what it is like to be a member of a sexual minority group, such as a lesbian, gay, bisexual, transgender, or queer person. They suggested they could readily experience this

difference by wearing rainbow wristbands and other recognizable symbols of lgbtq Pride. The teacher told them they would not be allowed to
do that because they were in a Catholic school, and Catholic schools do
not recognize sexual minorities. When the students pressed for a better explanation, the teacher switched to a different line of reasoning
and told them it was for their own safety because if they came to school
dressed like lgbtq people, they would "get beat up" by other students.
Mary tried to talk to the teacher about it later to understand further what
the problem was, but the teacher offered her only insubstantial explanations that made no sense. Frustrated, Mary dropped her request.

Mary also encountered opposition in her grade 7 physical education
class, which doubled as her health class. At the time, Canadians were
in the midst of debating same-sex marriage and Mary's phys ed teacher
took it upon herself to address the topic during a lesson on family life.
Conceding that "gay people are people too," the phys ed teacher nevertheless emphasized that they "shouldn't have the same rights as heterosexuals because marriage is a sacred vow and what homosexuals do
is wrong." Mary was not surprised by this because her gym teacher was
also very conservative about gender roles, specifically regarding two units
on gymnastics and wrestling. The girls knew the boys were taking up
wrestling at the same time that the girls were meant to do gymnastics,
and Mary and a handful of her friends asked the gym teacher if they
could do wrestling instead. The phys ed teacher told them they could
not choose wrestling, as that was for boys only. When the girls protested,
the exasperated teacher took away the gymnastics option and replaced
it with floor hockey.

When Mary got to high school, she found that the family life component of her religion class was not any more sophisticated than the junior
high version. She remembers receiving only 20 minutes of instruction on
this topic in the entire course. The focus was on abstinence and procreation, and Mary remembers specifically being told that "condoms are not
good because they are a contraceptive." She also recalls a time when one
of her classmates tentatively asked about homosexuality and, although
she does not remember the details of what the teacher actually said in
response, she does recall that the subject was tidily "turned into something else." The message Mary got from that exchange is that the subject
is taboo in a Catholic school.

Nevertheless, Mary could not ignore the way she was feeling about
other girls and she plucked up the courage to go in to see one of the
school counsellors to get advice about coming out as a lesbian. Rather

than attending to the immediate concern Mary raised by providing her with helpful information and resources designed for lgbtq youth, the school counsellor chose to tell Mary a story about how her son cross-dressed. Mary felt cheated that the counsellor was not taking her question seriously enough; it was certainly a serious matter to her. She felt the counselling services in her Catholic school "were not actually there" and that they were not "fulfilling the job requirements." Deciding she could no longer trust the services that were supposed to be in place to help her, Mary turned to one of her bisexual friends for advice.

This was how Mary first learned of a local support group for lgbtq youth. She had "no idea that a youth group even existed or to even search for one." Delighted in her discovery of the group, Mary started going right away and benefited immediately from the camaraderie of peer support. She also learned a great deal from guest speakers from various local agencies who came in to talk with the youth about queer history, healthy relationships, and emotional and psychological well-being. It was at the youth group that Mary first encountered comprehensive sexual health education. She remembers the stark contrast to the family life education she was also receiving in religion classes at her Catholic high school during the same period. Mary told her queer friends at school about the youth group, and many of them also started attending.

The youth group was a tremendous boost to Mary's self-confidence. She started dating girls at school and, together with a group of friends, tried to get a GSA started at the school. She was not too surprised when the teacher they approached immediately "skewered" the idea. She feels she was lucky to have learned about the lgbtq youth group from a friend and contends that counsellors in Catholic schools should not be allowed to withhold this lifeline from lgbtq youth who so desperately need it.

ESTHER

Growing up in a small town in northern Alberta, Esther attended two Catholic schools: one from kindergarten to grade 8 and the other until she graduated in 2010. She says in elementary school her classmates thought she was "weird" and she was teased a lot for being different. When she got a short haircut to begin her new high school life, the teasing turned to homophobic slurs. She was called "dyke" and "faggot" constantly from grade 9 to grade 11. The only reprieve from the homophobic bullying came when she entered grade 12, which Esther believes is simply due to the fact she was in her senior year and at the top of the school hierarchy.

It is not that Esther did not try to get help for the bullying. Shortly after arriving at the high school, she told the vice principal that some girls kept calling her a "dyke." He told her he would speak to the people involved, but Esther doesn't know if he ever did because "nothing ever changed." She got through that year by mostly ignoring the perpetrators. When school started up again in grade 10, so did the bullying. Esther continued to try to ignore it, but there were times when she got "really mad" about it. Once, for example, Esther was sitting in chemistry class and the teacher was explaining how two bonds come together like "a male and a female bond." One of her bullies was in the class and she and some of her friends turned around and glared at Esther saying, "Yeah, like a *normal* male-female bond, dyke!" Esther spoke to the principal about the incident, but she never saw any evidence of him doing anything about it.

The final straw for Esther came in grade 11 in an incident on the school bus. It was the end of the school day and Esther was sitting in the front of the bus with a female friend who was not her girlfriend (Esther did not have a girlfriend while in high school). Esther's friend was somewhat tired and started to lean into Esther's side. Esther responded by putting her arm around her friend. Immediately the yellow bus erupted in laughter and jeers of "look at the lezzies at the front of the bus making out!" Then the students on the bus started throwing things like apple cores and juice boxes at the two of them. There were no adults on the bus, except the bus driver who did not do anything about the bullying. In fact, when Ester and her friend went to get off the bus, the driver turned to them and said, "If you guys do that again, I'll kick you off the bus!" Astounded that they were being blamed for their own victimization, Esther and her friend filed a complaint against the driver, first with the bus company, then with the school.

This time when Esther spoke to the principal about homophobic bullying, he seemed to take it more seriously because an adult employed by the school board was involved who further victimized the students by blaming them for the bullying. The principal promised Esther he would talk to the bus driver but Esther does not know what happened because he never updated her. The principal then referred Esther to the school counsellor, who Esther found to be ill-suited to the task. "She wasn't the greatest counsellor," Esther said, "no one really talked to her about anything, and it was super hard trying to talk to her about this. She just didn't seem like the counselling type." Fortunately for Esther, the counsellor recognized her own limitations and called upon the town's human rights coordinator for guidance.

As an outsider, the human rights coordinator was not steeped in the Catholic school ethos. She made suggestions to the school counsellor that no one in the school system would ever dream of doing. In discussions with the school counsellor, the town's human rights coordinator learned that Esther had been experiencing homophobic bullying since she arrived at the school and had reported it to the vice principal and the principal to no avail. The human rights coordinator determined that the school climate was systemically homophobic and if the school administrators were not going to actively make the school safe for lgbtq youth, then one more subtle way to increase these vulnerable youths' perception of safety was by purchasing lgbtq-affirming books for the school library. Consulting with librarians from the town's public library system, the human rights coordinator presented the Catholic school counsellor with 20 titles of age-appropriate books that the Catholic school library should purchase for the school as a way of enabling lgbtq youth in the school to learn about themselves and feel less isolated in such a homophobic environment. Having no alternative solutions of her own, the Catholic school counsellor quietly purchased the books for the library. Esther knew the books were on their way to the school, so she regularly checked in with the school library to see if they had arrived. She was pleasantly surprised one day to find they had not only arrived but were on full display on the tops of bookshelves.

Another welcomed surprise came in the form of a GSA. As much as the town's human rights coordinator tried to convince the Catholic school to allow Esther and her friends to start a GSA, the school administrators were adamantly opposed to the idea. They finally compromised by saying Esther could start a GSA as long as it was not on school property. The town's human rights coordinator found a space for the GSA in the basement of the town's public library, and she convinced the Catholic school counsellor to display postcards advertising the GSA in the counselling office. While these are major victories for Esther, she wishes teachers and students could be better educated about the plight of sexual minority groups in Catholic schools.

Ontario students

GABRIEL

Gabriel attended two Catholic schools in southern Ontario: an elementary and middle school from grade 1 to grade 8 and an all-boys' school until he graduated in 2007. "I already came to terms with my homosexuality in middle school," Gabriel says, "and I wasn't in denial about it by the time

I entered high school." Accepting his sexuality to himself was one thing; being open about it in his all-boys' high school was something else entirely. Catholic schools often stress the importance of developing a strong mind and body, and this was especially true in Gabriel's high school, where physical fitness and athleticism reigned supreme. "There was a lot of testosterone at my school," Gabriel notes, "and it was not an environment conducive to being open to things like homosexuality. So, I really didn't want to go through the stress of being out in that kind of environment."

Gabriel played on various sports teams, but he always avoided the dominant sports like hockey and football. Sometimes, when badminton practice would end at the same time as hockey, he would overhear the hockey players uttering ferocious homophobic slurs in the locker room. Times like these reassured him that he had made the right decision to keep quiet about his homosexuality at school.

This decision was also reinforced whenever Gabriel attended a religion or philosophy class. According to Gabriel, the religion and philosophy teachers were the most socially conservative in the whole school and typically espoused beliefs on the far right of the political spectrum. They openly expressed their views on many social topics, including the idea that homosexuality is a choice and therefore a morality issue, which is why Catholics cannot support gay rights. It was not uncommon to hear a religion or philosophy teacher express his adamant opposition to same-sex marriage on the grounds that it "inhibits and damages the very fabric of family life." Sitting through these classes, Gabriel knew he was right to be secretive about his sexuality.

Classmates' regular use of the terms "gay," "fag," and "faggot," in the hallways, lunchroom, and even in the classrooms also solidified for Gabriel that he was safer being closeted. Peers used these terms a lot, "both casually and to actually mean it." Once, when Gabriel was volunteering in the yearbook office in the basement of the school, another volunteer was coming into the office and, as he did so, two football players passed by and shouted, "Yeah, go design some layout, you fucking faggot!" Gabriel believes his fellow yearbook club member was subjected to this kind of verbal abuse because his mannerisms made him appear stereotypically gay. Gabriel kept his appearance and demeanour in check precisely to avoid this kind of harassment. Even though Gabriel felt bad for his yearbook mate, he did not speak to him about the incident nor did he choose to come out to him about his own sexuality.

Gabriel was not closeted with everyone. He enjoyed the "good support of friends in that high school who weren't part of the typical makeup of the people there." Gabriel came out to a select few of his friends before grade 11. "They were a very understanding crew," he recalls. Gabriel also had a good network of support online. He joined an online dating service catering to young gay males whose average age was 18. Operated by a now defunct print magazine of the same name, the website featured some of the print magazine content, especially the arresting but not pornographic photographs of young men. The service required members to post their personal information, such as their age, location, and a photograph. This was how Gabriel got in contact with another gay male student at his own school. He remembers this experience with excitement. "I was really surprised! I certainly did not expect to meet anybody in my high school who was gay, considering the environment of my school, which was just too focused on being this masculine-acting individual. For someone to come out to me, even online, was pleasantly surprising!"

Gabriel was even more thoroughly surprised when he was given the opportunity to come out to one of the school's new administrators. Gabriel says he was able to become friends with this man "on a political basis because we had a mutual agreement on our support for a particular party." This administrator also functioned as a religious leader in the school because of his seminary training. Gabriel would "pop by his office" and they would discuss current events. They established a great rapport and a "certain level of trust." One day, the school administrator asked Gabriel directly if he was gay. When Gabriel hesitated, the school administrator assured him that it was OK to admit it because he was gay too. They became fast friends, and Gabriel is still in touch with him today. They occasionally have dinner together, and the school administrator even invited Gabriel to celebrate Christmas with him and his mother and siblings one year.

Befriending the school administrator changed Gabriel's perspectives on the Catholic Church, specifically the differences between the doctrine as laid out by the Vatican and the individuals who practise the faith. Although his high school had a venerable, ultra-conservative tradition and image, Gabriel found there was at least one dissenter among the faculty. Without any institutional supports in place for lgbtq youth in his Catholic school, Gabriel felt lucky to encounter this one maverick.

JONAS

Jonas attended Catholic schools in southern Ontario from junior kindergarten until he graduated in 2007. He remembers sitting through the heteronormative family life portions of his elementary and middle school religion classes and feeling tremendously alone. From a young age, he knew he was different, that he liked boys, and that he was gay. He saw no indication that other people in his school felt anything similar, so he was left to wonder, "Am I the only gay person here?"

When he started high school in grade 9, he visited the library often, searching through the psychology and spirituality stacks for anything that might help him understand himself better. He came upon a book about Christian ex-gays. The word "gay" in the title attracted him. When he opened the book, he saw a stamp that indicated it had been specially donated to the school library. As he read the table of contents, he started to understand that the book was about transforming from homosexual to heterosexual. He knew this was not what he needed, so he slammed the book shut and placed it back on the shelf.

Jonas felt alone about his sexuality, but at least one other person in his high school pegged him as gay. This classmate became Jonas's personal bully and stalker. Jonas referred to him by his last name – Gershom (not his real name). Whenever Gershom would see Jonas in the hallway, he would make his way over to him and whisper the word "fag" menacingly under his breath. Gershom seemed to be everywhere that Jonas was. Jonas was always hyperaware of Gershom's presence. "I was already looking at him the minute he would enter a room or hallway." One way Jonas diffused Gershom's power was to surround himself with a bevy of girlfriends and avoid being alone as much as possible. Although Gershom never stopped singling Jonas out in this way, his behaviour did become predictable enough that Jonas was able to downplay it by thinking, *Oh, that's just him. Prick! I will graduate and never have to see him again.*

Jonas remembers wishing in grade 9 that there were some resources available to him or "just material that I could read and understand that recognized homosexuality, that it did exist. Over time," he says, "I just kind of got used to the fact that it was a Catholic school and that they were probably not going to do anything." Then, towards the end of grade 9, Jonas developed a friendship with a boy called Ethan (not his real name) who also shared his cultural heritage. This turned out to be a momentous occasion for Jonas because the two of them were able to establish enough of a bond to come out to one another as gay in grade 10. Ethan became Jonas's major source of support, especially when it came to dealing with Gershom and Jonas's increasingly disapproving father. Jonas briefly considered approaching one of the school counsellors about the problems he was having but quickly concluded they would be of no help. Together with his great friend Ethan, Jonas explored the gay world both on the

Internet and in person at gay cafés and other hangouts during the summer between grades 10 and 11.

Returning to their Catholic high school in grade 11 was a breeze for Jonas and Ethan. They were both much more confident about themselves and decided to be open about their homosexuality. Other lgbtq students flocked to them and their circle of friends grew. One of Jonas's new gay friends suggested that they should try to start a Diversity Club at the school, but they dropped the idea once they learned the school would not allow it. Instead, in his final year of high school, Jonas observed the Day of Silence, an anti-homophobia campaign designed to show how lgbtq students must live in silence and fear to avoid harassment in schools. Even though his participation in this observance seemed to have little impact since none of the school faculty understood what he was doing, Jonas felt proud to take part in what he considered a very meaningful action. He knew what it was like to be closeted, and he was very relieved to be out at school.

Jonas's new openness about his sexuality did not stop Gershom from his daily harassment and actually invited new intimidating experiences. Once, when Jonas was walking alone past the smoker's corner, one of the smokers called out to him, "Hey, are you into guys?" Jonas froze and thought, "Uh-oh. What do I do now?" But, he just calmly replied, "Yeah," and then walked quickly away. Although Jonas was definitely scared, he was also proud of himself for answering honestly this first-ever direct question about his sexuality. This prepared him for another incident in grade 12 politics class when Jonas mistakenly picked up the wrong copy of the textbook *Canadian Civics*. The boy who owned the textbook shouted out, "Oh my God! Like, a fucking fag just touched my book. Like, now it has AIDS on it!" Jonas was pleased to see that the teacher dealt with the matter immediately by sending the student down to the office.

Jonas was even more pleased later in that politics class when he read in the textbook the case of Marc Hall, an Ontario high school senior who fought a successful legal battle in 2002 against his Catholic school in order to bring his same-sex date to his prom. Even though there was no classroom discussion of the case and the students were not tested on it, the teacher did assign it as required reading along with some written response for homework, and Jonas knew his homophobic classmate would have to read it and write about it. This made Jonas feel "kind of giddy," and he thought, *Cool. Like, it's actually in our textbook!* Jonas has great hope for change in Catholic schools.

SHILOH

Catholic schools were a big part of Shiloh's life in southern Ontario from junior kindergarten to his graduation in 2009. A self-described "un-athletic theatre kid," Shiloh was called "gay" innumerable times in elementary school. He remembers, "I did not know what they were saying, and I don't think they knew what they were saying, but I knew it was bad, and I knew what attributes they were calling me out on. Like, I hung out with a lot of girls. I did not think it was me liking boys. I thought it was me being girly." In an attempt to rid himself of the name-calling, Shiloh excelled at school, became involved in a variety of school clubs, and accepted any leadership opportunity that came his way.

As Shiloh grew older, his peers replaced calling him "gay" with direct questions about his sexuality. Upon being elected high school prime minister, classmates would openly ask him, "Hey, man, why don't you have a girlfriend?" to which he would always reply, "I'm too busy for a girlfriend." Students he barely knew would come up to him and ask, "Are you gay?" and his answer was always a patient "no." Shiloh recalls feeling "very, very, very, very uncomfortable with the idea of identifying as gay in high school." As a student leader, Shiloh felt obligated to uphold the code of student conduct written in the standard issue student agenda. "A graduating student is" the agenda read, "one who believes in the Lord and practices the Catholic faith." Shiloh felt a lot of pressure to be a high achiever and a role model. He thought, *If I am supposed to be a model student, I can't be an out gay person at the same time. Those two identities can't coexist in this school.* Shiloh found suppressing his sexuality consumed an inordinate amount of his energy, until he discovered the trick of keeping himself so tremendously busy that he would not have any time to deal with it.

In high school, Shiloh knew of two queer teachers who were also trying to pass as straight. One was the director of a play Shiloh was in who he discovered was gay through the many hours of rehearsal after school in a much less formal environment. The other was a French teacher who lived with her female partner in a house next door to one of Shiloh's friends. Shiloh was disappointed to discover, though, that he could not count on these two teachers to discuss anything vaguely related to homosexuality in the classroom. Nor could he count on the teachers whose subjects brought them close to the topic. Sexuality is overtly addressed in religion class, but only procreative heterosexuality, laments Shiloh. Homosexuality appears briefly in the curriculum of the Anthropology, Sociology, and Psychology (ASP) course, but Shiloh says all of his religion and ASP teachers were "ardently against discussing the topic."

In contrast to the general heterosexist norm of his high school teachers were two teachers that particularly stood out for Shiloh: his drama teacher and his English teacher. His grade 12 drama teacher was someone he could "really depend on giving progressive, new-age type of thinking that wasn't so muddled in Catholic tradition." Shiloh was excited when his closeted gay drama teacher tried to get permission from the school administration to produce *The Laramie Project*, a play about the 1998 homophobic murder of Matthew Shepard, a gay university student in Laramie, Wyoming. Although Shiloh was not surprised the play was refused, he was uncomfortable that his drama teacher told him to keep the news of the refusal in the strictest of confidence, which meant that Shiloh could not protest the decision. Shiloh also describes his grade 12 English teacher as "progressive," someone who "made a very, very welcoming environment," accommodated divergent thinking, and was "very open to suggesting homosexual themes in Shakespeare's work."

Another open-minded faculty member was one of the school's guidance counsellors. Although Shiloh did not seek the school's counselling services himself, he did suggest it to one of his friends who was trying to come out to him as gay. Shiloh's friend reported back to him that the counsellor was very helpful – she took his concern seriously, treated him like an adult, and, most importantly, did not "bring any Catholic themes or other religious connotations into the discussion." Shiloh was also surprised to learn that the guidance counsellor pointed out a hotline for gay youth to his friend. He is certain, though, that this is something she did "on her own initiative – the school certainly didn't give her any gay-positive materials to pass along to gay students."

These memorable faculty members were not the norm in Shiloh's school. According to Shiloh, "Homophobia was *everywhere*! The phrase 'that's so gay!' was thrown around like candy ... calling people fags ... it was pretty bad. Once in the locker room," Shiloh recalls, "a team captain got naked and touched this unpopular guy in the face with his genitals, basically teabagging him." Shiloh plucked up the courage to confront the team captain about it, but that was as far as it got.

Shiloh believes students will lead the revolution to combat homophobia in Catholic schools because most of the adults there are "constantly just pulling out the 'that's a sensitive topic' phrase, or 'that's just not what God intended' lines" whenever students ask a question related to homosexuality. He knows, though, that it is going to be "very hard to reach that state of liberation because of all the constant Catholic school administration resistance to any attempt at gay rights."

JUNIA

Junia attended Catholic schools in southern Ontario from grade 2 until her 2005 graduation. She waited until after graduation to come out as a lesbian because she felt that was the "safest route" for her. She had learned throughout all her religion classes that the only acceptable family structure was marriage between a man and a woman and that sexual intimacy between a married heterosexual couple was only for the purpose of procreation. When Junia started to develop romantic feelings for one of the girls in her small circle of friends, she did not know what to do about it. She knew her feelings did not fit the regular coupling and courting norms that would lead to the kind of marriage and family life that she had learned about in religion class, at church, and through her own family, so she kept them to herself. Her increasing desire for her friend just made her confused and unsure about herself, so it was easiest to just ignore it.

One day, while walking to the bus stop with three female friends, Junia was deeply surprised when one of them came out as gay. Although it was not the girl Junia had a crush on, she was thrilled to discover she was not alone. This female friend was the only non-heterosexual person, other than herself, that Junia knew of in her Catholic school.

Even though there was not anything queer-positive in her Catholic school, Junia kept abreast of developments for queer youth in schools throughout her province by following media reports. She was in grade 10 when the story broke about Marc Hall – an Ontario teen who fought a successful legal battle against his Catholic high school for the right to take his boyfriend to prom. She also followed closely the story of a local gay teen who managed to start a GSA in his public high school. Junia doesn't think there should be any "rules or regulations on who you can bring to your prom," but she does think trying to start a GSA in a Catholic school would not be wise because the students "would probably get bullied, or even beat up, or much worse."

Junia has good reason to be fearful of this kind of violence in a Catholic school. She was bullied to the point of receiving a death threat from the ringleader of her male tormentors. The bullies targeted her as soon as she entered high school in grade 9 sporting a super-short haircut after having had very long hair in middle school. She had also put on some weight and started favouring plain clothes, such as T-shirts, sweatshirts, and jeans. The bullies called her names that zeroed in on her gender nonconformity, specifically her masculine appearance, her inattentiveness to her looks, and her bigger size. The bullying would take place in the hallways and also in the classrooms.

The teachers did not seem to know it was happening. One time, it got so bad in a classroom that Junia approached the teacher and said, "You know what? I'm leaving because I'm not going to sit here in this classroom and be bullied like this." The teacher responded by allowing Junia to leave the classroom whenever the teasing got too bad and then the teacher would come and find Junia in the cafeteria and give her the day's homework.

Junia felt deeply unsafe in her Catholic high school. The environment did not make her feel welcomed and cared for and she felt no sense of belonging there. "I didn't even go to my prom," she says. According to Junia, resistance to the homophobia of her Catholic school is futile. "It would be impossible" for somebody to stand up for queer rights in a Catholic school because of the "fear of being bullied for their sexual orientation, or maybe even as far as getting kicked out of the school. You could get in a lot of trouble just for speaking up," she says.

ABIGAIL

Growing up in a Catholic family in northern Ontario, Abigail attended Catholic schools from kindergarten until she graduated in 2007. When religion teachers began to address the topic of human sexuality in the upper elementary grades and continued through to high school, they discussed only procreative heterosexual intercourse between married men and women. Looking back on what she learned in religion class, Abigail observes, "I think I could have come out as a lesbian a lot earlier if it had occurred to me that I could be gay, but it just wasn't talked about."

When Abigail's female friends started to date boys in middle school, she studiously avoided the topic by excelling in her classes and writing in her journal. Sometimes she would express her thoughts and feelings in simple diary entries, and other times she would create polished poems about alienation, isolation, and feeling different. She became so practiced at writing poetry that her grade 9 English teacher asked her if she could share it with the class. Hearing a teacher she respected read the poems she created aloud to the class was an instant boost to Abigail's self-esteem. She developed an immediate bond with this teacher and went to see her occasionally before class, after class, or at lunch to talk about her creative writing throughout the first three years of her high school career. It was not that Abigail needed a new friend – she had many friends, just none who appreciated poetry. "Poetry, for me, was really, really important," says Abigail, "because that was the way I expressed myself. Like, that was the way I carried on."

Eventually, Abigail finally agreed to a friend's frequent attempts to set her up with a particular young man in their grade. She liked him well enough, but after about a week into it she thought, "This isn't working. I don't like this," and she said to her friend, "I don't understand what is going on with me." She stopped dating the boy and started writing more in her journal.

Then there was a girl in her grade 11 English class that she really liked. They "started to hang out" and Abigail "really ended up having strong feelings for her." "Finally one day it just kind of clicked in my head," recalls Abigail, "I realized: Oh, OK, this is what it is supposed to feel like." This girl was the first person Abigail told about liking girls. Although she did not feel the same way, Abigail's friend from grade 11 English was "pretty cool" about it. Encouraged by this reaction, Abigail told all of her best friends that she was gay. She did not get a single negative response. "Once I realized I was gay," Abigail remembers, "I wanted to tell someone who wasn't just a friend. I wanted to tell an adult." So, Abigail told her former grade 9 English teacher and found that she, too, was "pretty cool" with it – initially. Then, something went terribly wrong.

To this day, Abigail still does not understand what happened with her former English teacher, but suddenly Abigail's mother was called into the school at the end of the day to have a discussion with the principal and Abigail's former English teacher while Abigail waited in a lounge chair outside the principal's office. On the way home, Abigail's mother told her, "They think that you're in love with her." Abigail protested that it was not true. She was 16 years old, secretly in love with a straight girl from her grade 11 English class, and only recently out to her close friends and one trusted teacher. "I definitely was *not* ready to tell my mom," Abigail remembers clearly. It turns out she did not have to tell her mom because the school already did that for her. Thinking back, Abigail remarks, "It was just a terrible time. It was bad for Mom, too. It really wasn't great to find out your kid's gay from the administration of the only Catholic high school in town. It *really* wasn't cool."

When Abigail returned to school the next day, she immediately sought out her former English teacher to tell her that she was not in love with her and the teacher responded by saying, "I know. Where did you ever get that idea?" Puzzled by this reaction, Abigail nevertheless thought "we were fine." Abigail visited her former English teacher less frequently for much of the rest of grade 11, but by the time grade 12 started, she was "writing again, giving her my poetry again."

It was not long before Abigail was called down to the principal's office at the end of the school day. When the secretary ushered her into the conference room, Abigail was surprised to see her mother, the school principal, and her former English teacher sitting around the oval table. In the ensuing discussion, Abigail discovered that her former English teacher started keeping anecdotal records about her behaviour at the beginning of her grade 12 year, kept some of the poems she shared with her, believed that Abigail wrote them about her, and claimed that Abigail "made her feel uncomfortable." Even though Abigail's principal "seemed just as perplexed" as both Abigail and her mom by what they were hearing from the English teacher, she decided nevertheless that Abigail had to stop going to see the English teacher to talk about poetry. In effect, a quasi-restraining order was placed on Abigail.

Abigail was outraged by the injustice of it all. She was not in love with her former English teacher; she was in love with a classmate from her grade 11 English class that was taught by a different teacher. She only wanted to continue getting encouragement on her poetry from her former grade 9 English teacher. Abigail felt deeply betrayed by this teacher whom she "totally trusted." "Not only had I already forgiven her for outing me," Abigail laments as she recounts the events, "but now *this* as well? It was just so bizarre!" Then Abigail had to endure walking past her former English teacher in the hallway and seeing a teacher she once held in such high regard act as though she did not exist. "She wouldn't even look at me," Abigail recalls bitterly. "I don't think any of that would have happened if I hadn't told her I was a lesbian," she notes.

Apart from the guidance counsellor, whom Abigail suspected was a secret, closeted lesbian, Abigail did not know of any other lgbtq people in her school. "Honestly, I felt, like, lost," she says. She visited the public library a lot and read every lgbtq-themed young adult novel on the shelves. She went online and learned about GSAs and then e-mailed an American young adult author she particularly liked to ask for advice about setting one up. When the author discovered that Abigail was in a Catholic school, she told her not to get her hopes up and that it might be better if she called it "Equality Awareness." Using the information she received from the author, Abigail designed a club that respected diversity and countered discrimination of all kinds – sexism, racism, classism, ableism, heterosexism – and successfully pitched it to a teacher sponsor. Much to Abigail's surprise, she got a core group of about 10 members who regularly attended the club.

They discussed "stuff that, like, nobody would bring up in the school." One student talked about how he was not allowed to wear the girls' kilt to school, and together they discussed freedom of expression versus social order. Along with the Equality Awareness club and her reading and writing, Abigail's "main outlet was pretty much the Internet." Online, she learned about the Day of Silence, the student-led action in which students refuse to speak for a day at school to draw attention to the need to make schools safer for all, regardless of sexual orientation, gender identity, or gender expression.

Abigail drafted a poster for the Day of Silence and brought it to the principal for approval. The principal told her the club was becoming too "gay centric" and that she "needed to tone it down." In the argument that ensued, Abigail retorted, "Well, I'm sorry, but this is personal to me. I'm a lesbian, you know? That's been established by now!" As a compromise, the principal said she could put up some posters as long as she changed the name from Day of Silence to "Oath of Silence" and removed the word "homophobia" from the draft sentence that read "Fight against sexism, racism, and homophobia!" When Abigail asked the principal what was the problem with the word "homophobia," the principal simply responded, "You know the Catholic stance: It's okay to be gay, as long as you don't act on it." In recounting this story, Abigail observes, "It was really bizarre because Catholics – they're so, like, sympathetic to you. So she wasn't mean. But, they don't understand that what they are saying is incredibly hurtful." In the end, Abigail's poster read: "Equality. Oath of Silence Day. Fight." She made sure students knew what the day was about by spreading the message through word of mouth.

In another stealthy act of resistance, Abigail convinced her school principal that the school should have a benefit concert along the lines of the *American Idol* Gives Back charity fundraiser. In selling the idea to the principal, Abigail said, "We have a lot of talented students in our high school – a lot of great singers and musicians. We could have a benefit concert like the *American Idol* one, but simpler. It would be another form of education. We could get an article in the local paper." The principal nodded her head in agreement and said, "Yeah, that's a great idea. So, go ahead. Do it." With only a few days remaining before the event, the principal asked Abigail what organization would be the beneficiary of the money. Abigail smiled and replied, "Oh, the local AIDS committee." The principal's smile disappeared from her face and she responded coldly, "Oh. OK." Later, when the AIDS committee representative came to pick up the cheque, he remarked to Abigail, "Yeah, you could just feel the tension of the place as soon as I walked in the door. I felt like I was getting death glares being from the AIDS committee."

Abigail devoted her final year of high school to actively combating her school's homophobia. Ever since she had been forced out of the closet by a teacher she once admired but who would no longer even look at her let alone talk to her, Abigail had developed a cavalier attitude. She knew she would be out of there soon and that they could not do much more than they already had to hurt her, so she defied her principal who told her, "It's OK if you are *quietly* a lesbian. *That's* fine." Now that she was forced out, the last thing Abigail was going to be was quiet about it. She thought, *I can't not be myself. If being myself was pissing them off, that's unfortunate because that's just the way it is.*

Abigail's last act of resistance was in the final semester of her graduating year. In her grade 12 English class, taught by a different English teacher, students had to pick one classic novel, complete an independent study on it, and present it to the class. Abigail chose Virginia Woolf's novel *Mrs Dalloway* and emphasized all the references to homosexuality in it. She was surprised that the teacher did not shut down her presentation.

Abigail is hopeful that more people will tackle homophobia in Catholic schools. She says, "The resistance is already starting to happen. People are starting to get upset, and not just gay people. It upsets a lot of people, like my mom. What happened to me upsets her. Same with my friends. It'll change one day, but *we* have to change it."

HANNAH

Born in 1991 into a tight-knit Catholic community in southern Ontario, Hannah went to Catholic schools from kindergarten until she felt compelled to drop out of high school after grade 11 because of her "being gay." She was an altar server at her local parish from grade 3 until grade 8, when she decided to stop. Back then, she worried: "My appearance! What are they going to think? They're going to know! They're, like, mind readers! They can tell!" Hannah was very active in her church, taking part in socials, afternoon teas with the "old ladies," and Catholic youth groups. In grade 7, she thought, *Yeah, I'm bisexual. Like, I really like this girl in my class and she likes me and this is hot!* In middle school, when Hannah cut her hair short and started dressing like a boy, she knew the "church ladies" would not approve, so she "completely withdrew from the parish – completely, 100% – no more youth groups, nothing."

On her withdrawal from church, Hannah comments, "I wasn't raised in the greatest of neighbourhoods, so I'd go to church and that was my *out* so I didn't get in trouble and, all of a sudden, that *out* was just taken from me ... I didn't go to church because I didn't feel safe anymore." On losing her religion, Hannah remarks, "It was really hard because it was my belief, something that was supposed to be my rock. Those beliefs

[were] what I was raised on ... they got me through. Then everything just turns around and then something you had – all this faith you based your whole life around – is ... not for you anymore, it's against you. And, you're like: 'Wow! What do I do?'"

If Hannah thought she was bisexual in grade 7, by the time she got to grade 10, she knew she was a lesbian. In the first semester of grade 10, Hannah signed up for automotives class. She was one of only two girls who registered in that class and, because there were only two girls, the male shop teacher decided no one would notice when he wouldn't let them participate in learning actual auto mechanics, so they "got stuck cleaning the tools in the tool room and washing the oil rags." Alone together for large chunks of time in the diesel-smelling tool room, Hannah and Jane (not her real name) got into some deep conversations in which Hannah learned that Jane had a girlfriend in the same school. It was the first time Hannah could envision a life for herself as a lesbian.

Jane was not the only great friend Hannah gained from shop class: "my two straight boys" – as she calls them, two boys from the school's junior wrestling team I will call Kevin and Liam – "stood up to the auto teacher's" sexist exclusion of the only female students in the class. They did this by wandering into the tool room, sitting on the floor with Hannah and Jane, throwing the oil rags all around the room, and lighting one of the rags on fire. When that got the teacher's attention, they said, "We don't want to do welding right now. We're not going to do anything until the girls can too." Realizing he was not going to win this battle, the shop teacher let the girls learn what the boys were learning and he never disciplined Kevin and Liam for setting a fire in the tool room. Hannah remembers thinking, *Yes! We're best friends!*

With this new group of friends, Hannah became more confident. In grade 11, She started dressing even more like a boy – wearing "the guys' school uniform, but with the girls' shorts" – and she began skipping school. This drew the attention of the vice principal and the school counsellor. In a meeting with the two of them over a forged field trip form she had made to get out of class, Hannah blurted out, "I'm gay and I don't know what to do." The guidance counsellor responded by suggesting they call Hannah's mother in to discuss it with them. Hannah protested, saying that was not a good idea because she had been trying to tell her mother throughout the summer between grade 10 and grade 11, but every time she brought it up, her mother shut her down saying, "No, it's just a phase. It's the friends you're hanging out with. Gay people go nowhere in life. You should just kill yourself now."

Impervious to Hannah's warnings, the school guidance counsellor called Hannah's mother into the school for a chat. Hannah remembers, "I sat in the guidance counsellor office while my guidance counsellor and my vice principal were in another room with my mom talking about [me being gay] and they came back and they're like: 'So, your mom knows now, but she's not very accepting of it,' and I said, 'I tried to tell you this one!'" Sitting in silence in the car with her mom on the way back home, Hannah thought her mother would eventually say, "You're an abomination! Go to church. Pray more, pray at home even. Go to church every Sunday. You're in deep crap!" Instead, she found her mother had something else in store for her.

After her discussion with the guidance counsellor and the vice principal in the guidance counsellor's office, Hannah's mother became deeply suspicious of the school. She didn't like how the mannish-looking guidance counsellor spoke so positively of the "homosexual lifestyle." She saw that poster of a rainbow flag on her office wall saying "be positive" and thought it was some vague gay message. She sent her daughter to this Catholic school to learn Catholic values, not this "it's okay to be gay" nonsense. Don't they know that "gay people amount to nothing in life because they go nowhere?" She also saw Hannah's new friends at school as "gay influences" and decided it would be best if Hannah just did not go back there. She decreed that not only was Hannah not allowed to go back to school, but she would be confined to her room and would not be allowed any outside contact whatsoever. Hannah was not going to be home-schooled – she was just going to be at home, period.

Not one to be easily confined, Hannah broke the new rules in a matter of days and her mother responded by kicking her out of the house. Hannah went to live at a friend's house and got a part-time job at a local coffee shop to pay for expenses like toiletries, bus passes, and lunches. Initially, she enjoyed her time away from her mom and attended school regularly. Even though her good friend, Jane, was a grade ahead of her, Hannah managed to take another class with her by signing up for the same option she was taking. One of the assignments for the class was doing a report on a local community association. The students were told to work in pairs and Jane and Hannah worked together on a project about the local lgbtq community.

While working in the school's computer lab, they discovered that all the websites affirming sexual minority groups were blocked while opposing websites, such as those of various Christian reform groups, with messages such as "Homosexuals should burn in hell" were fully accessible. Jane and Hannah went up to their teacher and said, "Ummm ... hello! We're trying to do our project and we can't do it because everything that [is gay] positive is blocked and everything that says 'gays should go die and burn in hell' we can access." The teacher referred the matter to the school administration, who referred it on to the computer support personnel, who then started to block and unblock certain sites from the school system. Hannah does not know if it was just a temporary fix so they could work on their project or if the changes are still in place, but she and Jane felt "triumphant ... like Rocky ... we were like: 'Yes! Yes! Projects! Queers are good!'"

Another change Hannah tried to make in her school before she dropped out had to do with opposing the removal of the only gay-positive book from the school's library. The parent council wanted to remove the book from the library and make it a teacher resource only. Hannah found out about this plan from the school guidance counsellor, with whom she had been in regular contact since "all hell had broken loose" and she was kicked out of the house. Hannah says the guidance counsellor might have felt a bit guilty: "She would come and talk to me every single day and pull me out of class and be all like: 'What's going on? Are you safe? Is there anything we can do?'"

Although the guidance counsellor never actually came out as a lesbian to Hannah and Jane, she did take them "under her wing" and told them about queer-themed events going on in town. When Hannah and Jane would show up to these events, the guidance counsellor would be there with a woman she would introduce as her "friend." On the guidance counsellor's desk in her office, Hannah also saw pictures of this same woman holidaying with the guidance counsellor. Hannah is certain they are a couple. Another detail that cemented Hannah's impression that the guidance counsellor is a lesbian was the fact that she advocated heavily for Jane to be able to take her girlfriend to prom and then showed up to the students' prom dance wearing a pants suit and necktie.

Hannah learned of the homosexual book controversy when the guidance counsellor came up to her at school one day and said, "Hey, hey! There's a meeting going on tonight for the board to take out this book that promotes homosexuality" and told Hannah how she could get involved. Hannah remembers, "I went to that board meeting and I put up my hand to speak ... and they looked directly at me and said: 'Oh, well, I guess if there are no more questions, or comments, we can close the meeting.'"

Despite getting involved in anti-homophobia activism during her grade 11 year, Hannah was not always up to being a courageous crusader. Getting kicked out of her family home was beginning to take its toll on her. She missed her mom (her father was living elsewhere) but would get news about her from her daily interactions with the school guidance counsellor. Having no other way to keep up with her child, Hannah's mom had taken to calling the school guidance counsellor on a regular basis. Eventually, the guidance counsellor told Hannah that Hannah's mother was harassing her at her place of work. "That's how bad it got," Hannah remembers, "my mom would call her and tell her that she didn't have her permission to talk to me and she shouldn't be speaking to me and she doesn't want her to be talking to me at all and to just leave me alone." The school guidance counsellor suggested that Hannah and her mother go to family counselling through a local Catholic agency.

In total, Hannah attended seven sessions with her mom at the Catholic family counselling services. Hannah says, "I didn't get to say much. I just shut up, sat there, listened for my 45 minutes, nodded my head, agreed, and left." The counsellor told her to "keep [your lesbianism] to yourself. You don't have to let everybody know. You shouldn't tell everybody. It's for selective people to know." When the Catholic counsellor tried to convince her that she should avoid gay people because they "are more promiscuous and [you] are more likely to get diseases," Hannah countered with "No, that's not true, actually." At the time, Hannah was also doing her own research online and she knew the counsellor was presenting a biased position. Hannah's outside research also came in handy during one of the counselling sessions when Hannah's mother suggested enrolling Hannah in a reparative therapy camp to transform her into a heterosexual. Hannah told her mother, "No. I'm not talking to you at all. This is the limit. This is the line. You're putting me as a person in danger doing this! It's not going to help me." That was the last family therapy session Hannah had with her mother and the Catholic counsellor.

Two days before Christmas, Hannah was invited to a family gathering at her maternal grandmother's house. There, she had to endure one of her uncles telling her, "You're not right, you're an abomination, and you weren't created in God's image." Then, Hannah says, "He went to punch me but didn't and [told] me to get out of the house." Shortly after this encounter, Hannah spiralled down into a deep depression and made her first of several suicide attempts. She stopped staying at her friend's place and "switched over and started staying at [her] other friend's place with him and his dad."

When school resumed in the new year, Hannah went in to see the school guidance counsellor and told her about the conversion camp her mother wanted her to go to and about the family gathering over Christmas. The guidance counsellor "felt really bad" for Hannah. Aware that all this had happened after she and the vice principal outed Hannah to her mother, the guidance counsellor met with the vice principal to work out a possible solution. The guidance counsellor assured Hannah, "I'm putting in all the supports I can," and made arrangements for an outside, queer-positive, counsellor to come to the school and offer Hannah therapy right at the school.

Hannah responded well to this new therapy. She considered seeking out a possible mentor in one of her three rugby coaches who was a lesbian, but she decided against it. "The lesbian coach," Hannah remembers, "kind of kept to herself ... she made it to practice, but she never really did get too involved with this commitment." Hannah thinks she did this "to cover her own ass" so that she would not risk being outed if she befriended a lesbian player. Hannah decided to leave her alone.

Back on the Internet, Hannah discovered another outlet she might be able to use to express herself at school: the Day of Silence. When she tried to observe it at her school, however, she "got in trouble." From what she read online, Hannah knew that observing the Day of Silence might provoke resistance from teachers or school administrators. She prepared for this, though, by asking for advice about it in advance from the school's closeted lesbian guidance counsellor. The guidance counsellor advised Hannah: "You can do it, I'm just not telling you that it's approved or anything, and it's off the record, as in, you can do it as an individual, but you have to follow rules, and, if a teacher asks you to speak, you should probably speak. It's not worth the fight." When Hannah participated in the Day of Silence, her teachers asked: "Why aren't you talking? Why aren't you answering questions?" Hannah explained she was trying to observe the Day of Silence, to which her teachers responded, "This is not approved by the administration, so you can't do it." Hannah was frustrated by her teachers' resistance to her peaceful protest because she was "just one person" and was not causing any trouble.

Just being herself got Hannah in trouble. As Hannah tells it: "One day, I was going to an acceptance assembly and one of the math teachers stopped me in the hallway because I was bugging her class and she told me to 'be on your way "mam" or "sir" or whatever you are!' And I brought that to the attention of administration, and they did nothing. And with this same teacher, I was pulled out of the washroom once, and

I was told that I was male and that I should be in the male washroom." Hannah did not know this math teacher – the first time she had ever met her was when she was called down to the guidance counsellor's office to receive the math teacher's "three-second apology" for harassing Hannah because of her gender nonconformity. Dissatisfied with the school administration's disregard of the matter, Hannah had previously mentioned it to the guidance counsellor who then met with the math teacher. After the two faculty members talked about the problem for approximately an hour, Hannah was called into the office to listen to the math teacher explain: "In no way was my remark meant to be hurtful towards you, or homophobic, or anything like that." As the two briefly shook hands, the math teacher remarked, "You should try out for wrestling," a sport she coached as part of her extracurricular duties.

Looking back on this experience, Hannah says she regrets "settling for a handshake from that teacher because that could have killed me and they never would have known." Hannah locates that incident as a pivotal encounter that "really sent [her] down." Hannah remembers thinking, "Wow! My family is not accepting me, I have no support, and now a random teacher comes up to me in the hallway and does this to me? She doesn't even acknowledge that I am a sex – she just calls me 'whatever you are' … I would have rather been called an *it*."

Shortly after this episode, Hannah went into a sharp decline emotionally and mentally. Fortunately, this was when the school's guidance counsellor had previously arranged for an outside queer-positive psychologist to provide therapy for Hannah at the school. Hannah remembers: "At one point, I was so down. I was sitting in front of my counsellor and I was looking at her and I was, like: 'My 17th birthday is coming up and I'm not going to be alive for it.' I was like: 'I'm telling you this right now. This is how it is going.'" Even though Hannah was doing much better with her new queer-positive counsellor than she was with the previous Catholic family counselling sessions, the stress of being rejected by her family, her church, and certain elements of her Catholic school began to have a cumulative effect on her. To ease the pain, she began making shallow cuts into her forearm. Hannah's self-harm trajectory escalated to attempts to take her own life by swallowing pills that were readily available to her. Once the outside psychologist and the school guidance counsellor discovered Hannah's emotional and mental state, they began the process of having her voluntarily committed to the psychiatric ward of the local hospital because she posed a significant danger to herself.

"When I got there," Hannah says, "the doctor tried to diagnose me with gender dysphoria because I looked like a man. He was like: 'You look like a man, you talk like a man, you want to be a man!' I was like, 'No! No! I really, really, really don't! I just like girls!'" Hannah remembers thinking, "Wow! What I just came out of and now you're telling me I want to be a man! No! Can't deal!" Because Hannah was under the age of 18, she required the consent of her mother to have any visitors while in hospital. Hannah notes, "So, of course, I saw none of my friends or anything, even though they attempted to visit." After a month and a half of being in the hospital, Hannah finally got out on a day pass in the care of her mother. As Hannah remembers it, "My mom just lit in to me and was like, 'See! Being gay is just causing more trouble! Do you really want to do this?' So, while I was out on the day pass, I ended up overdosing again and going back to the hospital [where] I was in isolation for a week and a half."

Hannah was in and out of the psychiatric ward for the remainder of her grade 11 year. When she was not in the hospital, Hannah was back living with her friend and his father. During this time, Hannah learned about a nearby lgbtq centre with specific programs for lgbtq youth and started getting additional counselling there. Despite all of these supports, Hannah still continued to make attempts on her life. Hannah concedes, "Without [the queer-positive counselling], I can guarantee that I would not be alive today, for sure." All of this turmoil and stress meant that Hannah did not have much of a chance at finishing her grade 11 courses. Hannah notes: "I was in the hospital and I missed the last month of school and I ended up failing my exams."

Hannah made a valiant effort to return to school the following September after her release from the hospital sometime over the summer. She "was in all of the sports teams and everybody knew [her]" so there was a lot of gossip circulating about her: "Oh, Hannah just dropped off of the face of the earth the last month of school." Hannah discovered that many people knew she was hospitalized because of her suicide attempts, but most people seemed to think she tried to take her own life because of her homosexuality, not because of the homophobia. Hannah remembers, "I got back and no one was talking to me anymore. We had to do projects and people didn't want to do a group project with a lesbian." Hannah recalls, "I [didn't] want to be the poster lesbian child at Catholic school."

A "poster lesbian" was exactly what the school newspaper wanted to make Hannah. One young writer, a girl in one of Hannah's classes, approached her and asked her if she could interview her as the "only lesbian in the school." She apparently did not know about Jane and her girlfriend, who had attended their prom together as a couple just four months previously. Hannah agreed, on the condition the interview take place in the presence of the school guidance counsellor. Hannah recalls, "The first question she asked ... was: 'Why did you choose to be gay?'" to which Hannah responded by standing up and saying, "If you're asking me that question, I'm not doing this interview." The school no longer seemed to be the right place for Hannah: "So, I ended up dropping out – I mean, I was like: 'I just can't deal with this!'"

Hannah moved from part-time at the local café to the full-time night-shift job. Eventually, she saved up enough money for first and last month's rent and got a bachelor apartment with a couple of friends: "It was good having three people in a bachelor. It was tiny. I slept in a closet, but we joked that I got to come out of the closet every morning!" She was just 16 years old when she got her first apartment.

The closeted guidance counsellor from Hannah's former high school approached Hannah at the café one night shortly after she dropped out of high school and asked her if she and her friend Jane might like to talk about their experiences of being lesbians in a Catholic school at an upcoming Catholic guidance counsellor convention in Toronto. The counsellor said, "You should speak there ... and just give us some insight and help us help the gay kids that are following you." Hannah responded, "Well, I think that, with students you need someone a little more stable and able to talk about experiences such as mine." The closeted guidance counsellor told Hannah to think about it, but Hannah says, "I didn't end up getting back to her because it was, like, just after I got out of the hospital and I still wasn't comfortable." She adds, "Like, now, I could do it fine. It's definitely needed."

Looking back at her Catholic high school, Hannah says, "There was a good mix of homophobia and acceptance. There was the staff that were willing to, like, try to make changes and stuff, and be like: 'No, this isn't how it should be. We really need to re-evaluate stuff.' And, then, there's the staff who are like: 'No. We're doing the Catholic teachings. These are our guidelines and this is what we are doing – no exceptions!'" On her outlook for less homophobia in Canadian Catholic schools, Hannah says, "I'm hoping that things are getting better and students are trying to get their voices out more because it needs to be done. But, there's been no change ... fear holds everybody back."

Hannah has done the hard psychological and emotional work of facing her fears and continuing forward in her life. She has been accepted as a mature student at a postsecondary institution and hopes to one day become a surgeon.

Concluding Remarks

Of the six teacher participants whose stories appear in this chapter, three said they were fired for behaving in ways that the Catholic school administrators deemed to be contrary to Catholic doctrine vis-à-vis sexual minority groups, and one reported such intense harassment that she only just managed to finish out the school year. Job said he was fired from his Catholic district in rural Alberta in 2008 because he was transitioning from female to male. Naarai said she was fired from her Catholic district in rural Alberta in 2009 because she was attempting to get pregnant so she could raise a child with her female partner. Anna said she was fired from her Catholic district in southern Alberta in 2004 for taking on the role of "straight ally" to the lgbtq students in her Catholic school and providing a "positive space" for them to meet in her classroom at lunchtime. Naomi said she was harassed by conservative residents in her northern Ontario town, and by certain colleagues at the elementary school where she had accepted a temporary teaching position, because of her suspected lesbianism. She said the harassment was so severe that she barely completed the school year in 2005.

The two other teacher participants, a male principal and a male teacher who have been teaching with their respective Catholic school districts since the mid-1990s, are able to do so only by remaining mainly closeted at work and by pretending to be bachelors unlucky in love, despite the fact that both men have long-term male partners with whom they have been living for several years. Mark is a principal at a Catholic elementary school in Alberta who has developed excellent coping skills in avoiding personal questions that might reveal his sexuality and marital status. Luke is a high school English teacher in Ontario who is fearful that the Catholicity clause in his employment contract might be used to fire him if it becomes known that he has been living with his male partner in a common law arrangement for more than a decade. Like Mark, Luke has developed coping skills to avoid the homophobic indoctrination that pervades his school atmosphere. Unlike Mark, Luke finds ways to express his sense of human rights activism in his Catholic school.

Of the 12 student participants whose stories are re-presented in this chapter, four chose to stay resolutely closeted while in their Catholic school. Judith witnessed the ridicule another transgirl faced in her school in southern Alberta and felt it would be safer to present as male rather than as the male-to-female transgender person she was discovering herself to be. Caleb tried to "butch it up" and date a girl in his Catholic school in northern Alberta, but he was called "faggot" anyway, and it was only when he was in treatment for his eating disorder that he was able to come out as gay. As a student leader in his southern Ontario Catholic school, Shiloh felt pressured to be an example of the Catholic faith, and this kept him closeted at school. Bullied for her gender nonconformity in her southern Ontario Catholic school, Junia decided it would be safer to wait until after graduation to come out as a lesbian.

One student participant, Gabriel, was semi-closeted in his southern Ontario Catholic school, coming out as gay to only a few trusted friends. The heteronormative environment of Gabriel's athletic Catholic school reinforced for him that it would be too stressful to come out at school. Gabriel was able to be out to some select friends at school, online through a website for young gay males, and also to one of the school's clergy administrators who asked Gabriel about his sexuality while reassuring him it was safe to talk about it with him because the administrator revealed that he was gay too.

The three student participants who were out about their sexuality to themselves and some of their friends had the disastrous experience of their Catholic school administrators outing them to their parents. Jacob now identifies as a "queer trans-guy," but back when he was in grade 7 at his Catholic junior high school in southern Alberta, he identified as a lesbian. Jacob came out as a lesbian at the age of 12 to a trusted religion teacher who told the principal of the school who then called in Jacob's parents for a meeting so Jacob could come out to them at the school. Jacob's parents reacted by sending him to reparative therapy. Abigail had such a positive experience coming out as a lesbian in grade 11 to her best friends in her Catholic high school in northern Ontario that she decided to tell a trusted teacher with whom she had bonded over poetry. That teacher informed the principal of the school who then called in Abigail's mother to apprise her of Abigail's disclosure of her lesbianism. Reflecting on this experience, Abigail says she "definitely was *not* ready" to tell her mom and that it was a "terrible time" for both her and her mother. While being disciplined for not wearing the full girl's uniform and for making a forged form to get out of one of her grade 11 classes, a frustrated Hannah told her vice principal and guidance counsellor that she was gay. These administrators of her southern Ontario Catholic high school decided it was best to call in Hannah's mother so that she could be informed of this. Hannah's mother responded by pulling Hannah out of the school to keep her away from what she regarded to be "gay influences," and by eventually expelling Hannah from the family home.

One student participant, Esther, was outed as a lesbian by bullies in her northern Alberta Catholic high school who had been tormenting her since she arrived in grade 9. Esther reported the bullying to her administrators early on, but the only action she ever witnessed was in grade 11 after she complained to the school board about an incident on the school bus in which the bus driver tried to blame Esther and her friend for the homophobic bullying they endured. Following Esther's complaint, the school's guidance counsellor was persuaded to purchase several lgbtq-affirming books for the school library and Esther was allowed to run a GSA off school property. The bullying stopped in Esther's senior year.

Three student participants in this study were able to be fully out about their non-heterosexuality while in their Catholic schools. Jonas knew from an early age that he was gay. When he started grade 9 at his southern Ontario Catholic high school, at least one other student knew Jonas was gay, too. This student became Jonas's personal bully and stalker who followed Jonas around and called him a "fag" whenever he could. Together with a close friend, Jonas found ways to cope with his bully. Eventually, Jonas came out as gay to his close friend who responded by also coming out as gay. Drawing strength from one another, the two friends came out to others in their Catholic school at the same time and their openness earned them a new set of friends. Like Jonas, Simon also knew he was gay from a young age. He came out as gay to his friends in his northern Alberta Catholic high school at the beginning of grade 9. His friends reacted positively but the assistant principal/school counsellor did not. He asked Simon to "rein in" his "behaviour" because he said it was making some parents uncomfortable. Simon told his parents, who threatened to sue the school, and Simon was able to carry on being himself. Mary remembers realizing she liked girls at the beginning of junior high but it was not until high school that she came out as a lesbian. She sought guidance about coming out from the counsellor at her southern Alberta Catholic high school and, when she did not receive any help or encouragement, she confided in a friend who informed her about a local support group for lgbtq youth. The youth group gave Mary the confidence she needed to be more and more out about her sexuality at school.

Of the six teacher participants whose stories are recounted in this chapter, four are no longer teaching with their original Catholic school board (three said they were fired for not conforming to Catholic doctrine regarding sexual minorities, and one said she was harassed about her lesbianism until she finished her temporary contract). The three who said they were fired still continue to assist sexual minority groups in other school districts, and one is still fighting his wrongful dismissal through legal channels. The one teacher participant who said she was harassed about being a lesbian until she left the town where she was fulfilling a temporary teaching assignment is now pursuing graduate studies. Of the remaining teacher participants, two continue to teach with their original Catholic school boards but remain closeted about their homosexuality. One of the closeted teachers is in a leadership position as a principal and is therefore reluctant to openly question the homophobia of the system in case his actions draw attention to his own homosexuality, thereby jeopardizing his employment. The other closeted teacher has received a continuous contract and feels confident enough in his role as a regular classroom teacher to question his board's systemic homophobia.

Of the 12 student participants whose stories appear in this chapter, five felt too closeted to be able to take any action against the homophobia around them. Of the others, four were outed at school, either by school personnel or by bullies, and were able to transform their anger over this experience into positive steps to combat homophobia in their schools. The remaining three student participants were able to be out about their non-heterosexuality while studying in Catholic schools and, while they experienced both positive and negative reactions to their openness about their sexuality, their courage in being out likely had incalculable effects on those around them in their Catholic schools.

The majority of teacher participants in this study experienced objectively greater degrees of doctrinal disciplining than the student participants, even though the harm to the students may seem more devastating. Nevertheless, some of the teacher participants who were disciplined by being fired were able to find alternate ways to still serve the cause of equality and justice for all in their new school districts or through legal avenues. The two teacher participants who remain employed by their original Catholic school districts engage in a kind of strategic self-disciplining designed to shield their homosexuality from others. One of the closeted teachers is able to find ways to circumvent his doctrinal disciplining and thereby feel less oppressed by the system.

The doctrinal disciplining that the majority of the student participants experienced came in two forms: (1) feeling afraid to come out about their sexuality while still in school and (2) being outed to their parents by school personnel or being forced out of the closet by bullies. Even those student participants who were able to be out about their sexuality of their own volition when they were students in their Catholic schools still did not feel entirely safe about being out in such an environment.

This summary of the participants' experiences helps to answer the research questions posed at the beginning of this book. For the first question: "How does power operate within and across Alberta and Ontario Catholic schools?" it appears from the participants' experiences that the power that originates with the Catholic doctrine operates primarily by means of discipline and repression. However, another form of power originates with people in the ways they are able to resist the dominating force of Catholic doctrine.

Regarding the second question: "How do Catholic documents portray teachers and students as subjects?" it appears from the participants' experiences that Catholic documents, such as curriculum and policy documents (discussed in Chapter 4) designed to disseminate Catholic doctrine about sexual minorities, try to cast lgbtq students and teachers as "persons with same-sex attraction" whose behaviour should be closely monitored, controlled, and disciplined. The documents portray teachers and students as sick subjects in need of pastoral care from the Church. They provide a roadmap of sorts showing Catholic education leaders how to manage gender and sexually diverse students and teachers. The connection between the Catholic documents and the behaviours of Catholic education leaders depicted in the narratives is not explicit but is implied through ideology.

This chapter's answer to the third research question, "What effects do Catholic documents have on the experiences of lgbtq individuals in Alberta and Ontario Catholic schools?" is overwhelmingly negative – most student participants felt it would be safer to stay in the closet, some student participants were outed by the school to their parents, and most teacher participants were apparently fired or forced out for behaving in ways considered contrary to Catholic doctrine regarding non-heterosexuals.

There is hope, however, in that this chapter answers "yes" to the final research question: "Is resistance possible in an education context so dominated by the repressive force of religiously inspired homophobia?" Yes, some participants resisted the doctrinal disciplining of their Catholic schools, although the evidence of resistance among participants is not as strong as the evidence of their domination.

The participants' experiences begin to gesture towards ways in which the three data sets that compose this book intersect with one another. The majority of the participants' experiences overwhelmingly show how the Catholic doctrine (examined in Chapter 4) asserts its disciplining force against sexual minorities in some Alberta and Ontario Catholic schools. However, some participants' experiences show alternative ideologies competing with the dominant ideology of homophobia that pervades the Catholic school system.

For example, Simon, an out gay student who attended Catholic schools in northern Alberta from kindergarten until he graduated in 2010, was able to counter the homophobic effects of the curriculum that excluded information about non-heterosexuals by attending queer youth groups and camps, where he learned about lgbtq history, such as the Stonewall Riots, and famous gay people like Harvey Milk.

Simon's autodidactic drive also led him to the Internet where he filled in the gaps of his formal education by learning about the social justice issues underlying several media accounts about lgbtq youth throughout North America who were subjected to homophobic discrimination by their schools. Online, Simon read news stories such as that of Constance McMillan, the Mississippi high school student who was refused permission to bring her girlfriend as her date, and to wear a tuxedo, to her high school prom.

These kinds of news stories about homophobic discrimination against students that Simon read on the Internet show the important role the news media can play in disseminating news stories about lgbtq youth to other lgbtq youth, which can have the powerful effect of making these youth feel less alone and more connected to other lgbtq youth of their generation. Simon said this kind of alternative information made him feel more confident about his sexuality and capable of taking on the role of mentor to younger gay youth in his Catholic school. If reading a news media story can have the effect of instilling confidence and a sense of belonging among lgbtq youth, it is not inconceivable to imagine the media accounts igniting the spark that starts a resistance movement. Simon's experience highlights an important connection between this chapter and the next.

3

Media and the Law:
Allies in Resisting Homophobia

The role of religion in public education in Canada has been a contentious topic since the nineteenth century, eventually resulting in the formation of two separate school systems for the two dominant religions of early Canada: Protestant and Catholic (Lawr & Gidney, 1973). Upon the establishment of the Canadian Confederation, the denominational rights of these two school systems were enshrined in the *British North America Act* of 1867 (Wilson, Stamp, & Audet, 1970). This is an important detail because it is to these denominational rights that Catholic education leaders point when defending their adherence to Catholic canonical law rather than to Canadian common law.

Questions rarely arise about the operation of Catholic schools, however, because of the increasing secularization of Canada, and Canadians' deep respect for the fundamental freedom of religion, which is a constitutionally protected right guaranteed by Section 2 of the *Canadian Charter of Rights and Freedoms* (1982). Before 1971, less than 1% of Canadians selected the box beside "no religion" on national surveys; today, that number has risen to 23% (Valpy & Friesen, 2010). Canadians who are not Catholic are often unaware of special concessions regarding curriculum that Catholic schools enjoy, as well as the structures in place that enable the continued public funding of Catholic schools in Alberta, Ontario, and Saskatchewan. Canadians who are not Catholic are often equally unaware of the discriminatory ways in which Catholic doctrine disciplines sexual and gender minority groups in Canadian Catholic schools. This lack of awareness could be attributed to what communications scholar Dane Claussen (2002) has identified as a failure on the part of North American journalists to take on and competently cover news stories that involve both religion and sexuality. The media coverage

Leanne Iskander received – the story of her attempts to establish a bona fide GSA in her Ontario Catholic high school opened this book – suggests the failure Claussen (2002) identifies may be turning around. Media accounts have recently been more instrumental in disseminating information to the general public about the mistreatment of sexual and gender minority groups in Canadian Catholic schools. Without this important media coverage, very little would be known of various clashes between Catholic canonical law and Canadian common law in relation to non-heterosexuals in Canadian Catholic schools. The news media, the law, and the acts of individuals all play important role in raising awareness leading to social change. The role of the news media is especially important where Catholic schools are concerned because of the Catholic Church's historical and theological preoccupation with avoiding scandal (McBrien, 1995). This, in practical terms, has often produced reticence and secrecy around its administrative inner workings.

Catholic schools seek to manage such conflicts between Catholic canonical law and Canadian common law vis-à-vis sexual and gender minorities "in-house" – that is, away from the critical eyes of student groups, teachers' associations, the news media, human rights tribunals, and courts of law. However, ever since the Gay Liberation Movement of the 1960s swept through parts of the Western world such as Australia, New Zealand, North America, and Western Europe (Carter, 2004), members of sexual minority groups in those areas have become increasingly aware of their legal rights and started to demand respect in public institutions, including Catholic schools. Students and teachers who have experienced homophobic harassment in Canadian Catholic schools, but who can get no satisfactory resolution to the problem through the school system, often turn to the media to express their frustration.

The following collection of Canadian media accounts range from media coverage of important court cases to individual homophobic school policies. The stories are not meant to be an exhaustive list, or a representative sample, but rather a snapshot of homophobic incidents occurring in some Canadian Catholic schools. They are meant to provide a context for the stories shared by the participants in this study. Some of the media accounts offer a rare glimpse into the inner workings of Canadian Catholic schools, such as in this brief example: Ontario Catholic education leaders have gone on public record explaining that their denominational rights exempt them from fully adhering to governmental policies calling for diversity, equity and respect in relation to sexual minority groups and from completely implementing provincial curricula that addresses sexual orientation or gender identity. Regular lay Catholics, such as parents or teachers, who are interested in learning more about the process of revamping provincial curricula or educational policies to suit Catholic codes of morality cannot easily access high-ranking Catholic education leaders through normal channels. However, various Canadian media outlets, such as the CBC, *The Globe and Mail*, the *Ottawa Citizen*, the *Toronto Star*, and *Xtra! Canada's Gay and Lesbian News* have been able to interview Catholic education leaders and have provided the general public with direct quotations of their views and rationales. This is an immeasurably valuable exchange that sheds light on a hitherto obscure element of Canadian schooling – the behind-the-scenes decisions of Catholic education leaders that adhere to Catholic canonical law while contravening Canadian common law pertaining to sexual and gender diverse individuals.

Relatively speaking, matters related to Catholic schools and non-heterosexuals rarely appear in the media, and those that do tend to be negative. This focus on negative news is reflected in the topics that tend to dominate the global news agenda, such as crime, violence, politics, and government. A limitation, then, of this media section is that it does not contain direct examples of positive experiences lgbtq people may have had with their Canadian Catholic schools. However, this research does reveal suggestions of queer-positive activism occurring at the trustee level of one Catholic school board in southern Ontario. More details on this little-publicized activism can be found in the section "Banning an inclusive education book that mentions homophobia." Discussion of its significance are in the "Concluding Remarks" section.

My data collection methods were as follows: starting in 2006, I began amassing media reports on the topic of homosexuality and Canadian Catholic schools dating back to 2000. I did this by subscribing to the paper version of *The Globe and Mail* newspaper and reading other Canadian newspapers online, such as the *Ottawa Citizen*, the *Toronto Star*, and *Xtra!* – I read these print and electronic versions of Canadian newspapers daily for relevant stories. I also set up electronic alerts through Google and some media outlets. I used search strings containing variations on such words as homosexuality, same-sex, sexual minority, lesbian, gay, bisexual, transgender, queer, and homophobia, combined with the standard "Canadian Catholic schools." This process continued until 2011 and yielded a significant number of stories, not all of which I could use.

Because this is study regards the treatment of sexual minority groups in the Catholic schools of Alberta and Ontario, I limited the media accounts to these two provinces primarily. Two exceptions are references to one story from British Columbia and another from Saskatchewan, which I included for contextual and illustrative purposes. In my search for teacher participants to interview for this study, more came forward from Alberta than Ontario. I decided therefore that I needed more data from Ontario in this study, and so I have included more media stories from this province. Ontario also generated more news reports on the topic than Alberta. This could be due to a number of factors, including a more active Ministry of Education in Ontario that works harder to effectively implement progressive policies on equity and inclusivity – policies that have become problematic for Ontario Catholic boards because of ideological clashes with Catholic doctrine. Because of some high-profile clashes and controversies, and particularly the infamous *Hall* case (discussed later in this chapter), there are more media accounts from Ontario than from Alberta.

Turning to the Canadian Court System to Fight Homophobia

Two significant court cases involving homosexuality and Christian educational institutions caught the public's attention. The first court case involves a gay male teacher who was fired in 1991 from his teaching position at King's College, a private postsecondary Christian institution in Edmonton, Alberta, because of his sexual orientation. The second involves a gay male student whose school administration refused him permission in 2002 to take his same-sex date to the prom at his publicly funded Catholic high school in Oshawa, Ontario.

These two cases underscore a potential *Charter* conflict between Section 2, freedom of religion, and Section 15, the equality clause. Although Canada has yet to experience a *Charter* challenge between Sections 2 and 15 involving the denominational rights of Catholic schools and the equality rights of lgbtq Canadians, a recent Saskatchewan Court of Appeal ruling that marriage commissioners cannot claim freedom of religion to deny marriages to same-sex couples (discussed later in this chapter) suggests current Canadian judicial leanings on this particular intersection.

A pivotal court case in Alberta: Delwin Vriend

The fact that this Alberta case did not take place in a Catholic school setting is insignificant given the powerful ramifications it has had for same-sex legal advances in Canada. Peter W. Hogg, the former dean of

Osgoode Hall Law School at York University in Toronto, Ontario, has ranked this Alberta case as one of three all-time important Supreme Court of Canada decisions since the *Charter* became law in 1982 (Saunders, 2002). Indeed, it would be highly unusual to discuss the effects the advancement of same-sex legal rights have had on Canadian lgbtq schoolteachers without addressing the landmark *Vriend* case. The case is important to this study because it shows the Canadian legal precedence requiring provincial human rights protection acts to reflect the *Canadian Charter of Rights and Freedoms* (1982) by including sexual orientation as prohibited grounds for discrimination.

As I have briefly described elsewhere (Callaghan, 2007b), the Alberta case concerns Delwin Vriend, a chemistry laboratory instructor at King's College, who was hired in 1988 then fired in 1991 when he was 25 years old because his openness about his homosexuality violated the college's newly drafted policy statement on homosexuality (Lahey, 1999). Disapproval of Vriend's "openly gay" behaviour in a Christian educational setting eventually made its way to the president of the college who called Vriend in for a meeting in 1990 to ask him directly if the rumours about his sexuality were true. Following this meeting, the college president drafted a policy on homosexuality reflecting the college's Christian beliefs that would tidily exclude Vriend (Pratt, 2008). Because Vriend had earlier admitted that he was gay and that he had a boyfriend, the college president then asked Vriend to resign on the grounds that he was not complying with the college's newly drafted policy on Christian religious beliefs vis-à-vis homosexual behaviour.

After his termination, Vriend attempted to file a complaint of discrimination on the basis of sexual orientation with the Alberta Human Rights Commission but was informed that Alberta's *Individual Rights Protection Act* (IRPA) (now called the *Human Rights, Citizenship and Multiculturalism Act*) did not include sexual orientation as a prohibited ground for discrimination (Hiebert, 2003).

The *Vriend v Alberta* case was eventually heard by the Supreme Court of Canada, which decided unanimously in 1998 that the omission of sexual orientation from Alberta's IRPA infringed upon Section 15 of the *Charter* and ordered that sexual orientation be "read in" to the legislation (Hurley, 2005). In its written decision, the Supreme Court of Canada commented that this omission was as good as "condoning or even encouraging discrimination against lesbians and gay men" and that it revealed a "sinister message" that gays and lesbians are less worthy than others (cited in Hiebert, 2003, p. 12).

As a result of the *Vriend* decision, all Canadian provinces and territories were required to include sexual orientation as a prohibited ground of discrimination in their human rights codes. The discussions and debates that surrounded these legislative changes called upon Canadian people to re-examine the cultural and social practices that have discriminated against and excluded their fellow lgbtq citizens simply because lgbtq people live and love outside the heterosexual norm (Grace, 2004).

Not only did the *Vriend* decision confirm equality rights for lesbian and gay Canadians, but it also attracted the attention of teachers' associations across Canada, which realized the need to develop policies protecting the rights of lgbtq teachers and students in Canadian schools (Grace, 2004). In its *Vriend* decision, the Supreme Court of Canada made plain that lgbtq teachers and students have a right to pursue their educational goals in Canadian schools free from fear of discrimination on the basis of sexual orientation.

It is unclear how many lgbtq students and teachers in Alberta are aware of this protection, however, because Alberta took several years to actually write the words "sexual orientation" into the re-named *Human Rights, Citizenship and Multiculturalism Act.* This omission existed for those years despite the fact the Supreme Court of Canada's 1998 decision in the *Vriend* case ordered the province to include sexual orientation as a prohibited ground of discrimination in its provincial human rights act. The Alberta legislature had many opportunities to do so.

The *Vriend v Alberta* case, which began as Delwin Vriend's attempt to file a complaint with the Alberta Human Rights Commission, ended with a monumental step forward throughout Canada in recognizing sexual orientation as grounds for protection from discrimination.

Although Delwin Vriend was ultimately successful in his court challenge to have sexual orientation included as a protected ground, he declined to proceed with his original complaint against his former employer. Vriend had been fired in 1991, and it was not until 1998 that he learned the Alberta Human Rights Commission could legally hear his complaint about wrongful dismissal. Sadly, the intervening seven years had taken their toll on Vriend and he no longer had the energy for, or interest in, pursuing another legal battle (Pratt, 2008).

Catholic teachers fired for behaving in a manner contrary to Catholicity

Complainant burnout is not uncommon in cases of teachers who say they are being fired because of their sexual orientation. In 1997, Joseph Stellpflug said he was fired from his position as lay chaplain and religion teacher in the York Region of Toronto, Ontario, because he took part in a commitment ceremony with his same-sex partner (DiManno, 1997). An unknown person had passed one of Stellpflug's commitment ceremony invitations to the archdiocese offices in Toronto, and the bishops responded by conducting an investigation. Their investigation concluded that Stellpflug's commitment ceremony was analogous to a wedding (this was before the 2005 legalization of same-sex marriage in Canada) and was therefore contrary to the teachings of the Catholic Church. Stellpflug tried to fight his dismissal, believing that the *Ontario Human Rights Code* would protect him because it forbids discrimination on the basis of sexual orientation. He gave up his fight, however, once he learned that courts had interpreted Catholic separate school systems as benefiting from a legal loophole due to their denominational rights, guaranteed by the *Canadian Charter of Rights and Freedoms* (1982), and their occupational hiring rights assured to them by the Ontario *Education Act* (Young & Ryan, 2014).

The teachers who took part in this study said they are aware of other Canadian teachers who have been fired from their Catholic school systems because of their sexual orientation or gender identity, and they lament that these stories are not widely known. Those who took their cases to the media did not follow through with a human rights complaint or lawsuit. One example is Lisa Reimer. A music teacher at a Catholic school in Vancouver, she said she was fired in April 2010 for what her Catholic administrators regarded as living outside Catholic doctrine after her female partner gave birth to their son (Matas, 2010). Although Reimer informed the media about the discrimination she said she experienced, she did not pursue legal action. Like Stellpflug and Reimer, two teachers I interviewed for this study, whose stories are recounted in Chapter 2 under the pseudonyms Naarai and Anna, also chose not to contest their wrongful dismissals through legal channels. First, both teachers could foresee they would not have the necessary mental and emotional stamina, not to mention the financial resources, to withstand such a battle while simultaneously looking for other work. Second, Naarai's Catholic school board offered her a lump sum payment to settle the matter out of court. Third, the lawyers that both teachers engaged through their Catholic teacher associations discouraged them from proceeding further because they believed the case was not winnable because of previous legal precedent that sided in favour of the Catholic school boards (Young & Ryan, 2014).

Indeed, though Canadian educational theorist James Covert (1993) makes clear that Canadian Catholic school systems have a long history of firing their heterosexual teachers for not upholding specific aspects of Catholic doctrine, most cases Covert describes took place in the 1970s and 1980s, before the institution of the *Canadian Charter of Rights and Freedoms* (1982), and tended to involve teachers who got pregnant outside of marriage, teachers who left Catholicism to join another faith, and teachers who married a non-Catholic. Given that these types of cases are no longer appearing in the Canadian news media and the Canadian courts, it appears as though dismissals of heterosexual teachers on these grounds occur less frequently in Canadian Catholic schools today. This is likely due to shifting societal values and morals related to marriage and selective observance of Catholic doctrine. Many of the dismissals Covert describes from the 1970s and 1980s would not withstand a *Charter* challenge today.

Enforcement of Catholic doctrine on Catholic schoolteachers seems to have shifted from regulating the coupling arrangements and sexuality of heterosexual teachers to ensuring that non-heterosexual teachers strictly comply with the Catholic doctrine that calls upon them to remain celibate. Indeed, Catholicity, or the state of being in accordance with Catholic doctrine, is increasingly invoked as a reason for discriminating against non-heterosexuals (Baird, 2007).

Catholic education leaders appeal to Catholicity and enforce select elements of Catholic doctrine to punish non-heterosexual teachers who are too open not only about their lesbian, gay, bisexual, transgender, or queer status but also about the fact that they have partners, are legally married, or are raising children in their families. The apparent public aspect of living this way catches the attention of the Catholic education leaders, and they respond by questioning the teachers' degree of Catholicity and punishing them accordingly. Not everyone agrees that people's private lives are a public matter, however. For example, once Joseph Stellpflug (the Catholic teacher described above who said he was fired in 1997 for having a commitment ceremony with his male partner) took his case to the media, interested parties began to share their thoughts on the matter. Pearl Eliadis, who was at the time the director of public policy and public education for the Ontario Human Rights Commission, openly questioned how far denominational rights should extend. Eliadis asked, "Can the board or the archbishop fire a male teacher who's had a vasectomy? A female teacher on the pill?" (cited in DiManno, 1997, p. 1). A Toronto archdiocese spokesperson responded, "Nobody is going to go snooping after people – that would be absurd. But if something is extremely public, that's different" (cited in DiManno, 1997, p. 1). As

Covert's (1993) description of wrongful dismissal cases from the 1980s shows, some Canadian Catholic school districts regarded the "mortal sin" of getting pregnant out of wedlock "extremely public" enough to warrant firing a female Catholic teacher. A male Catholic teacher's violation of the same doctrine regarding premarital sex would presumably go unpunished because his sin would be undetectable and therefore would not carry the same "extremely public" shame.

Similarly, lgbtq teachers in Canadian Catholic schools are not technically at risk of being fired today as long as they portray the image of complying with Catholic doctrine; that is, being gay but not acting on it, essentially living a celibate life. Entering into a same-sex relationship (as Vriend did), marrying a same-sex partner (as Stellpflug did), becoming a parent and raising a family in a same-sex relationship (as both Lisa Reimer and this study's participant Naarai did) are all life decisions that can still put lgbtq teachers at risk of being fired if they teach for a Canadian Catholic school. True, if lgbtq teachers are able to be less public about these aspects of their lives (as this study's participants Mark and Luke are able to do), then their risks of being fired from their Catholic school diminish significantly. But who among us can be easily secretive about falling in love or silent about bringing a child into the world? Even if a Catholic teacher manages to be closeted about his or her same-sex relationship and new family, young children may inadvertently out the family.

If the dismissals from Canadian Catholic schools throughout the 1970s and 1980s were primarily about regulating the "extremely public" aspects of heterosexual teachers' sexuality, the focus in the 1990s and beyond has been directed towards the "extremely public" aspects of non-heterosexuals' sexuality, namely commitment ceremonies, marriages, and raising children. The shift in Catholic dismissals means only that the focus has moved from particular members of the heterosexual dominant culture to members of sexual minority groups, already the subjects of religiously inspired homophobic harassment, hatred, and violence.

The Canadian Charter of Rights and Freedoms:
Potential conflicts

Canada has yet to see a *Charter* challenge that pits Section 2, the section pertaining to fundamental freedoms including freedom of religion, against Section 15, the equality clause, in cases where lgbtq teachers have been fired from their Catholic schools because of their sexual orientation or gender identity. However, a recent case in Saskatchewan highlights this particular battle, albeit in the civil service arena of marriage commissions. On 10 January 2011, the Saskatchewan Court of Appeal unanimously ruled that marriage commissioners cannot claim freedom of religion to deny marriages to same-sex couples (Graham, 2011). The case began in 2009, when the Saskatchewan Minister of Justice asked the province's highest court to rule on the constitutionality of a law proposed by the ruling right-of-centre Saskatchewan Party that would have allowed marriage commissioners to cite their religious beliefs as a bona fide rationale for refusing to marry lgbtq couples (Christopher, 2011).

In its unanimous decision in January 2011, the court ruled that the proposed legislation is unconstitutional – such a law would violate the equality rights of lgbtq people, which are safeguarded by Section 15 of the *Canadian Charter of Rights and Freedoms* (1982). Writing on behalf of three of the five judges on the Saskatchewan Court of Appeal, Justice Robert Richards notes, "Persons who voluntarily choose to assume an office, like that of marriage commissioner, cannot expect to directly shape the office's intersection with the public so as to make it conform with their personal religious or other beliefs ... the law is supreme over officials of the government as well as private individuals, and thereby preclusive of the influence of arbitrary power" (Saskatchewan Court of Appeal, 2011, p. 40).

The decision of the Saskatchewan Court of Appeal has some interesting implications for the problem of homophobia in Canadian Catholic schools. Like marriage commissioners who provide the service of officiating weddings for members of the general public, publicly funded Canadian Catholic schools provide an education to the general public, including students who may not subscribe to the Catholic faith. Publicly funded Catholic schools increasingly cater to a diverse cross-section of the general public, many of whom are under the age of majority and did not choose to attend a Catholic school or follow the Catholic faith of their own volition. After I read the decision in the Saskatchewan marriage commissioner case, it struck me that the logic of this decision can be applied to the problem of homophobia in Canadian Catholic schools. That is, Canadian Catholic schools should not have the arbitrary power to force the selective observance of particular religious beliefs that directly infringe upon the *Charter* rights of minority groups among the school's population, namely lgbtq individuals.

The Saskatchewan court case that ruled marriage commissioners cannot refuse to marry same-sex couples on religious grounds because this would violate Section 15 of the *Canadian Charter of Rights and Freedoms* (1982) reverberates in other notable ways with the issue of discrimination against sexual minority groups in Canadian Catholic schools. Canadian Catholic schools that receive government monies and provide educational services to the general public must respect all aspects of the *Canadian Charter of Rights and Freedoms* – including the equality rights provision – even if it poses problems for the selective observance of particular Catholic doctrine related to non-heterosexual behaviour. Canadian Catholic school boards and Catholic education leaders must be reminded that the Catholic Church is not the sole arbitrator when it comes to the daily operations of publicly funded Catholic schools. School trustees make important decisions that directly impact how Catholic schools are run, and they are answerable to many authorities: the Roman Catholic Church, by tradition; parents, taxpayers, provincial school acts, the provincial Ministry of Education, provincial human rights legislation, and the *Charter*, by law. Publicly funded Canadian Catholic schools are part of an historical separate school system enshrined in the Canadian Constitution of 1867 and are operated by a civil authority called a separate school board comprising municipally elected school trustees. Because of trustees' publicly elected status, Canadian Catholic schools are therefore legally accountable to provincial governments rather than to church authorities.

In the case of Saskatchewan marriage commissioners attempting to exercise their freedom of religion rights in refusing to marry same-sex couples, one of the judges on the Saskatchewan Court of Appeal arrived at the same conclusion as the majority but with a different rationale. Justice Gene Ann Smith argued Section 2 of the *Charter* – religious freedom – is not violated by the court's finding that the proposed law is unconstitutional because "interference with the right of marriage commissioners to act in accordance with their religious belief ... is trivial or insubstantial, in that it ... does not threaten actual religious beliefs or conduct" (Saskatchewan Court of Appeal, 2011, p. 65). Discussing circumstances in which the expression of particular religious beliefs should not require the suppression of the equality rights of certain groups, Justice Smith concluded: "The legislative objective in this case cannot be found to be of sufficient importance to permit the infringement of the Charter rights of others" (Saskatchewan Court of Appeal, 2011, p. 67). Essentially, lgbtq people should be treated equally when attempting to receive government services, in this case having a civil marriage performed by a marriage commissioner, even if the marriage commissioner objects to the federal marriage equality law on religious grounds. The logic outlined in Smith's decision has enormous wider implications – perhaps as far-reaching as the 1998 *Vriend* case discussed above – for lgbtq teachers who have been fired from a Canadian Catholic school because of their sexual orientation or gender identity on the grounds that Section 2 of the *Charter* should not trump Section 15. Sexual and gender diverse teachers working in publicly funded Canadian Catholic schools should be equal before and under the law and should have the right to the equal protection and equal benefit of the law without discrimination on the basis of sexual orientation or gender identity because of perceived conflicts with the religious beliefs of the Catholic education leaders.

A notable legal battle in Ontario: Marc Hall

Although Canada has yet to see a *Charter* challenge in cases involving lgbtq teachers who have been fired from their Catholic schools because of their sexual orientation or gender identity, *Hall v Durham Catholic District School Board* almost reached this level. Marc Hall was a 17-year-old gay Catholic student enrolled in his senior year at Monsignor John Pereyma Catholic Secondary School – a publicly funded Catholic school in Oshawa, Ontario. He was successful in obtaining an interlocutory injunction on 10 May 2002 to take his boyfriend as his date to the prom (Grace & Wells, 2005). Earlier, on 25 February 2002, the principal of the school had refused Hall permission on the grounds that interacting with a same-sex partner at the prom would constitute a form of sexual activity that was contrary to Catholicity (MacKinnon, 2002).

Experiencing the sting of discrimination, Hall discussed the school's decision with his family and together they rallied the support of several community organizations who believed in Hall's fight for equality rights. David Corbett, a well-known lawyer and gay activist who was involved with several Canadian advances in same-sex legal rights, offered to represent Hall free of charge (Huber, 2002). Two main pillars supported Corbett's legal arguments. First, as a publicly funded institution, Hall's Catholic school had to respect the same secular laws as other publicly funded institutions, specifically those pertaining to anti-discrimination. Second, by refusing Hall permission to take his boyfriend as his date to prom, Hall's Catholic school contravened the anti-discrimination sections of the *Ontario School Act*, which governs all school boards in the province, as well as the *Ontario Human Rights Code* (MacKinnon, 2002).

Canadian children's rights advocate and scholar Katherine Covell (2007) has pointed out that in discriminating against Hall, Monsignor John Pereyma School also violated several articles of the United Nations Convention on the Rights of the Child, which Canada ratified in 1991 and is bound by international law to uphold. Specifically, the school's homophobic discrimination against Hall violated Hall's article 13 right to freedom of expression, article 14 right to freedom of thought and conscience, and article 15 right to freedom of association (Covell, 2007, p. 250). Covell underscores that in picking on a member of a sexual minority group, the Catholic school sends the dubious message that it believes it has the authority to discriminate against, and otherwise mistreat, lgbtq individuals in its midst.

Authority, history, and tradition form the main pillar of the counter argument put forth by the lawyers for the Catholic school in the 2002 *Hall v Durham Catholic District School Board* case. Legal counsel for the Catholic school argued that Section 93 of the Canadian Constitution assured the school of its denominational rights to make curricular and policy decisions that are in line with Catholic doctrine. Furthermore, the Catholic school legal team argued that any secular interference with its reliance upon Catholic doctrine to conduct its affairs would constitute a violation of its religious freedom, as guaranteed by Section 2 of the *Canadian Charter of Rights and Freedoms* (MacKinnon, 2002).

At the end of the two-day hearing, Justice Robert MacKinnon ordered that Hall be allowed to attend his high school prom with his boyfriend as his date. MacKinnon had the foresight to stipulate that the school could not circumvent his ruling by cancelling the prom (MacKinnon, 2002). The hearing's purview did not encompass the wider issues the case raised in terms of Section 2 of the *Charter* versus Section 15 – MacKinnon left those arguments to be addressed by a higher court. Although both parties expressed an interest in fighting further in a court of appeal, Hall ultimately did not pursue a lawsuit.

The *Hall v Durham Catholic District School Board* case is well known among Canadians because it was widely covered in the Canadian news media (Canadian Broadcasting Corporation News, 2002; Oziewicz, 2002). Hall became a minor celebrity after filmmaker Larry Peloso cast Hall to star as himself in a one-hour documentary about his case called *Prom Fight: The Marc Hall Story* (Peloso, 2002). The *Hall* case became even more widely known after filmmaker John L'Ecuyer created a made-for-television movie called *Prom Queen: The Marc Hall Story*, which received even more distribution than the previous documentary (L'Ecuyer, MacLennan, Staines, K. Haldane, & Young-Leckie, 2004).

When the creators of *Queer as Folk*, the television series about a group of gay men, learned of Hall's plight, they invited him to appear in a cameo role as a reveller on the dance floor of the series' fictional bar Club Babylon, set in an actual Toronto gay bar called Woody's (Cowen & Lipman, 2002). This cameo appearance cemented Hall's status as a folk hero among lgbtq people in Canada and abroad. One young lgbtq Canadian I interviewed for this study who regularly watched the *Queer as Folk* series said he learned from the television program that "there is nothing wrong with being gay" (quotation from the narrative vignette about the participant referred to by the pseudonym Jacob in this study). Hall's brief appearance on *Queer as Folk* shows the interconnectedness between an increased cultural acceptance of non-heterosexuals and the advancement of their legal rights.

The 2002 *Hall v Durham Catholic District School Board* case received tremendous media coverage, spurred the production of two films, caught the attention of a television drama about the lives of gay men, and even influenced the content of a Canadian law textbook. Hall's influence on young lgbtq Canadians has the potential to endure much longer than in the fleeting world of popular culture now that his case is outlined and explained in the textbook *Canadian Civics*, which was written by two Catholic educators and is used in secondary schools throughout Ontario (Ruypers & Ryall, 2005). One young Ontarian I interviewed for this study (referred to by the pseudonym Jonas) spoke about how encouraged he was to see the *Hall* case in his textbook while in Catholic school, and he noted that this case made him more interested in following other lgbtq human rights cases occurring in schools throughout the world.

Homophobia Making Headlines: Examples from Ontario Catholic Schools

Catholic school boards in Canada have not only drawn unwanted media attention for the cases involving Joseph Stellpflug, Lisa Reimer, and Marc Hall; they have also made national headlines for a myriad of other homophobic incidents. In Ontario, some of these incidents include Catholic school boards banning a book called *Open Minds to Equality* because it discusses homophobia; disregarding the aspects of the Ontario Ministry of Education's Equity and Inclusive Education Strategy that attend to homophobia and circumventing the parts of the Ontario Ministry of Education's 2010 health and physical education curriculum that address gender identity and sexual orientation; declining to participate in a national survey on homophobia in schools; and banning GSAs from forming in Catholic schools. Each will be briefly described in turn.

Banning an inclusive education book that mentions homophobia

In November 2007, during the height of the fallout surrounding the 2005 legalization of same-sex marriage in Canada, Waterloo Catholic District School Board (WCDSB) in southern Ontario succumbed to pressure from Defend Traditional Marriage and Family (DTMF), a Christian organization serving the Kitchener, Waterloo, and Cambridge area of southern Ontario, to remove a controversial book from circulation (Kawawada & Mercer, 2007). The book, *Open Minds to Equality*, is a teacher resource that provides learning activities designed to affirm diversity and promote equity in schools (Schniedewind & Davidson, 2006). DTMF opposed the book's circulation in Catholic schools because it lists homophobia as being on par with other types of discriminatory practices in schools, such as racism, ageism, sexism, and anti-Semitism (Kawawada, 2007). Jack Fonseca, communications director for DTMF, said the "clever subtlety" of the book is that it "hooks the immature Catholic reader by mixing homosexuals and children of homosexuals into the list of racial/ethnic groups who suffer 'institutional discrimination'" (as cited in Kawawada, 2007, p. 1).

Although his original complaint was about the presence of *Open Minds to Equality* in Waterloo Catholic schools, Fonseca also tried to broaden his concern to include objections to the WCDSB's approved referral of Catholic students to queer-positive therapists and organizations (O'Brien & Westen, 2007). Queer youth who come from devoutly religious homes often have fewer supports than those who come from nominally religious or non-religious homes and receive less affirming information about sexual orientation or gender identity. In recognition of this added stress and safety issue, in 2006 the WCDSB's Family Life Advisory Committee approved of referring troubled queer youth throughout the district to a local, queer-positive, and provincially certified psychotherapy organization called Rainbow Therapist and to a local support group for lgbtq youth called OK 2B Me (O'Brien & Westen, 2007).

In addition, in 2006 the WCDSB approved of referring Catholic parents of lgbtq youth to PFLAG (Parents, Families and Friends of Lesbians and Gays), a well-established support group that promotes the health and well-being of lgbtq individuals by actively supporting their friends and family. DTMF was opposed to the WCDSB's approval of referrals to the above-noted queer-positive services, and Fonseca tried to raise these concerns along with his original complaint about the queer-positive book. However, the WCDSB's Family Life Advisory Committee informed Fonseca that their meeting was arranged to solely attend to his original complaint and that other matters would have to be raised in future complaints (O'Brien & Westen, 2007).

Trustees for WCDSB, inundated with requests to keep the book *Open Minds to Equality* away from students, devised a compromise whereby the book would be available only as an optional teacher resource in a designated teacher resource library, which is housed in the Catholic Education Centre in downtown Kitchener, off limits to students (Kawawada & Mercer, 2007).

Circumventing curriculum about sexual orientation and gender identity

In 2008, Ontario's minister of education, Kathleen Wynne, recognized a need to take action against all forms of discrimination in schools and consulted with a diverse group of educational stakeholders to develop what is now known as the Equity and Inclusive Education Strategy for Ontario schools (Ontario Ministry of Education, 2009a). The Equity and Inclusive Education Strategy describes homophobia as being at the "forefront of discussion" (Ontario Ministry of Education, 2009a, p. 7). To realize the government's vision of an equitable and inclusive education system, future curricula revisions would have to reflect the guiding principles outlined in the Ontario Ministry of Education's Equity and Inclusive Education Strategy. Accordingly, Ontario's health and physical education curriculum, which was slated for revision in 2007 after not having been updated since 1998, attempted to redress homophobic discrimination in schools by actively discussing gender identity and sexual orientation.

As with the Equity and Inclusive Education Strategy, the development of the health and physical education curriculum was a lengthy consultative process involving many educational leaders and specialists, including the education division of the Assembly of Catholic Bishops of Ontario (ACBO), the Institute for Catholic Education (ICE) (Craine, 2010). ICE's executive director, Sister Joan Cronin, was not overly concerned about the more controversial aspects of the new curriculum – such as appreciating invisible differences in others and recognizing that some people are raised in families led by two mothers or two fathers – because the Catholic education system enjoys a long-standing tradition of reworking ministry curriculum so that it can be appropriately presented from a Catholic faith perspective (Greenberg, 2010b). That is, Sister Cronin knew Catholic school boards would be exempt from having to present this contentious curriculum so there was no real need to spend energy opposing it.

When the Ontario Ministry of Education posted the revised health and physical education curriculum on its website in January 2010, a coalition of religious and family-values organizations – with the notable exception of Catholic education stakeholders because they would have special exemption status – vocally opposed it (Hammer & Howlett, 2010). The coalition's opposition involved a threat to keep their children home from school on 10 May 2010, as a form of protest to the new curriculum unless Ontario Premier Dalton McGuinty agreed to abandon the changes. Caught off guard, Premier McGuinty defended the new Ontario health and physical education curriculum, saying it had gone through a rigorous two-year consultative process involving parent groups and a wide variety of education experts (Babbage, 2010). When pressed as to whether Ontario's publicly funded Catholic schools would also have to teach aspects of the new curriculum that were affirming of sexual minority groups, Premier McGuinty asserted that Catholic schools would not be able to opt out of the revamped curriculum because of conflicts with Catholic doctrine (Babbage, 2010; Greenberg, 2010b). McGuinty's new education minister, Leona Dombrowsky, a former Catholic school board trustee, confirmed that educational experts from Ontario's Institute for Catholic Education were involved in the development of the new curriculum and therefore endorsed it (Babbage, 2010; Greenberg, 2010b).

Premier McGuinty erroneously believed the Ontario provincial curriculum applied equally to all publicly funded schools in the province, saying, "We have a single curriculum when it comes to mathematics, when it comes to history, when it comes to world studies and when it comes to sex education" (as cited in Howlett, 2010b, p. A5). Similarly, education minister Leona Dombrowsky went on public record saying, "This is the Ontario curriculum, and it's the curriculum for all schools and all students" (as cited in Greenberg, 2010a, p. 1). Ontario's premier and minister of education can be forgiven for being unaware of a rarely discussed special arrangement for publicly funded Catholic schools in Canada – even education experts and specialists are surprised to learn of the little-known practice in which the ICE "interprets" provincial curricula to reflect Catholic doctrine.

In a rare public explanation of the situation, Ottawa Archbishop Terrence Prendergast told the *Ottawa Citizen,* "Whatever is prescribed by the government on issues of sexuality, life and faith – these are to be understood in the rights that Catholics have by the denominational school system to apply them and to interpret them in their own way" (as cited in Greenberg, 2010a, p. 2). The ICE's executive director, Sister Joan Cronin, clarified that Catholic education consultants were developing their own human sexuality program that deviated significantly from the new provincial one because of conflicts with Catholic doctrine. Sister Cronin confirmed that the Catholic version of the new provincial health and physical education curriculum would simply be a supplement of the current Catholic curriculum for family life education called the Fully Alive series (Greenberg, 2010b). "When it comes to matters like faith and morality," Sister Cronin explained, "the denominational rights accorded to the Catholic schools supersede any Ministry of Education policy directive" (as cited in Howlett, 2010a, p. A5).

Once his "misunderstanding" was pointed out to him, Premier McGuinty arranged to have a statement of clarification issued from his office. Signed by James Ryan, president of the Ontario English Catholic Teachers' Association, together with Paula Peroni, president of the Ontario Catholic School Trustees' Association, and Thomas Collins, Archbishop of Toronto and president of the ACBO, a portion of the statement reads, "We want to be clear: Ontario's Catholic schools teach the provincial curriculum from a Catholic perspective and have done so successfully" (as cited in Howlett, 2010b, p. A5). The McGuinty government succumbed to the religious right's objections and subsequently changed course, agreeing to release the new health and physical education curriculum in the fall of 2010 without the contentious components having to do with homosexuality and gender identity. Accordingly, the Ontario Ministry of Education withdrew the newly approved curriculum from its website in April 2010, just a few weeks following the initial opposition from the conservative religious coalition (Howlett & Hammer, 2010).

Declining to participate in a national survey on homophobia in schools

Recognizing a lack of comprehensive data on levels of homophobia in Canadian schools, critical pedagogue Catherine Taylor devised a national climate survey in 2007 to assess the situation (University of

Winnipeg, 2009). An education and communications professor at the University of Winnipeg, Dr Taylor also serves on the education committee of Egale Canada (formerly Equality for Gays and Lesbians Everywhere), an advocacy association that strives to advance equality for lgbtq individuals and their families across Canada (Egale Canada, 2005). Egale Canada showed interest in assisting with anti-homophobia education in Canadian schools, but its resources were exhausted by the long campaign to legalize same-sex marriage in Canada. Once Egale Canada was able to regroup and refocus following the successful legalization of same-sex marriage in Canada in 2005, it turned to its education committee for ideas, and Dr Taylor suggested a collaborative study with her team at the University of Winnipeg and Egale Canada.

Launched in January 2008, Dr Taylor's Internet-based survey was completed by students from St John's to Victoria to Iqaluit. Dr Taylor and Egale Canada invited all school boards across the country to participate in the survey, but not all accepted. Absent from the study are Catholic school boards throughout Canada – all declined to take part (Egale Canada, 2009). Father Dennis Noon, former chair and trustee of the Wellington Catholic District School Board in Guelph, Ontario, made national headlines for responding to Egale Canada's invitation to take part in the nationwide survey with a capitalized, "not interested thank you" (as cited in Kawawada, 2008, p. 1). When reporters pressed for an explanation, Noon simply stated that homophobia was not a big issue for his board. Apparently, homophobia was not a concern for any other Catholic board in the country either, given that no bishop gave his assent for any Catholic board to take part in the study (Egale Canada, 2009). The uniformity of this response suggested a centralized directive from within the upper echelons of the Catholic Church in Canada.

Despite the fact that no Catholic school boards in Canada agreed to officially participate in the national survey on homophobia in schools, some Canadian Catholic school students participated on their own by visiting the Egale Canada website and following the links to the survey. An initial report on the survey shows that the few students from Canadian Catholic schools who did participate were much more likely than their counterparts in non-Catholic schools to feel that their school was not supportive of lgbtq people, that teachers were ineffective in addressing homophobic harassment, and that they could not talk to at least one adult in their school about issues facing sexual minority groups (Egale Canada, 2009). Because of the lack of involvement from Catholic boards throughout the country, Dr Taylor and her research team are not be able to provide any further data on the situation in Catholic schools for lgbtq students (Egale Canada, 2009).

Banning Gay-Straight Alliances from Catholic schools

In keeping with its Equity and Inclusive Education Strategy, launched in the fall of 2008 and available in an abridged version on its website (Ontario Ministry of Education, 2009b), the Ontario Ministry of Education released a policy statement in the fall of 2009 intended for all administrators in all publicly funded schools throughout the province. This policy statement, which the ministry refers to as "Policy/Program Memorandum No. 145," addresses the topic of "progressive discipline and promoting positive student behaviour" (Ontario Ministry of Education, 2009c, p. 1). This policy statement specifically names GSAs as important student-led initiatives that should be encouraged: "In order to promote a positive school climate, school boards must provide opportunities for all members of the school community to increase their knowledge and understanding of such issues as homophobia ... Boards must also help school staff to give support to students who wish to participate in gay-straight alliances and in other student-led activities that promote understanding and development of healthy relationships" (Ontario Ministry of Education, 2009b, p. 1). Government support for GSAs could not have come at a more opportune time.

During 2010, a dramatic rise in the suicide rates of gay youths in North America prompted human rights activists to launch a grassroots Internet campaign titled It Gets Better, urging suicidal queer youth to "hang on" until they can leave high school (Savage, 2010). At that time when the need for GSAs could not be more profound, the Halton Catholic District School Board (HCDSB) revealed its disconnect from larger cultural shifts by voting to ban GSAs in their schools (Houston, 2011a). One of Ontario's 29 Catholic school boards, HCDSB serves 29,000 students in several suburbs of Toronto, such as Milton, Halton Hills, Burlington, and Oakville (HCDSB, 2010). HCDSB chose to ban GSAs in deference to the wishes of their local bishop. In a 19 January 2010 letter to all Ontario Catholic school board directors, Bishop Paul-André Durocher discouraged the establishment of GSAs in Catholic schools claiming that they "imply a self-identification with sexual orientation that is often premature among high school students" (Durocher, 2010, p. 1). As the chair of the Education Commission within the ACBO, Bishop Durocher is an important authority for Catholic education in Ontario. Intrepid reporters for *Xtra!*, Canada's leading source of lgbtq news, confirmed Durocher's powerful influence by contacting all 29 of Ontario's Catholic school boards to see if any of them maintained some form of a GSA – not one of them reported having a GSA in any of their schools (Stayshyn & Houston, 2011).

Bishop Durocher, and the other bishops before him who served as Catholic education leaders, provide Catholic perspectives and guidance for revised versions of Ontario education curricula and policy that may clash with Catholic doctrine (Collins, 2011). On the matter of implementing the Ontario Ministry of Education's Equity and Inclusive Education Strategy, a Catholic consortium of education leaders worked closely with members of the Ontario Education Services Corporation to design what is known as a "Catholic template" of the ministry's equity policy (Ontario Education Services Corporation, 2010a). The Catholic version is similar in content to the original provincial ministry's equity policy, but it reserves the right to implement the policy "in a manner which is consistent with the exercise of the Board's denominational rights" (Ontario Education Services Corporation, 2010b, p. 1). The denominational rights of Catholic schools in Canada form the main pillar of the Catholic template, with its authors invoking these rights seven times using variations on the above-quoted phrase throughout the 16-page document. There is no requirement that Catholic boards throughout Ontario adopt the Catholic template; however, doing so would assure Catholic boards that they are implementing a Catholic version of the ministry's equity policy that has been approved by the province's highest bishops and Catholic curriculum and educational policy leaders.

Written into the Ontario Ministry of Education's Equity and Inclusive Education Strategy was a list of action items requiring all school boards in the province to develop their own equity and inclusive education policies that had to comply with the ministry's overarching strategy and be ready for implementation by 1 September 2010 (Ontario Ministry of Education, 2009a, p. 21). In an attempt to follow this directive, HCDSB met in November 2010 to review the existing Catholic equity template provided by the Ontario Education Services Corporation and voted to adopt the bulk of the document with the notable removal of "gender" and "sexual orientation" from the list of prohibited grounds of discrimination (Houston, 2011a). During the same November 2010 meeting, the HCDSB also took a conservative reading of the letter from Bishop Durocher in which he discouraged the establishment of GSAs in Catholic schools, and HCDSB voted to ban GSAs outright from all schools in its jurisdiction (Houston, 2011a). When members of the press asked Alice Anne LeMay, the chair of HCDSB, for a rationale of the ban, she retorted, "We don't have Nazi groups either. Gay-straight alliances are banned because they are not within the teachings of the Catholic Church. If a gay student requests a gay-straight alliance, they would be denied" (as cited in Houston, 2011a, p. 1). This ban earned HCDSB international notoriety as people around the world struggled to understand this particular form of institutionalized homophobia (Hammer, 2011).

Students responded by leading a challenge against the ban. Specifically, two grade 12 HCDSB students contacted the York Federation of Students and a member of provincial parliament to prepare a human rights challenge to the ban on the grounds that HCDSB's local equity and inclusive policy – the tool the board created to prohibit GSAs in all its schools – is in violation of the Ministry of Education's Equity and Inclusive Education Strategy and the *Ontario Human Rights Code* (Houston, 2011b). The students eventually chose to withdraw their human rights challenge, however, since HCDSB trustees voted 6–2 in favour of rescinding the ban during an emergency board meeting in Burlington on 18 January 2011 (Houston, 2011c).

Removing the official ban does not automatically ensure clearance to establish a GSA. Even though GSAs are not explicitly banned, they are still not allowed. Speaking to *Xtra!* reporters, Gerald Casey, superintendent of education for the Bruce-Grey Catholic District School Board in southern Ontario, remarked, "No, I wouldn't say we ban them. We support student clubs that support inclusiveness, especially for students who might otherwise feel marginalized. But all our clubs must, however, adhere to the Catholic teachings and values" (as cited in Stayshyn & Houston, 2011, p. 1). When the reporters asked Casey if students at a Bruce-Grey Catholic school could start a GSA, he admitted, "The answer would be no" (as cited in Stayshyn & Houston, 2011, p. 1). The Canadian Civil Liberties Association (CCLA) continues to monitor HCDSB to ensure that an unwritten ban does not replace its written one and that students will not be precluded from exercising their equality rights guaranteed by the *Canadian Charter of Rights and Freedoms* (1982), as well as their Charter rights to freedom of expression, association, and speech (CCLA, 2011).

The students' potential court challenge would have been a difficult battle, as leaders of Catholic education in Ontario regularly rely on a liberal interpretation of their denominational rights. For example, in referring to the right of Catholic schools to disregard progressive curriculum on sexual education, Lou Piovesan, the general secretary of the ACBO, stated, "In particular, when it comes to matters of faith and morality, the ... denominational rights accorded to Catholic schools in Ontario would supersede Ministry of Education proposed curriculum content ... accordingly, if some content related to faith and morality matters is indeed determined to be at variance with [Catholic] principles, it would not be endorsed for use in Catholic schools" (as cited in Artuso, 2010, p. 1). Students' human rights challenges on the grounds described above would more likely be successful if lawyers are able to point out to Catholic education leaders, as well as to members of the tribunal hearing the case, that the Roman Catholic Church is not the only authority on Catholic education in Ontario.

Concluding Remarks

This collection of media accounts reveals a progression in terms of same-sex legal rights in Canada. The accounts also show, however, a subtle and determined Catholic backlash to those same legal advances. In the *Vriend* case, the Supreme Court of Canada decided in 1998 that the omission of sexual orientation as a prohibited ground of discrimination under the Alberta IRPA infringed upon Section 15 of the Charter. This decision represents a logical first step in ensuring that Albertans who have experienced discrimination on the basis of sexual orientation now have an avenue for legally filing a complaint. The *Vriend* decision did not, however, attend to the larger issues raised by his wrongful dismissal in terms of how far religious freedom can extend when intersecting with equality rights.

Canadian educational researcher James Covert (1993) shows a history of Canadian legal precedent that has almost always decided in favour of the denominational rights of Catholic schools over the individual rights of Catholic teachers. Despite the fact that most of the cases Covert describes took place in the 1970s and 1980s, this record of past legal proceedings serves as a guide for subsequent cases of a similar kind and successfully discourages new complainants from proceeding. Joseph Stellpflug eventually dropping his 1997 wrongful dismissal complaint after learning that his lawyers were not confident they could win his case because of legal precedent is a prime example. This legal precedent was powerful enough to dissuade Stellpflug from seeking a legal remedy for the discrimination he endured, despite the fact that his province's human rights code had already included sexual orientation as a prohibited ground of discrimination in the years before his wrongful dismissal.

No legal precedent exists that shows Canadian judges deciding in favour of Catholic school leaders who wish to use Catholic doctrine to legally discriminate against students. Hence human rights lawyers were not deterred from taking on the 2002 *Hall v Durham Catholic District School Board* case resulting in the Ontario Superior Court granting an interlocutory injunction so that Mark could take his boyfriend to his high school prom. As in the *Vriend* case, the presiding judge did not decide on the broader issues the *Hall* case raised in terms of Section 2 versus Section 15 of the Charter. A higher court would have addressed these issues and, although both parties were interested in arguing their case further, Hall eventually dropped the matter because of the stress it caused and his desire to move on with his life.

The Education Commission of the OCCB did not drop the matter, however. Instead, the OCCB held a two-day conference in the fall of 2002 – four months following Hall's successful court challenge – to strategize ways to make clear the official Catholic stance on homosexuality and avoid such embarrassing student challenges in the future (Borst, 2003). The product of the bishops' conference was a brief pastoral guideline, written in the form of a letter, called *To All Involved in Catholic Education*, which it released on its website and sent out to all Catholic schools in Ontario (OCCB, 2003). A footnote at the end of the OCCB pastoral guideline states, "The controversy leading up to and resulting from the interim decision of the Ontario Superior Court in the case of *Hall v Durham Catholic District School Board* showed that this pastoral instruction is opportune" (OCCB, 2003, p. 5). Essentially, the OCCB pastoral guideline reiterates the official Catholic doctrine on homosexuality and informs teachers that they must enforce the doctrine in Catholic school settings. More disturbingly, it harbours a conversion agenda in that it asks teachers to "try to lead the homosexual student to a progressively better sexual morality" (OCCB, 2003, p. 4).

With this kind of leadership from the Education Commission of the OCCB in 2002, it is not surprising that the homophobic school policies described in this chapter soon spread to other Catholic school boards of Ontario, notably HCDSB and the WCDSB. One important example noted was the 2007 banning of a book called *Open Minds to Equality* because of its frank discussion of homophobia. Although on the surface this media report recounts a negative news event (WCDSB's banning of an equity book that attends to homophobia), the subtext of the media report contains some surprising references to lgbtq positive activism occurring within this school board's Family Life Advisory Committee. That is, this media report also contains references to WCDSB's authorization of its counselling staff to refer lgbtq students and their families to queer-positive therapists (the Rainbow Therapist) and community organizations (a local lgbtq support group called OK 2B Me and the local chapter of PFLAG).

Through this media report, we can see instances of queer-positive resistance to repressive Catholic doctrine about non-heterosexuality and the importance of individual activism in leading progressive change. WCDSB would have been familiar with the Ontario bishops' pastoral guideline *To All Involved in Catholic Education,* which clearly lays out the official Catholic teaching about "persons with same-sex attraction." Nevertheless, the school board authorized its counsellors to provide referrals to local queer-positive services – services that affirm gender and sexual diversity, services that are therefore *not* aligned with Catholic teaching on non-heterosexuality. This anomaly suggests a fissure between what the Catholic bishops want and what the Catholic schools are willing to do. It is one thing for the Ontario bishops to remotely declare that lgbtq youth must be called to a lifetime of celibacy; it is something else altogether for educators in Catholic schools to condemn students they work with on a daily basis to such a sentence. The media account ostensibly about the banning of the book also reveals resistance by some individuals within the Waterloo Catholic board who recognized the grave consequences of callously calling lgbtq youth to a lifetime without intimacy and romantic love and offered instead some affirming resources for students and their families.

Although the Waterloo banning of *Open Minds to Equality* is, for the most part, a depressing media account, the tangential reference it makes to resistance to homophobic Catholic directives is hopeful. If negative stories about homophobia in Canadian Catholic schools rarely appear in the media, then positive stories about resistance to homophobic policies and curricular revisions in Catholic schools are even rarer. The infrequent appearance of stories describing resistance to homophobia in Canadian Catholic schools is not only due to the tendency of the media to report on negative stories but also because any kind of resistance movement, no matter what its size or scope, must initially be clandestine lest it draw the attention of the oppressive force and incur sanctions and other forms of retaliation. If WCDSB's Family Life Advisory Committee sent out a press release outlining its new policy of offering queer-positive referrals to queer and questioning youth and their families, then surely other staunchly Catholic factions within the board or the ACBO would exert power and reverse the decision. It is vital to be stealthy when first resisting homophobic school policies and curricular revisions.

The good news is just because few direct media reports exist on *specific* resistance to homophobic school policies, it does not mean that resistance is not occurring. The blogosphere is jammed with comments on media stories from Catholic school stakeholders and members of the general public who are disgruntled with homophobic school policies and curricular decisions related to sexual and gender diversity. Many regular lay Catholics I have worked with and spoken with over the years disapprove of bishops targeting vulnerable sexual and gender minority groups. Media reports, the law, and individual acts of resistance work in tandem to ignite the online debate and raise general awareness of this disturbing little-known aspect of public education in Canada.

When Canadian media sources, such as the *Ottawa Citizen* and *The Globe and Mail*, asked Catholic education leaders why they feel they can openly disregard aspects of the Ontario Ministry of Education's Equity and Inclusive Education Strategy or why these same Catholic education leaders carefully circumvent the parts of the Ontario Ministry of Education's 2010 health and physical education curriculum that raise the topics of gender identity and sexual orientation, they invariably replied that it is within their denominational rights to do so. For example, as mentioned earlier in this chapter, Ottawa Archbishop Terrence Prendergast told the *Ottawa Citizen* that Catholic schools have the denominational right to interpret governmental policy on matters of sexuality through a Catholic lens. Similarly, the ICE's executive director, Sister Joan Cronin, concurred with Prendergast, telling *The Globe and Mail*, "When it comes to matters like faith and morality, the denominational rights accorded to the Catholic schools supersede any Ministry of Education policy directive" (as cited in Howlett, 2010a, p. A5).

Ontario Catholic education leaders and bishops might believe that the Roman Catholic Church is the only authority on Catholic education in Ontario, but the fact is, Catholic schools in Ontario are also expected to answer to the Ontario Ministry of Education and its Equity and Inclusive Education Strategy, which reflects the *Ontario Human Rights Code*, which itself in turn is modelled after the *Canadian Charter of Rights and Freedoms* (1982). Section 93 of the Canadian Constitution and Section 29 of the Charter outline the need to establish and maintain particular denominational schools; they do not provide provisions for Catholic schools to use selective aspects of Catholic doctrine to discriminate against groups of people. Denominational rights do not mean the right to openly discriminate against ill-protected sexual or gender minority groups, even though this is precisely how Catholic education leaders have been interpreting these sections of Canadian law. This is not exclusively an Ontario problem – Alberta was in an even more precarious position in terms of respecting the equality rights of lgbtq people in Catholic schools because, up until the 2015 historic toppling of the provincial Progressive Conservative Association of Alberta's 44-years of uninterrupted rule in Alberta, Alberta's provincial Ministry of Education had been less modern and forward-thinking than Ontario's. Furthermore, as will be discussed in Chapter 4, Catholic bishops in Alberta write pastoral guidelines and make statements about how to manage lgbtq people in Catholic schools that are heavily influenced by similar documents and policies authored by the ACBO.

Ironically, separate schools in Canada – established in the nineteenth century because of the perceived need to protect Catholic faith minorities from a hostile Protestant majority – are now often culpable in the twenty-first century of similar hostility towards minority groups (Callaghan, 2009). Resistance is not futile, as one media report's oblique reference to Waterloo Catholic school officials' referral of queer youth and their families to queer-positive support services suggests. Marc Hall was successful in reversing his Catholic school's homophobic policy that forbade same-sex dates at his high school prom. Two grade 12 students in the Halton Catholic District School Board mustered the courage to consider mounting a human rights challenge to their board's equity policy on the grounds that it explicitly excludes sexual orientation from the list of prohibited forms of discrimination, which is in direct violation of the Ministry of Ontario's equity policy.

Without question, media accounts have played an instrumental role in getting this much needed discussion started. Without the news media, Catholic school districts throughout Ontario would have been able to quietly continue suppressing same-sex legal advances in Canada by continuing to draft unnoticed and unresisted homophobic school policies and curricular revisions. Without the media, regular Canadians, Catholic and non-Catholic alike, would have remained in ignorance. It is fair to say that the media have been and continue to be important "first responders" to instances of homophobic discrimination in Canadian Catholic schools. Media reports on these kinds of stories have the power to set in motion a far-reaching chain of events that can bring about progressive change. The Halton situation involving the banning of GSAs is a case in point. It was only after the media reports drew unwanted attention to the Halton Catholic board's discriminatory equity and inclusive education policy that the chair of that board called an emergency board meeting resulting in a removal of the official written ban on GSAs in all of its schools. The important role the news media can play in highlighting legal cases that effect positive change is also evident in one of the student participant's stories. Jonas, who attended Catholic schools in southern Ontario from junior kindergarten until he graduated in 2007, remembers feeling "kind of giddy" upon discovering the *Hall* case in his politics textbook. It is not likely that the *Hall* case would have appeared in an Ontario high school politics textbook if it were not for the amount of attention drawn to this case by the Canadian media.

In both the Halton and the Jonas examples, we can see one of the ways in which the different types of data collected for this study overlap and inform each other. The Catholic doctrine (to be discussed in Chapter 4) asserts its disciplining force against non-heterosexuals in Catholic schools. The Canadian news media learn of these homophobic and discriminatory practices and disseminate them to the general public. Members of the general public respond with such outrage in various forms that the Catholic school districts in question are compelled to reverse or at least revise their homophobic policies. In this way, media reports together with individual activism have the potential to play a crucial role in influencing school policy and, by extension, improve the school experience of non-heterosexual students and staff in Canadian Catholic schools.

Of course, informing the public about discriminatory practices does not mean that once members of the public are more aware they will necessarily be moved to take action to redress the discrimination. However, a news media report does have the potential to be the impetus behind the drafting of a protest petition, the establishment of a letter-writing campaign to elected officials, and other forms of public demonstrations designed to bring about change. Journalism scholar Dane Claussen (2002) notes that journalists often avoid covering stories that involve the intersection of religion and sexuality. The fact that the stories showcased in this chapter received any kind of media coverage at all is significant and points to a change in practice among Canadian journalists regarding these types of stories. Such an increase in media coverage is important because Canadian mainstream media reports have the power to sway public opinion and lead to progressive change.

So, in summary, How does power operate within and across Alberta and Ontario Catholic schools? The majority of news media reports show that Catholic doctrine originating from the Vatican asserts a dominant force within Alberta and Ontario Catholic schools. In fact, in terms of policing the sexual conduct of non-heterosexuals, Catholic canonical law prevails over Canadian common law. As they struggle with how to respond to lgbtq people in their schools, Catholic education leaders tend to abandon the tradition of Catholic social teaching involving justice for the weakest and turn instead for guidance to the formidable Catholic canonical law on the topic of homosexuality. In so doing, they also disregard Canadian human rights legislation at the provincial and federal levels. The Vatican's power is not absolute, however, as is evidenced by those media reports describing successful acts of resistance to the doctrinal disciplining of non-heterosexuals. How do Catholic documents portray teachers and students as subjects? The majority of news media reports suggest that Catholic documents, such as curriculum and policy documents (discussed in Chapter 4) designed to disseminate Catholic doctrine about sexual minorities, are an attempt to portray lgbtq students and teachers as "persons with same-sex attraction" whose behaviour should be closely monitored, controlled, and disciplined. What effects do Catholic documents have on the experiences of lgbtq individuals in Alberta and Ontario Catholic schools? Predominantly negative – most of the media reports outline stories of students and teachers in Catholic schools experiencing discrimination on the basis of sexual orientation because of directives originating with homophobic Catholic doctrine. Other media reports describe stories of homophobic school policies that were drafted specifically so that the Catholic schools in question would be properly aligned with Catholic doctrine. Is resistance possible in an education context so dominated by the repressive force of religiously inspired homophobia? Tentatively, yes, but unfortunately, the evidence of resistance is not as strong as the evidence of domination.

4

Catholic Documents:
Doctrinal Disciplining

When I first saw one of the documents that will be discussed in this chapter, *Pastoral Guidelines to Assist Students of Same-Sex Orientation*, the word "pastoral" jumped out at me, and I was briefly transported back to my English 30 classroom where one of my students asked the meaning of the word. "Serenity," I said. "Imagine the protected idyllic life of a flock of sheep being cared for by a loving shepherd." And I proceeded to teach one of the Western world's most famous pastoral poems, "L'Allegro" by John Milton. It's a poem that begins with Darkness and Melancholy (in which, interestingly, the word "holy" resides) but moves quickly to Joy "Untwisting all the chains that tie/The hidden Soul of Harmony." For reasons that will become clear, it was therefore with a growing sense of irony and unease that I read *Pastoral Guidelines to Assist Students of Same-Sex Orientation*.

This chapter examines two obscure but extremely important primary texts. They are obscure because they are known almost solely in Catholic education circles. The first text is the original 2004 document called *Pastoral Guidelines to Assist Students of Same-Sex Orientation* written by several Catholic education leaders from Ontario in collaboration with members of the Education Commission of the OCCB. A pastoral guideline is normally a sanctioned letter from a bishop, or group of bishops, outlining official policy on a topic involving the moral care of a congregation. The second text is an original 2007 workbook for Catholic educators called *Towards an Inclusive Community* written by Catholic education leaders from Alberta. Its purpose was to ensure that the ACB's 2001 pastoral guideline called *A Resource for an Inclusive Community: A Teacher's Guide for and about Persons with Same Sex Attractions* is read and understood by Alberta Catholic educators and that the bishops' message is disseminated in Catholic schools throughout Alberta.

The Ontario text is a pastoral guideline commissioned, written, and approved by Ontario bishops for mandatory use in Ontario Catholic schools. The Alberta text is a workbook for Catholic educators (similar to a teacher resource manual, a teacher in-service/workshop manual, or a policy and curriculum document) written by and for Catholic educators in Alberta for required use in Alberta Catholic schools. Both texts are little-publicized documents intended primarily for Catholic educators, and they have a powerful influence on the educational policy and curriculum decisions Catholic education leaders make regarding sexual minority groups in the Catholic schools of Alberta and Ontario. This study of homophobia in the Catholic schools of Alberta and Ontario must necessarily examine the written *sources* of homophobia. These sources can be found in elements of Catholic doctrine regarding non-heterosexuals about which the Catholic bishops write. The Ontario text is a good example of Catholic bishops' attempts to draw the attention of Catholic school staff to the official Catholic doctrine on homosexuality. It is one thing for the bishops to write a pastoral guideline about sexual minorities – it is something else entirely to get that message communicated in Catholic schools. The Alberta text is a good example of conservative Catholic educators' attempts to ensure the bishops' message reaches teachers and students in Alberta Catholic schools. A close examination of both the Ontario text and the Alberta text is necessary to understand how homophobia is institutionalized and how it serves as the underpinning for the education administered in these provinces' Catholic schools.

Both texts are obscure in the sense that they are not available in public or academic libraries, and very few lay Catholics (i.e., Catholics who are not members of the clergy) or non-Catholic educational stakeholders and experts know of their existence. They are normally distributed "in-house," that is, from the Catholic committees that created them to the Catholic education leader hierarchy within each province. Ontario is different from Alberta in that the Ontario bishops designed a course called Teaching in Ontario Catholic Schools: A Religious Education Course for Initial Teacher Education Candidates, which is offered in Ontario faculties of education and is required by Ontario Catholic boards as a prerequisite for a job interview and a condition of employment. Such courses are also available in Alberta, but they are not mandatory. I first came across the 2004 Ontario text *Pastoral Guidelines to Assist Students of Same-Sex Orientation* (PGASO) in 2005 when it was posted on the OCCB's website. Since then, the OCCB has changed its name to the Assembly of

Catholic Bishops of Ontario (ACBO), and its new website intermittently provided a link to this 2004 publication. That is, sometimes it would be posted on the website and other times it would be removed. The Education Commission of the ACBO, and the Institute for Catholic Education in Ontario, did not provide a reliable link to it either, despite the fact that they were both heavily involved in creating it. Given that PGASO was occasionally removed from the ACBO website, it appears the Ontario bishops wanted, at times, to limit the general public's knowledge of and access to it. I was able to get a copy from one of the Catholic diocese centres I had contacted throughout Ontario. A Sister of St Joseph of Toronto sent me a paper copy of it via Canada Post. The PGASO is now readily available via a simple Google search.

Similarly, the complete Alberta text *Towards an Inclusive Community* is not available online. Its principal author, the Council of Catholic School Superintendents of Alberta, does not provide a link to this 2007 publication on its website either. However, a revised version of the PowerPoint presentation contained in the *Towards an Inclusive Community* workbook is available as a PDF online (Council of Catholic School Superintendents of Alberta [CCSSA], 2007b). I first became aware of an early version of the *Towards an Inclusive Community* workbook when I attended a teacher in-service in 2004 called Sensitive Issues in Our Catholic Schools in my capacity as a high school teacher employed by a Catholic school district in Alberta. The first edition of *Towards an Inclusive Community* was issued in October 2005 to all Catholic school jurisdictions in Alberta. Two minor amendments were made to the workbook, and it was subsequently reissued in 2007 (CCSSA, 2007b). I obtained a copy of the complete 2007 edition from one of my contacts in an Alberta Catholic school district.

A characteristic of Catholic documents that address non-heterosexuality is to refer to other Catholic documents that have also addressed it and to appeal to the authority of official doctrine from the Vatican. Therefore, a study of one Catholic document, such as the Ontario text, for example, is often a study of several other similar Catholic documents. As indicated, both the Ontario text and the Alberta text refer to several other Catholic documents and the authority of the Vatican's official doctrine, and both use language to describe sexual minority groups that is considered antiquated by today's standards. For example, the authors of both the Ontario text and the Alberta text use the term *homosexual* as a universal term to refer to all lgbtq individuals because the other Catholic documents and doctrine use the term liberally. Furthermore, as I discuss in more detail below, a prevalent Catholic belief is that it is "reductionist" and "problematic" to use "politically charged language," such as *lesbian* or *gay*, not only because the authors believe such labels are "inaccurate" but also because the labels have the power to "reinforce" and "legitimate an arrested psycho-sexual development" (as cited in CCSSA, 2007, sec. 3). Accordingly, the Alberta bishops advise Catholic educators to refer to lgbtq students and teachers as "persons with same-sex attractions" (as cited in CCSSA, 2007, sec. 3), while the Ontario bishops prefer the phrase "students of same-sex orientation" (OCCB, 2004a, p. 26). Phrases such as "students of same-sex orientation" already suggest the homophobic underpinnings of both the Ontario text and the Alberta text.

Ontario's *Pastoral Guidelines to Assist Students of Same-Sex Orientation*

Chapter 3 refers to an increase in same-sex legal rights in Canada. And these changes directly affect public schools in a positive way. The 2002 case of *Hall v Durham Catholic District School Board*, which decided in favour of Hall taking his boyfriend as his date to prom, is particularly far-reaching and influential. On the secular side, the *Hall* case drew attention to homophobic discrimination against lgbtq students occurring in publicly funded Catholic schools and prompted social justice activists to ensure educational policies were in place to safeguard the equality rights of sexual minority groups in all publicly funded schools, including Catholic ones. On the Catholic side, the *Hall* case prompted the bishops of Ontario to react by holding conferences and producing documents designed to "be clear about the authentic teaching of the Church on sexual morality and in particular in the area of homosexuality" (OCCB, 2003, p. 1). Suddenly the issue was being openly addressed for school contexts.

While the secular arguments relied upon the authority of Canadian common law, specifically the *Canadian Charter of Rights and Freedoms* (1982), the Catholic arguments referred to the tradition of Catholic canonical law, specifically the *Catechism of the Catholic Church*. The secular and the Catholic positions are at odds with one another, and this led to several power struggles captured by news media reporters and described in Chapter 3.

On the part of anti-oppression educators and proponents of equal opportunity and social justice within Ontario's Ministry of Education in 2008, one tactical move following the *Hall* case was to develop a province-wide Equity and Inclusive Education Strategy (Ontario Ministry of Education [OME], 2009a). This policy's most important feature was its recognition that "homophobia has risen to the forefront of discussion"

(OME, 2009a, p. 7) and that school boards throughout Ontario "must also help school staff to give support to students who wish to participate in gay-straight alliances" (OME, 2009c, p. 1). HCDSB responded to this directive from Ontario's Ministry of Education with a tactical move of its own – it banned gay-straight alliances from all of its schools in 2011. As Chapter 3 describes, a flurry of media reports ensued.

Unaccustomed to so much media attention to curriculum and policy decisions taken by Catholic schools in Ontario, Father Thomas Collins, President of the ACBO (formerly the OCCB) and Archbishop of Toronto, issued a formal statement on the Halton matter (Collins, 2011). In defending the willingness of Catholic schools throughout Ontario to recognize that "bullying is wrong under any circumstances and all schools should provide a safe and welcoming environment for each student," Collins declared, "In 2004 the bishops sponsored the development of pastoral guidelines to ensure that such an environment was in place in Catholic secondary schools for students dealing with the issue of same-sex orientation, long before the government mandated an equity and inclusivity policy" (Collins, 2011, p. 1). An exegesis of PGASO (OCCB, 2004a), the text to which Collins refers, shows that lgbtq students are taught that they must remain celibate for life and that a corrective 12-step program called Courage will help them attain this exalted state. This message is the very opposite of a "safe and welcoming environment" the bishops purported to be proposing for lgbtq students in PGASO. It is to this document that I now turn.

PGASO is a lengthier and more detailed version of an earlier pastoral guideline from the Catholic bishops of Ontario called *To All Involved in Catholic Education* (OCCB, 2003), which I discussed in Chapter 3. A pastoral guideline is an official message from a bishop, a group of bishops, or a group of bishops in collaboration with other clergy members or laypersons who have expertise in a subject. The intended audience of a pastoral guideline can be other clergy members, members of a bishop's diocese, or those under an archbishop's authority within a province. The pastoral guideline functions as a directing principle or policy pertaining to the spiritual or moral care of a congregation.

PGASO is a 75-page document, arranged in seven sections, formatted with sequential page numbers, hole-punched for easy storage in a school binder, and contained by front and back covers made of hard stock paper. Its seven sections are labelled as follows: (1) Letter from Bishop Paul-André Durocher; (2) Letter from Ontario bishops, Spring 2003; (3) Introduction; (4) Personal Stories; (5) Pastoral Practices;

(6) Appendix – Theological Foundations; and (7) Catholic Church Teachings: Resources. Although various Catholic clergy members refer to pastoral guidelines as "letters," the sheer bulk and complexity of PGASO makes it more reference manual than letter.

PGASO can also be regarded as a curriculum and policy document given that its writing team comprises members of various Catholic education organizations. Although the copyright of the Ontario 2004 PGASO rests with the OCCB (now known as the ACBO), and it is essentially the Ontario bishops' document, the Ontario bishops consulted several other Catholic education leaders for their expertise. In addition to its own Education Commission, which monitors the development of curriculum for both the English and French Catholic schools of Ontario, the OCCB also sought the advice of members from leading Catholic education organizations, such as the Institute for Catholic Education in Ontario, the Catholic Association of Religious and Family Life Educators of Ontario, the Faculty of Theology of St. Michael's College at the University of Toronto, and educators from four Catholic district school boards in and near Toronto (Dufferin-Peel, Durham, Toronto, and York) (OCCB, 2004a). On 3 August 2004, the Education Commission of the OCCB officially approved PGASO and directed that it be used within all Ontario Catholic schools (OCCB, 2004a, p. 1).

The Ontario pastoral guideline advocates celibacy and reparative therapy

PGASO opens with a letter from Bishop Paul-André Durocher followed by the complete 2003 pastoral guideline from the Ontario bishops, *To All Involved in Catholic Education.* I analysed the contents of this 2003 pastoral guideline closely elsewhere (Callaghan, 2007b), so I will not attend to it in detail here, except to point out that the 2004 PGASO is a more thorough condemnation of lgbtq people to a lifetime of celibacy, and a more prolonged – yet subtle – promotion of "therapy directed toward changing a homosexual orientation" (OCCB, 2004a, p. 60), than is the 2003 pastoral guideline. In his opening letter for PGASO, Bishop Paul-André Durocher acknowledges in blatant understatement that "we have not always been sensitive to the particular needs of students with a same-sex orientation" (OCCB, 2004a, p. 1), yet he goes on to introduce a pastoral guideline steeped in Catholic doctrine that condemns homosexuality.

PGASO is replete with the Catholic doublespeak I have elucidated elsewhere (Callaghan, 2007a), which is characterized, on the one hand, by repeated emphasis on the need to protect non-heterosexuals from "unjust" discrimination, while, on the other hand, actively contributing to that very same discrimination by referring to the authority of Catholic doctrine that condemns homosexuality, and by advocating for reparative therapy. Reparative therapy, also known as reorientation therapy or conversion therapy, is employed by some mental health professionals and religious pastoral caregivers to convert gay men and lesbians into heterosexuals by using aversive treatments – such as electric shock – and spiritual interventions (Haldeman, 2002). As I have discussed in a previous publication (Callaghan, 2010), scientific, medical, legal, and academic experts have soundly denounced reparative therapies as unethical, discriminatory, and abusive (Canadian Medical Association, 1999; Grace, 2005; Hicks, 2000; Just the Facts Coalition, 2008). Furthermore, in June 2015, Ontario made into law the *Affirming Sexual Orientation and Gender Identity Act* (Bill 77), which bans conversion therapy for minors and ensures that public health insurance will not cover it for any Ontario citizen regardless of age. Cheri DiNovo, a member of the provincial Parliament of Ontario and a member of the Ontario New Democratic Party, introduced the bill, and the Ontario Legislative Assembly passed it without any opposition (Strapagiel, 2015). Manitoba also banned conversion "therapy," and there have been calls to ban the practice in other Canadian provinces. It remains unclear if Ontario Catholic education leaders will revise their pastoral guidelines to ensure that they comply with Ontario law.

Despite the dangers posed by reparative therapy, PGASO nevertheless refers to it as a viable option. PGASO is not a specialized publication that is read only by clergy members. On the contrary, PGASO is the Ontario bishops' directive to all Catholic schools in Ontario and is distributed to every school administrator (principals, vice principals, assistant principals), school guidance counsellors, school chaplains, school pastors, secondary school department heads for every school subject, and teachers responsible for teaching the course simply called Religion (OCCB, 2004b; Dufferin-Peel Catholic District School Board, n.d.). As Chapter 3 demonstrates, Catholic doctrine pertaining to "homosexuality," described in great detail in PGASO, informs school policy on matters related to sexual minority groups and underpins the sexuality component of the religion class every student in every Catholic school in Ontario must take to graduate.

Unlike non-Catholic public schools where the topic of human sexuality is covered in various non-religious classes, Catholic public schools relegate lessons on sexuality to religion class where the topic can be presented within the confines of Catholic doctrine. Textbooks intended for the religion classes taught in Canadian Catholic schools are developed by the National Office of Religious Education, an organization within the Canadian Conference of Catholic Bishops (CCCB), located in Ottawa. A grade 9 religion textbook called *Be With Me*, used extensively throughout Catholic high schools in Ontario, teaches, for example, that "love, commitment and procreation don't go together for [homosexuals]; therefore love, commitment and genital sex don't have to go together either" (CCCB, 1997a, p. 93)

The Ontario pastoral guideline cites condemning Catholic doctrine

In the formal introduction to their pastoral guideline, the authors of PGASO acknowledge their obligation to adhere to Canadian common law in the following passage:

> As publicly funded institutions, Ontario Catholic schools have a legal obligation to provide equal access to education and equal protection under the law for all students. Catholic schools, and Catholic school boards must ensure that legislation, including legal requirements addressing professional responsibility, issues of confidentiality and the protection of privacy, are adhered to in board policy and school practice. The right of each student to be free of harassment, violence or malice in speech or in action is unequivocal, and schools carry the clear obligation to provide a positive school environment for all students and staff. As faith-based communities, Catholic schools carry an even more compelling obligation to protect the most marginalized within their care. (OCCB, 2004a, p. 10)

Although this introduction gives the impression the Ontario bishops are concerned for the safety of "marginalized" lgbtq students and staff, and want to ensure a positive environment for everyone in their schools, their continued dissemination of homophobic Catholic doctrine in all Catholic schools throughout Ontario belies this caring impression. It is doubly disquieting to administer such sanctioned homophobic discrimination under the guise of compassionate rhetoric.

In addition to relegating non-heterosexuals to a lifetime of celibacy and promoting reparative therapy, the Ontario 2004 PGASO contains references to Catholic doctrine such as, "Although the particular inclination of the homosexual person is not a sin, it is a more or less strong tendency ordered toward an intrinsic moral evil; and thus the inclination itself must be seen as an objective disorder" (as cited in OCCB, 2004a,

p. 45). Directing Catholic school boards in Ontario to inform students in their schools that falling in love with a person of the same sex and physically expressing that love is an "intrinsic moral evil" and an "objective disorder" is not only contrary to the Ontario Ministry of Education's Equity and Inclusive Education Strategy but is also an insidious form of discrimination against a sexual minority group, which contravenes the Canadian Charter's guarantee of equality for every individual in Canada.

The Ontario bishops' pastoral guideline contains many references to the *Catechism of the Catholic Church* (CCCB, 1997b) that describe "homosexual acts" as "intrinsically disordered," "contrary to the natural law," and therefore "under no circumstances can they be approved" (as cited in OCCB, 2004a, p. 53). Variations on this phrasing describe "homosexual practices" as being "among the sins gravely contrary to chastity" (as cited in OCCB, 2004a, p. 53). The authors of PGASO vaguely define chastity as "the holy and holistic approach to sexuality" (OCCB, 2004a, p. 42), though non-religious definitions are clear that it refers to virginity and celibacy.

This is an important distinction because the authors of PGASO try to argue that it is not an undue punishment to expect gender and sexually diverse individuals to live a life devoid of romantic love and physical intimacy since Christians believe that "each [Christian] is called to live chastely, whether married, single, celibate, widowed or divorced" (OCCB, 2004a, p. 12). However, this call to "live chastely" cannot apply to heterosexual Christians who are married within the Catholic Church because they are also called to the goal of procreation. So even if a person were to adhere to their unsubstantiated, self-created definitions, it is not true, according to them, that all Christians *are* called to chastity all the time. Expecting non-heterosexual people who are born into Catholic families and, by extension, the Catholic faith to remain chaste, virginal, and celibate for the rest of their lives is not only a double standard but also a harmful form of discrimination. I would be remiss if I did not point out the hypocrisy that the Catholic Church expects even married people to be chaste when it takes little to no action against priests caught in one of the biggest child sexual abuse scandals.

The Ontario pastoral guideline references a similar American guideline

In addition to referencing the *Catechism of the Catholic Church* and other Vatican encyclicals, it is not uncommon for bishops, and other Catholic education leaders who have been commissioned to write guidelines like PGASO, to reference their colleagues in other parts of the world. Accordingly, the authors of PGASO include in their text the full length of another pastoral guideline called *Always Our Children: A Pastoral Message to Parents of Homosexual Children and Suggestions for Pastoral Ministers* written by the United States Conference of Catholic Bishops (USCCB, 1997). The introduction to *Always Our Children* begins on a positive note, informing parents of lgbtq youth that "the Church offers enormous spiritual resources to strengthen and support them at this moment in their family's life and in the days to come" (as cited in OCCB, 2004a, p. 56). However, just a few paragraphs later the authors of *Always Our Children* make it clear that their pastoral message is "not to be understood as an endorsement of what some call a 'homosexual lifestyle'" (as cited in OCCB, 2004a, p. 56).

The Church resources referred to by the authors of *Always Our Children* are not only the usual pertinent passages of scripture, Vatican encyclicals, and excerpts of selected Catholic doctrine pertaining to homosexuality, but also information about "special" parish resources in the form of a "parents' support group," a "retreat designed for Catholic parents of homosexual children," and a "special diocesan ministry to gay and lesbian persons" (as cited in OCCB, 2004a, p. 63). This additional information is listed under the heading "Pastoral Recommendations to Parents" (as cited in OCCB, 2004a, p. 62). The American bishops are careful not to name the "special" parish resources, opting instead to invite parents of lgbtq youth to contact their parish for further information.

The Ontario bishops' PGASO is issued to Catholic schools throughout Ontario with an accompanying eight-page pamphlet called *Pastoral Guidelines to Assist Students of Same-Sex Orientation: A Parent's Guide* (OCCB, 2004b). This parents' guide also obliquely refers to the same Catholic resources alluded to in the American pastoral guideline *Always Our Children.* Appealing to distressed parents, the Ontario bishops' guide to help parents understand PGASO uses the same sentences as the authors of *Always Our Children* to advise Ontario parents to participate "in a retreat designed for Catholic parents of homosexual children" and directs them to contact their "diocesan family ministry office" for more information on "a special diocesan ministry to gay and lesbian persons" (OCCB, 2004b, p. 4).

These same Catholic resources are also mentioned in a three-page brochure issued to teachers employed by the Dufferin-Peel Catholic District School Board (DPCDSB) in Mississauga, Ontario (DPCDSB, n.d.). The DPCDSB designed the brochure, *Building Safe, Nurturing, Inclusive*

Communities, to advertise its teacher in-service that helps teachers understand PGASO (DPCDSB, n.d.). But, unlike the American bishops' pastoral guideline *Always Our Children* and the Ontario bishops' parents' guide to PGASO, the DPCDSB brochure actually names the umbrella Catholic organization that offers the above-mentioned Catholic resources as Courage. A brief reference to Courage also appears in a section of testimonials called "Personal Stories" in PGASO. Directly following the first testimonial, the authors of PGASO include a small note that describes Courage as "an apostolate of the Roman Catholic Church [that] ministers to those with same-sex attractions and their loved ones" (OCCB, 2004a, p. 14).

Ontario bishops endorse Courage, a 12-step program for homosexuals

According to its website (Courage Apostolate, 2011), Courage International operates as a 12-step support group modelled after the original 12-step program, Alcoholics Anonymous, but instead of sobriety, Courage promotes chastity for "same-sex attracted" Catholics. The first step members must take is to admit "we are powerless over homosexuality and that our lives have become unmanageable" (Courage Apostolate, 2011). Subsequent steps require members to pray to God to "restore us to sanity," and to admit "the exact nature of our wrongs," "defects of our character," "shortcomings," and the "persons we had harmed" (Courage Apostolate, 2011). Along with Courage is another 12-step support group called Encourage, which is intended for friends and relatives of Catholics with same-sex attractions and has a similar supporting function as Al-Anon within the Alcoholics Anonymous program. Fully endorsed by the Holy See in Rome (i.e., the Vatican), Courage hosts annual conferences, regular retreats, and a summer sports camp (Courage Apostolate, 2011).

I have already covered the function of Courage in a previous publication (Callaghan, 2007a), so I will not analyse it in great depth here except to underscore that although Courage is, for the most part, carefully reticent about its conversion agenda, it does publicly acknowledge that it supports its members who choose to seek reparative therapy to explore the possibility of developing a heterosexual orientation. Available on the Courage International website are the "success" stories of its members who have managed to convert to a heterosexual orientation to varying degrees and for fluctuating periods by following the 12-steps and by living a chaste life. Courage operates a Courage Reparational Prayer Group for its members who "seek to make reparation for sins against human sexuality" in which its "weak" and "suffering" members pray "for the conversion and healing of those who struggle with same-sex desires" (Courage Apostolate, 2011). The Courage International website provides a link to Narth (the National Association for Research and Therapy of Homosexuality), Exodus International, and Homosexuals Anonymous – all organizations devoted to reparative therapy. Courage also lists books on reparative therapy in the resources section of its website.

Always Our Children, the American pastoral guideline fully reproduced in the Ontario bishops' PGASO, advises parents of lgbtq youth to respect "a person's freedom to choose or refuse therapy directed toward changing a homosexual orientation ... though some might find it helpful" (OCCB, 2004a, p. 60). The footnote that appears at the end of the first testimonial in the Personal Stories section of PGASO recommends Courage as a valuable resource and informs Ontarian readers that individual chapters of the 12-step support group do operate in Ontario with the permission of each diocesan bishop (OCCB, 2004a, p. 14). Furthermore, the authors of PGASO assure readers in Ontario that local Courage chapters are fully endorsed by the Pontifical Council for the Family, which is part of the Curia, or administrative apparatus, of the Roman Catholic Church in Rome (OCCB, 2004a, p. 14).

Although the authors of PGASO provide no introduction to, or explanation of, the three testimonials they apparently collected from three citizens of Ontario, their purpose in including them in PGASO becomes immediately clear: to encourage the reader that people can progress from non-heterosexuality to a better, more acceptable form of sexuality. The first story, titled "No One By My Side," is a two-page account from "a member of Courage, Toronto, ON" (OCCB, 2004a, pp. 13–14). The second testimonial, simply called "Michael's Story," is also two pages long, and a note at the end indicates that "Michael attends an Ontario Catholic high school" (OCCB, 2004a, pp. 15–16). The third story, titled "Take Time to Discover," is three pages long and offers no information about its origins (OCCB, 2004a, pp. 17–19).

Each testimonial describes a difficult period for the protagonists as they became aware of their "same-sex attractions" while in Catholic school (OCCB, 2004a, pp. 13–19). Each story culminates in a new beginning for the protagonists: a young homosexual male who joined Courage progresses to the morally superior sexuality of celibacy (p. 14); a young man who was able to find a way to feel more attracted to females than to males advances to having a girlfriend and admits to bisexuality rather than homosexuality (p. 16); and a formerly homosexual young woman eventually marries a man and is expecting her first child at the time her story is written (p. 19). Like many of the testimonials available on the Courage Apostolate website, the three testimonials presented in PGASO all neatly end with smoother, less complicated existences for the no-longer-homosexual protagonists.

Contradictions in the Ontario pastoral guideline

PGASO contains a section called "Pastoral Practices," which offers practical guidelines for "creating a safe school environment for students of a same-sex orientation" (OCCB, 2004a, pp. 23–4), and a section that offers answers to "most commonly asked questions about same-sex orientation" (OCCB, 2004a, pp. 25–7). The Pastoral Practices section of PGASO opens with an address to guidance counsellors, chaplains, pastors, and teachers in Catholic schools throughout Ontario. Included in the list of values the authors of PGASO believe people holding such positions in Catholic schools should possess is the value of "conversion" (OCCB, 2004a, p. 20). Although the authors of PGASO do not elaborate on what they mean by conversion, it is conceivable that they are referring to the more morally acceptable forms of sexuality (celibacy and heterosexuality) available through conversion therapy alluded to elsewhere in the pastoral guideline. The authors of PGASO go on to caution pastoral caregivers that "the process of assimilation into Christ is ... unique ... for each individual" (OCCB, 2004a, p. 20). Controlling words such as "conversion" and "assimilation" reveal a very specific vision of how "students of same-sex orientation" should be "assisted" in Ontario Catholic schools: they should be carefully absorbed, transformed, and otherwise indoctrinated into a Catholic and heterosexual way of life.

In the Guidelines for Administration segment within the Pastoral Practices section of PGASO, administrators are advised to familiarize themselves with the Catholic teaching on human sexuality. Catholic school administrators would not have to look much further than PGASO itself since approximately 70% of the document contains all of the relevant Catholic doctrine and theological foundations on the topic of homosexuality. Once they have familiarized themselves with this Catholic teaching, Catholic school administrators are expected to "actively promote a welcoming, safe environment rooted in gospel values of love, justice, and compassion" (OCCB, 2004a, p. 23). These two guidelines, needless to say, are at severe cross purposes. There is no "love," "justice" or "compassion" in singling out members of a sexual minority group by disseminating homophobic Catholic doctrine in a public school setting, nor by trying to eradicate the core of who a person is. Circulating this kind of material in a Catholic school promotes the grim opposite of a "welcoming and safe environment" for lgbtq people.

Catholic school administrators are also encouraged to "be involved in working for school-wide support and education for understanding and tolerance of sexual minorities" (OCCB, 2004a, p. 23). Unfortunately, these administrators seem reluctant to use already existing school resources and strategies, such as the Positive Space Campaign or the active encouragement of student-initiated GSAs.

The Positive Space Campaign is an initiative undertaken by lgbtq activists in North American universities in the 1990s to disrupt the heteronormativity of institutional spaces by raising awareness of sexual and gender diversity through the placement of small stickers – bearing the inverted triangle that has come to symbolize non-heterosexuality and the phrase "This is a positive space" – on the office windows and doors of campaign participants (Burgess, 2005). The goals of a Positive Space Campaign are to create a positive and welcoming environment for non-heterosexuals, and to reduce discrimination on the basis of sexual orientation and gender identity in educational settings (Tate & Ross, 2003). In the United States, the Positive Space Campaign is referred to as the Safe Space Campaign (Gay, Lesbian and Straight Education Network, 2011a).

Variations of the Positive/Safe Space Campaign also operate in some primary and secondary schools, with funds from diversity and equity programs available in certain school boards and teacher federations whose members oversee the design, development, and distribution of their own versions of Positive Space stickers, posters, and training programs (Elementary Teachers' Federation of Ontario [ETFO], 2010). The Positive Space Campaign can take different forms in different schools, but it generally involves designating a Positive Space–trained staff member for the school who places a small sticker bearing an inverted triangle, the rainbow colours of the Pride flag, and a message stating a variation of "This is a positive and inclusive space for lgbtq students and their allies" in his or her classroom window or on the office door (ETFO, 2010). The Positive Space–trained staff member is often the first point of contact for students struggling with homophobia or transphobia and can be instrumental in providing support for the establishment of a GSA in the school (ETFO, 2010).

The various configurations of Positive/Safe Space campaigns and GSAs that have existed in some North American secular schools since the early 1990s have effectively improved understanding of sexual minority groups (Blumenfeld, 1995; Uribe, 1995). However, as Chapter 3 attests, both initiatives are rarely, if ever, approved by the administration of Ontario Catholic schools. It is difficult to imagine how administrators of Catholic schools can follow the Ontario bishops' guideline to "be involved in working for school-wide support and education for understanding and tolerance of sexual minorities" (OCCB, 2004a, p. 23) when the chair of the Education Commission of the ACBO actively discouraged the establishment of GSAs in Ontario Catholic schools (Durocher, 2010). Without Positive Space Campaigns and GSAs, working towards school-wide support of lgbtq people is far more difficult than it need be.

The Guidelines for Administration section of PGASO also advises Catholic school administrators to "provide grade level assemblies to address zero tolerance for discrimination of any kind as outlined in the Charter of Rights and Freedoms ... [including] sexual orientation" (OCCB, 2004a, p. 23). Yet the Catholic bishops of Ontario seem oblivious to the ways in which their dissemination of homophobic Catholic doctrine encourages various forms of discrimination on the basis of sexual orientation in Catholic schools. Circulating Catholic doctrine to parents, teachers, and administrators who deal directly with students – doctrine that decrees physical love between people of the same sex is an "intrinsic moral evil" and an "objective disorder" (as cited in OCCB, 2004a, p. 45) – contributes to a homophobic school environment and leads to homophobic school policies that periodically cause children to take their own lives.

These kinds of glaring contradictions are lost on the authors of PGASO. A final example of how the Ontario bishops overlook their contributions to homophobic discrimination in Catholic schools can be found in the section of PGASO called "Answers to most commonly asked questions about same-sex orientation" (OCCB, 2004a, pp. 25–27). This section is fraught with contradiction and misinformation. The most obvious example is the fifth question, "What is homophobia?" (OCCB, 2004a, p. 25). In describing the many forms of homophobia, the Ontario bishops list "vulgar and abusive language and jokes about homosexuals, condemnation, discrimination, persecution and even murder of homosexuals" (OCCB, 2004a, p. 25).

However, in the Catholic Church Teaching section of PGASO, the Ontario bishops cite Catholic doctrine that describes homosexual acts as "acts of grave depravity" that are "intrinsically disordered," which count among the list of "sins gravely contrary to chastity" (as cited in OCCB, 2004a, p. 53). These references to Catholic doctrine condemn with language that is, itself, if not abusive, then certainly condoning, perhaps even inviting, abuse. Yet these homophobic citations appear in the same pastoral guideline as do their calls to accept and protect.

Likewise, "condemnation" of homosexuals takes place when the Ontario bishops cite Catholic doctrine that states, "under no circumstances can [homosexual acts] be approved" (as cited in OCCB, 2004a, p. 53). This citation is a clear, strong judgment of homosexuality, an example of the homophobia described in the Ontario bishops' pastoral guideline intended for use in Catholic schools.

The very existence of PGASO constitutes a form of religiously inspired maltreatment of a vulnerable minority group. PGASO does not offer the assistance to lgbtq people in Catholic schools that its title promises. On the contrary, it singles out sexual minorities and subjects them to a thinly disguised guide to the ill treatment of, and hostility towards, "students of same-sex attraction." PGASO cites Catholic doctrine that lists "homosexual practices" as being among the "sins gravely contrary to chastity" (as cited in OCCB, 2004a, p. 53), but – interestingly – also included in that list is pornography. It is unclear why Catholic leaders have written so much about homosexuality and so little about pornography, when they regard both as "sins gravely contrary to chastity." This persistent singling out of sexual minorities is a clear example of the behaviour that the authors of PGASO identify as homophobic, yet they do not recognize their culpability in this regard.

Similarly, the authors of PGASO seem unaware that their pastoral guideline contains references to specific Catholic doctrine that appear to be condoning violence against non-heterosexuals. The Catholic doctrine in question is an earlier pastoral guideline published in 1986 called *Pastoral Care of Homosexual Persons,* which was issued by the Congregation for the Doctrine of the Faith (CDF), an office in the Vatican responsible for the development and promotion of official Catholic doctrine. The CDF has had many name changes over the centuries, but it is perhaps best known by its sixteen-century name, the Supreme Sacred Congregation of the Roman and Universal Inquisition, which is often shortened to the Holy Roman Inquisition or simply the Inquisition (Vatican, 2011). Given its long history of developing and safeguarding Catholic doctrine and Catholic morality throughout the Catholic world, the CDF is the oldest and most active of the nine congregations that form the administrative apparatus (also known as the Roman Curia) of the Vatican (Vatican, 2011). The CDF writes prolifically on matters of sexuality, including homosexuality. This example of Catholic doctrine from the CDF – the *Pastoral Care of Homosexual Persons* – has the distinction of being co-authored by Pope Benedict XVI, who served as the Pope of the Catholic Church from 2005 until he resigned in 2013, when he was still Cardinal Ratzinger, the Prefect of the CDF ("Prefect" is the title given to a cardinal in charge of a congregation of the Roman Curia). The fact that a recent pope is the principal author of a highly influential pastoral guideline containing some of the most spurious language about non-heterosexuals offers some explanation for the conservative direction of a recent Vatican administration on the matter of sexual minorities. The violent tone of the *Pastoral Care of Homosexual Persons* is particularly alarming given that it is reprinted in PGASO, which is disseminated in Catholic schools throughout Ontario. In discussing the "violent malice" against homosexuals, the authors of *Pastoral Care of Homosexual Persons* state:

> The proper reaction to crimes committed against homosexual persons should not be to claim that the homosexual condition is not disordered. When such a claim is made and when homosexual activity is consequently condoned, or when civil legislation is introduced to protect behaviour to which no one has any conceivable right, neither the Church nor society at large should be surprised when other distorted notions and practices gain ground, and irrational and violent reactions increase. (as cited in OCCB, 2004a, p. 48)

This passage of Catholic doctrine from the Vatican decries civil legislation that decriminalizes homosexuality and lays the blame of violence against non-heterosexuals directly with the advancement of same-sex legal rights via civil legislation. According to the authors of this passage (Bovone and Ratzinger), the quest for increased protection from discrimination on the basis of sexual orientation rightfully infuriates the general population to such a degree that no one should be surprised when violence against sexual minority groups increases. In other words, no one has any "conceivable right" to live as a non-heterosexual.

The fight on the part of lgbtq activists for human rights for non-heterosexuals stresses the equality of persons before the law and rejects homophobic Catholic doctrine that claims homosexuality is "disordered." According to the authors of *Pastoral Care of Homosexual Persons*, when human rights activists – such as those in Canada who fought in the mid-1960s for the Canadian Parliament to decriminalize homosexuality (Rayside, 2008) – respond to violent homophobic hate crimes by stressing the need to protect the equality rights of non-heterosexuals, they invite even more violence against sexual minority groups. The solution offered in this papal passage, then, is to accept the authority of Catholic doctrine that describes the "homosexual condition" as "disordered," and to denounce the advancement of same-sex legal rights because it is this agitation of the status quo that increases violence against non-heterosexuals, not the homophobic Catholic doctrine itself. This passage of Catholic doctrine represents a tacit endorsement of violence against non-heterosexuals, a form of homophobia described by the authors of PGASO, to which they seem to be unaware that they are contributing.

In their description of homophobia, the Ontario bishops state that "sometimes homophobia exhibits itself in silence, ... [which] can be perceived as compliance to continue discrimination" (OCCB, 2004a, p. 25). As Chapter 3 demonstrates, there are many examples of how homophobic silence furthers discrimination against sexual minority groups in Catholic schools. Catholic doctrine that requires non-heterosexuals to remain celibate for the rest of their lives means that, as long as they work for Catholic schools, lgbtq teachers, counsellors, chaplains, pastors, and administrators must remain silent or lie about their same-sex partners and any children they may be raising with their same-sex partners. This deception not only wreaks havoc on the mental, emotional, and physical health of lgbtq staff in Catholic schools (Callaghan, 2007b) but also deprives lgbtq students of important positive role models. Other forms of homophobic silence manifest themselves in curriculum and policy decisions taken in Catholic schools that would eliminate or at least reduce the circulation of positive information about sexual orientation and gender identity through the banning of books, the editing of provincial curriculum, and the banning of GSAs. The authors of PGASO mention homophobic silence, but they seem oblivious to the ways in which their pastoral guideline keeps such silence alive in Catholic schools.

In spite of these disturbing examples of the many ways in which PGASO contributes to homophobia in Catholic schools, its authors contend "it should not be assumed, however, that to guide others away from the practice of homosexual genital activity comes out of homophobia" (OCCB, 2004a, p. 25). The authors of PGASO can state that their pastoral guideline is not homophobic, but the document's many contradictions suggest otherwise. In their answer to the question, What is homophobia? in PGASO, the Ontario bishops state, "Unlike homosexuality, homophobia

can be 'cured' through education, experience, reflection and prayer"
(OCCB, 2004a, p. 25). It is conceivable then, that the authors of PGASO
may be cured of the homophobia expressed in the document, if only
they would follow their own advice and reflect on the ways their pastoral
guideline contributes to homophobia in Catholic schools.

The Ontario bishops' references to vilifying Catholic doctrine, their
emphasis on the homophobic Catholic requirement that non-heterosexual lay Catholics must remain celibate for the rest of their lives, and
their recommendation of the corrective 12-step program Courage as a
viable option for non-heterosexuals are all forms of discrimination that
contribute to the institutionalization of homophobia in Catholic schools
throughout Ontario. These examples of discrimination may not be as
obvious as firing lesbian and gay teachers, barring same-sex dates at the
high school prom, or banning GSAs, but they nevertheless constitute a
form of discrimination that violates the equality rights provision (Section
15) of the *Canadian Charter of Rights and Freedoms* (1982). Many of these
examples, especially the endorsement of Courage, can be regarded as
more subversive and even more harmful for their insidiousness and for
their call to treat a huge, healthy, and contributing segment of the population inhumanely.

The authors of PGASO state that they are aware of the legal obligation
Ontario Catholic schools are under to uphold Canadian law affecting
sexual minority groups in public schools, yet they have designed a pastoral guideline that encourages Catholic schools in Ontario to disregard
these very pieces of Canadian law. In so doing, PGASO does not assist
lgbtq students in Ontario Catholic schools at all – on the contrary, it
actively encourages further discrimination to be levelled against them.
This kind of homophobic curricular and policy document encourages
an unsafe, uncaring environment for sexual minority groups in Ontario
Catholic schools.

Alberta's *Towards an Inclusive Community Workbook for Catholic Educators*

In his essay on Christian churches and homosexuality, Wolfgang Lienemann (1998), an ethics professor at the University of Bern in Switzer-
land, documents an unusual proliferation of official church studies,
declarations, and pastoral guidelines on the topic of homosexuality
since the 1970s. In the case of the Roman Catholic Church, the defini-
tive doctrine is a pastoral guideline from the Vatican to all bishops of

the Catholic Church, titled *Pastoral Care of Homosexual Persons* (Vatican Congregation for the Doctrine of the Faith, 1986). This is the example of Catholic doctrine, discussed above, that refers to homosexuality as "an intrinsic moral evil" and "an objective disorder" (as cited in OCCB, 2004a, p. 45).

To ensure that this message from the Vatican reaches young people in Catholic schools, different associations of local Catholic bishops throughout North America started to write their own pastoral guidelines with the audiences of Catholic school administrators, teachers, and students in mind. One American example discussed above is *Always Our Children: Pastoral Message to Parents of Homosexual Children and Suggestions for Pastoral Ministers* (USCCB, 1997). This was followed by a Canadian example, the Alberta bishops' 2001 pastoral guideline called *A Resource for an Inclusive Community: A Teacher's Guide for and about Persons with Same Sex Attractions* (ACB, 2001).

The Alberta bishops' 11-page pastoral guideline predates the Ontario bishops' PGASO (OCCB, 2004a) discussed above and can be therefore regarded as a model for the much lengthier and more detailed Ontario 2004 pastoral guideline. As I discuss further below, there is some evidence of the Ontario and Alberta bishops working together on the development of their pastoral guidelines. I have previously examined the contents of the Alberta bishops' 2001 pastoral guideline *A Resource for an Inclusive Community* elsewhere (Callaghan, 2007b), so I will not analyse it closely here, except to underscore that it refers to the same largely anti-lgbtq Catholic doctrine found in the Ontario bishops' 2004 pastoral guideline, and it also recommends Courage, the reparative 12-step program covered above, as a supportive pastoral ministry for "those with same-sex attractions and their loved ones" (ACB, 2001, para. 56–8). Unlike the ACBO, the ACB has no centralized office or online presence, though their spokesperson is Calgary Bishop Frederick Henry, who functions as a liaison bishop to the Alberta Catholic School Trustees' Association (ACSTA, 2004).

One problem ACSTA noticed about the Alberta bishops' 2001 pastoral guideline was that although ACSTA promptly posted that pastoral guideline on its website, the Alberta bishops' message was slow to reach the Catholic schools of Alberta. To rectify this, during the 2002–3 academic year, the Council of Catholic School Superintendents of Alberta (CCSSA) struck a subcommittee called Inclusive Communities that was charged with devising a province-wide implementation plan for the guideline (CCSSA, 2007, sec. 2). The Inclusive Communities implementation plan was the development of a workbook called *Towards an Inclusive Community* (CCSSA, 2007), designed to teach Catholic educators about the Alberta bishops' 2001 pastoral guideline. The focus in this chapter is to closely examine this workbook to understand how members of the CCSSA have received the pastoral guideline and how they envision it being used in the Catholic schools of Alberta.

The authors of Towards an Inclusive Community

According to its website, the CCSSA is "a community of disciples" whose vision is to "influence the development and direction of Catholic education in Alberta" (CCSSA, 2011b). Most of the CCSSA's 34 educator members hold administrative positions within the central administrative offices of their school districts, including – but not limited to – superintendent or director of their Catholic school districts (CCSSA, 2011a). Many of CCSSA's 34 members are Catholic school administrators from the Calgary Roman Catholic Separate School District No. 1 and the Elk Island Catholic Separate Regional Division (representing areas east of Edmonton). Of the 22 Catholic school districts in Alberta, 17 send a representative to the CCSSA (CCSSA, 2011a). The CCSSA is not a governmental organization; it receives its funds through member fees and donations from member school jurisdictions (CCSSA, 2011c). Members of the CCSSA are bound by a code of ethics that requires them to "be aware that all actions are for the benefit of the students and for the glory of God"; "hold to the ideals of the Christian family, promote these ideals through commitment to family life"; and "participate actively in the advancement of the Catholic faith at the parish and diocesan levels" (CCSSA, 2011d, p. 1).

The mandate of the CCSSA's Inclusive Communities subcommittee was twofold: (1) to provide a practical manual for teachers and counsellors in Alberta Catholic schools to consult when implementing the Alberta bishops' pastoral guideline for persons with same-sex attractions; and (2) to develop standard, predictable answers to possible media questions about the treatment of sexual minority groups in Alberta Catholic schools (CCSSA, 2004a). The CCSSA's Inclusive Communities subcommittee was comprised of eight members, four of whom are also members of the CCSSA's Religious Education Network, which is described on the CCSSA website as "a community of Catholic educators providing support and opportunities for collaboration ... in teaching through the eyes of Faith in the Province of Alberta" (CCSSA, 2011c,

p. 1). CCSSA's Religious Education Network is similar in function to its counterpart in Ontario, the Education Commission of the ACBO. The difference in Alberta is that the CCSSA's Religious Education Network is made up of Catholic educators from Catholic school districts throughout the province in collaboration with representatives from each Catholic diocese (i.e., lay or religious members of a parish within a district overseen by a bishop) (CCSSA, 2011c). In Ontario, the Education Commission is part of the ACBO, comprising predominately clergy members. The advantage of the CCSSA's Religious Education Network over the Ontario bishops' Education Commission is that its members are also Catholic educators and can readily disseminate directives from the ACB in Alberta Catholic schools.

Although the authors of *Towards an Inclusive Community* were a group of eight committed Catholic educators, they did not work alone. They sought the guidance of Bishop Frederick Henry, Liaison Bishop to ACSTA and the principal author of the ACB's 2001 pastoral guideline *A Resource for an Inclusive Community: A Teacher's Guide for and about Persons with Same Sex Attractions*. Bishop Henry is from Ontario and was a member of the OCCB Education Commission. An internal memorandum of the Alberta Catholic School Trustees' Association (ACSTA, 2004) shows Bishop Henry's influence on the *Towards an Inclusive Community* workbook, as well as the involvement of Bishop Thomas Collins, Archbishop of Toronto. Based on the similarities between the Alberta and Ontario pastoral guidelines (such as citations of the same Catholic doctrine, references to the corrective 12-step program Courage, and a similar question and answer section), as well as the fact that Bishop Henry and Bishop Collins (both of Ontario) were consulted on the development of the Alberta educators' *Towards an Inclusive Community* workbook, it appears the organizations of Catholic bishops from Alberta and Ontario worked closely together in the development of their separate pastoral guidelines for managing sexual minority groups in the Catholic schools of Alberta and Ontario.

A brief description of Towards an Inclusive Community

Towards an Inclusive Community is a Catholic teacher in-service manual designed to ensure Catholic educators throughout Alberta are trained on the contents of the ACB's 2001 pastoral guideline *A Resource for an Inclusive Community: A Teacher's Guide for and about Persons with Same Sex Attractions*. Written by devout Catholic educators, whose membership in the CCSSA requires them to be family oriented and active in their Catholic parishes, *Towards an Inclusive Community* represents a particularly conservative Catholic perspective on the topic of sexual minorities in Alberta Catholic schools. The *Towards an Inclusive Community* teacher workshop manual is intended to be used by senior Catholic administrators in various Catholic school districts throughout Alberta to train their district personnel (teachers, counsellors, administrators) on the contents of the Alberta bishops' 2001 pastoral guideline so that its message can inform curricular and policy decisions on the topic of sexual minorities in Alberta Catholic schools. In terms of curriculum, the Alberta bishops' 2001 pastoral guideline is distributed directly to students as a course text within high school religious studies courses (CCSSA, 2007, sec. 7) and religious studies teachers therefore need to be trained on its contents. In terms of school policy, counsellors facing students who are questioning their sexual orientation, or administrators trying to determine if students should be granted a GSA, are trained on the contents of the Alberta bishops' pastoral guideline so that its message may direct how to proceed in these matters.

Along with their professed goal of supporting students "with compassion and respect as they develop on their faith journey," the authors of *Towards an Inclusive Community* wish to ensure "that there is clear direction in this sensitive issue" of sexual minority groups in the Catholic schools of Alberta (CCSSA, 2007, sec. 2). Furthermore, a memorandum from the CCSSA's Inclusive Communities subcommittee to all Catholic school superintendents of Alberta lists their rationale for developing the *Towards an Inclusive Community* workbook as follows:

> There is mounting pressure from special interest groups outside of our school jurisdictions to be involved in providing "support" to young people in our schools. Much of that is based on seeing same-sex attraction as a reality with no specific call to chastity. Added to that is the overwhelming exposure of the issue of same-sex aspirations. Facing the situation directly, discreetly and deliberately would ensure that the moral teachings of the Church be upheld. (CCSSA, 2005, p. 2)

Compiled in an unassuming, school-friendly binder with eight section dividers, *Towards an Inclusive Community* is a collection of approximately 95 unnumbered pages of articles and other miscellaneous material the authors deem will be of use to Catholic educators working with lgbtq individuals in Catholic schools. Among the miscellaneous materials included in the *Towards an Inclusive Community* workbook are needs assessments and pretests for the Catholic educators taking the workshop in order to determine how much the workshop participants already know about Catholic perspectives on non-heterosexuality. Since there are no consecutive page numbers in this unbound resource for Catholic educators, references to its contents in this study will necessarily have to be to its sections. The authors divide *Towards an Inclusive Community* into eight sections: (1) PowerPoint Presentation; (2) Opening and Closing Prayer; (3) Catholic Perspective; (4) Student and School Perspective; (5) When Students Disclose; (6) Parental Support; (7) Curriculum Support; and (8) Media Questions. Sections 3, 4, 7, and 8 are the most illuminating for this study.

Towards an Inclusive Community – *Section 3: Catholic Perspective*

Section 3 of *Towards an Inclusive Community*, labelled "Catholic Perspective," opens with the complete text of the Alberta bishops' 11-page pastoral guideline *A Resource for an Inclusive Community: A Teacher's Guide for and about Persons with Same Sex Attractions*. Presumably for those Catholic educators who do not have the time to read the Alberta bishops' pastoral guideline in its entirety, the authors of *Towards an Inclusive Community* also include a five-page summary of its salient points, which directly follows the original bishops' text. Insisting "this is a document of HOPE!" (uppercase letters in the original), the authors' summary of the Alberta bishops' pastoral guideline declares that it "offers to teachers, support staff, parents and students a vision of Christian community which calls for holiness and accountability, compassion and justice" (CCSSA, 2007, sec. 3). However, a close reading of the complete Alberta bishops' pastoral guideline shows the same fundamental lack of justice for sexual minority groups that exists in the Ontario bishops' PGASO (OCCB, 2004a).

It is not surprising that Catholic educators who compiled *Towards an Inclusive Community* can attempt to cast the Alberta bishops' 2001 pastoral guideline as a "document of hope" given that the most contentious segments have been omitted from their five-page summary. In their 2001 pastoral guideline, the Alberta bishops reference the same Vatican encyclical called *Pastoral Care of Homosexual Persons* that the Ontario bishops reference in their 2004 pastoral guideline, which reads as follows: "Although the particular inclination of the homosexual person is not a sin, it is a more or less strong tendency ordered toward an intrinsic moral

evil; and thus the inclination itself must be seen as an objective disorder" (as cited in CCSSA, 2007, sec. 3). However, the authors of *Towards
an Inclusive Community* have removed this reference to Catholic doctrine
from their summary of the Alberta bishops' 2001 pastoral guideline. Also
absent from the authors' five-page summary is the following question
from its "Questions and Answers about Same-Sex Attraction" section:
"Where can a homosexual person go for information and support?"
Answer: "Courage is an apostolate of the Roman Catholic Church whose
purpose is to minister to those with same-sex attractions and their loved
ones" (CCSSA, 2007, sec. 3). As discussed above, the Ontario bishops also
suggest Courage, a corrective 12-step program that tries to "cure" people
of their non-heterosexual orientation, as a viable option for lgbtq persons. One can imagine why this question and its suggested answer were
not included in the summary.

The Alberta and Ontario bishops may not be willing to recognize or
admit the dangers of reparative therapy apparent in Courage, but they
do seem to be aware of the controversy associated with this corrective
12-step program. Both Alberta and Ontario bishops suggest Courage in
a decidedly understated way in their pastoral guidelines, which signals
the bishops' awareness of possible controversy surrounding the Catholic
endorsement of Courage. The Alberta and Ontario bishops try to avoid
this controversy by mentioning Courage only briefly in their pastoral
guidelines and by embedding it discretely within questions and testimonials that are not set apart under headings with the word Courage in their
titles. Despite their attempts to downplay their advocacy for Courage, the
Alberta and Ontario Catholic bishops do favourably suggest Courage as a
resource for Catholic educators to pass along to lgbtq students and their
families. Rather than address the dangers that Courage represents, the
Alberta and Ontario bishops chose to downplay the fact that Courage is
associated with reparative therapy.

Similarly, the Catholic clergy members in Alberta and Ontario who
were involved in the development of the pastoral guidelines for each
province overlooked and continue to overlook how their continued push
for the dissemination of homophobic Catholic doctrine in both provinces' Catholic schools contributes to the very "hostile environments"
from which they say they seek to save lgbtq students. All lgbtq teachers
and students who participated in this study found their Catholic school
to be hostile to non-heterosexuals. The authors of *Towards an Inclusive
Community* included in their summary of the Alberta bishops' pastoral guideline the above-noted quotation that "homosexuality is [not]

something that can or should be fixed" because this perspective aligns with the image of "HOPE" they were trying to depict in their workbook for educators. The authors' emphasis on the quotation that "homosexuality is [not] something that can or should be fixed" also ties in neatly with their pretest designed to be given to workshop participants at the start of the *Towards an Inclusive Community* in-service. Arranged in a true or false chart, the pretest states, "The Church encourages the homosexual person to seek therapy to change their orientation," to which the correct answer is meant to be false (CCSSA, 2007, sec. 1). However, in their pastoral guidelines to "assist" sexual minorities in Catholic schools, both the Ontario bishops and the Alberta bishops suggest the corrective 12-step program Courage as a support for lgbtq people. Therefore, the Church is, in fact, encouraging reparative therapy. This is just one of many semantic games the authors of *Towards an Inclusive Community* play in order to detract from the overall disturbingly homophobic message contained in the Alberta bishops' 2001 pastoral guideline.

The Alberta bishops wrote their 2001 pastoral guideline *A Resource for an Inclusive Community: A Teacher's Guide for and about Persons with Same Sex Attractions* for educators in Alberta Catholic schools, and Catholic educators wrote their 2007 teacher in-service manual *Towards an Inclusive Community* to ensure the Alberta bishops' message is properly disseminated among educators in Alberta Catholic schools. The further away from the bishops the message gets, and the closer it comes to reaching lgbtq students, the greater the need on the part of the authors who developed the *Towards an Inclusive Community* workbook to deny its homophobic message. To soften the Alberta bishops' message, the authors of *Towards an Inclusive Community* summarized the Alberta bishops' 2001 pastoral guidelines in a way that carefully expunges Catholic doctrine that describes "homosexuality" as an "intrinsic moral evil" and an "objective disorder," and, as I said, makes no mention of the bishops' recommendation of the 12-step rehabilitation program Courage.

Section 3 of *Towards an Inclusive Community* concludes with three supplementary resource materials the authors included in the binder under the heading "backgrounders": (1) a 1997 statement from the CCCB called "The Catholic Church's Teaching on Homosexuality"; (2) an essay titled "Chastity – A Universal Christian Call," excerpted from a 1999 book called *Catholic Moral Teaching*; and (3) an article titled "Psychology and the Church's Teaching on Homosexuality" by Stephen J. Rossetti and Gerald D. Coleman, both American priests, published in 1997 in the journal *America* (CCSSA, 2007, sec. 3). With the exception of the essay on chastity, the "backgrounders" are essentially apologies – formal defences, justifications, and excuses – for the contentious piece of Catholic doctrine from the Vatican that both the Ontario and the Alberta bishops cite in their pastoral guidelines, which I previously pointed out, but bears looking at again: "Although the particular inclination of the homosexual person is not a sin, it is a more or less strong tendency ordered toward an intrinsic moral evil; and thus the inclination itself must be seen as an objective disorder" (as cited in CCSSA, 2007, sec. 3). By including these apologies in their teacher in-service manual, the authors of *Towards an Inclusive Community* show they are aware this particular example of Catholic doctrine from the Vatican may cause alarm among the Catholic educators who take part in their workshop, and, ultimately, harm to their students. Including essays from prominent Catholics who try to justify and excuse this official Catholic doctrine will, they must be thinking, hopefully assuage any concerns raised by educators who participate in the *Towards an Inclusive Community* workshop.

For example, the CCCB's statement titled "The Catholic Church's Teaching on Homosexuality" denies the meaning of the above portion of Catholic doctrine, claiming instead "when the Church speaks about homosexuality as an 'objective disorder,' it is speaking not of the tendency but of genital acts between people of the same sex" (as cited in CCSSA, 2007 sec. 3). This same statement also included in the OCCB's PGASO. However, the original Catholic doctrine from the Vatican, quoted in the previous paragraph above, is clearly referring to the homosexual "inclination" or "tendency." Even if it were true that the Church is not referring to a "homosexual" identity when it says the "homosexual inclination" or "tendency" is "an intrinsic moral evil" and an "objective disorder," but is referring instead to "homosexual genital acts," the Church is still singling out non-heterosexuals and condemning them to a lifetime of celibacy in an overtly homophobic manner.

In a similar vein, the two American priests, Stephen Rossetti and Gerald Coleman, who wrote the article "Psychology and the Church's Teaching on Homosexuality" also try to defend the official Catholic doctrine from the Vatican, cited above, that refers to homosexuality as "an intrinsic moral evil" and "an objective disorder" by claiming that lay Catholics and others are "citing isolated phrases and concepts that, taken out of context, are not in harmony with a comprehensive view of church teaching" (as cited in CCSSA, 2007, sec. 3). According to Rossetti and Coleman, the trouble non-clergy Catholics have been having with this official statement on homosexuality from the Vatican is not what it actually says but rather that it is not taken within a broader view of all that the Church has to say on the matter. However, it is incongruous for the Catholic Church to say on the one hand that homosexuality is "an objective disorder" and, on the other, to say that "it is deplorable that homosexual persons have been and are the object of violent malice in speech or in action" (as cited in CCSSA, 2007, sec. 3). The problem is not that these statements are taken out of context; rather, it is that the statements are themselves contradictory and some are clearly inflammatory.

The authors of *Towards an Inclusive Community*, faced with the monumental task of having to implement the Alberta bishops' pastoral guideline that contains contradictory Catholic doctrine on homosexuality, chose instead to remove some of the most problematic portions and – in their place – include various defences from Catholic clergy members who twist themselves into semantic pretzels to explain the condemning Catholic doctrine and try to convince non-clergy Catholics that Catholic doctrine does not discriminate against non-heterosexuals but affirms their dignity and right to the "pastoral care" of the Catholic Church.

Towards an Inclusive Community – *Section 4:*
Student and School Perspective

Section 4 of *Towards an Inclusive Community* is a collection of three journal articles and one compilation of excerpted portions of a book titled *Being Gay and Lesbian in a Catholic High School: Beyond the Uniform*. The first journal article is titled "Gay Adolescents in Catholic Schools: Avoiding the Topic Won't Make It Go Away," written by Robert Mattingly, a priest and admissions director at a Catholic high school in the United States. It was published in 2004 in two parts in two separate editions of *Momentum*, the official journal of the National Catholic Education Association of the United States. Part 1, which appeared in the September/October 2004 edition of *Momentum*, examines research and church teaching about homosexuality. Part 2, which appeared in the November/December 2004 edition, attends to the research that shows a majority of lgbtq students in Catholic schools report being harassed without any intervention from staff.

The second journal article is titled "How Catholic Schools Are Creating a Safe Climate for Gay and Lesbian Students," written by two authors: Sister Mary Ellen Gevelinger, the director of personnel and planning for Catholic schools in the St. Paul and Minneapolis Archdiocese, and Laurel Zimmerman, the chair of the guidance department in a private Catholic high school within the St. Paul and Minneapolis Archdiocese.

Both authors are adjunct professors at two separate Catholic universities in the state of Minnesota. The Gevelinger and Zimmerman article was published in the October 1997 edition of *Educational Leadership*.

The third journal article is titled "Reflecting on Shattered Glass: Some Thoughts about Gay Youth in Schools," written by Dr Kevin Alderson, a clinical hypnotist and adjunct associate professor in applied psychology at the University of Calgary. The Alderson article was published in the summer 2002 edition of *The Alberta Counsellor*.

This collection of essays that the authors of *Towards an Inclusive Community* included in Section 4, Student and School Perspective, is followed by 12 pages of excerpts they selected from a 169-page Catholic study conducted in the United States titled *Being Gay and Lesbian in a Catholic High School: Beyond the Uniform* (Maher, 2001). Forgoing a formal conclusion, the authors chose to close Section 4 simply with excerpts from this book.

The first article by Mattingly offers a similar defence of contentious Catholic doctrine from the Vatican as the CCCB, cited above. In his discussion of the Vatican's 1986 document *Pastoral Care of Homosexual Persons* that describes homosexuality as "intrinsically disordered," Mattingly admits that this phrase "may not sound pleasing to the ear" but he attempts to minimize its sting by arguing that the phrase "must be seen as precise philosophical terms" having to do with the "immorality" of any sexual act that does not lead to the begetting of children (as cited in CCSSA, 2007, sec. 4). These "precise philosophical terms" that underscore the "immorality" of non-procreative sex do little to detract from the powerfully oppressive phrase "intrinsically disordered." In effect, Mattingly sends the same message as the Vatican, except with less explosive language.

The overarching thesis of Mattingly's defence of contentious Catholic doctrine is his misleading declaration that "no modern church document labels a homosexual orientation as sinful" (as cited in CCSSA, 2007, sec. 4). As in the OCCB's 2004 pastoral guideline, discussed in the first part of this chapter, Mattingly praises the American Conference of Catholic Bishops' 1997 pastoral guideline called *Always Our Children*. Skipping over the sections of *Always Our Children* that recommend *Courage* for lgbtq people, Mattingly insists that "the church does not call for a homosexual to be 'fixed' but rather to be met with pastoral respect and care" (as cited in CCSSA, 2007, sec. 4).

Characteristic of writings from Catholic clergy members on the topic of homosexuality is their inability, or refusal, to acknowledge Catholic doctrine as contributing to societal homophobia. Mattingly's article is no exception. He recognizes "religions that communicate negative messages about homosexuals are destructive and can contribute to the young gay listener's self hate" but he does not admit that the Catholic religion is a contributor of these negative messages. Another common element of writings from Catholic clergy members on the topic of homosexuality is their protestations that they have nothing but love, compassion, and justice to offer homosexuals. In this vein, Mattingly states, "Gay teens need to feel loved and accepted as they are by family, friends, school and church. Nothing could be more in keeping with church teaching" (as cited in CCSSA, 2007, sec. 4). Mattingly's reading of Catholic Church teaching is a selective one that denies the existence of damning Catholic doctrine on the topic of homosexuality.

One refreshing element of Mattingly's article is his conditional acceptance of the idea of an in-school support group for lgbtq students. He acknowledges that "bringing students questioning their sexual identity together provides a powerful sense of support for these students, while it can also raise their visibility in the school" (as cited in CCSSA, 2007, sec. 4). Yet he cautions that "careful attention should be given to the name of the group, what external organization it affiliates with, how public the group is, and what guidelines the local Catholic School Office may have" (as cited in CCSSA, 2007, sec. 4). According to Father Mattingly, lgbtq students can have a support group as long as they are not too obvious about it and do not draw too much attention to themselves with provocative names or associations with outside lgbtq-rights organizations. This American Catholic priest and Catholic school administrator's concern over the name of an in-school support group for lgbtq students is also reflected in Canadian Catholic education leaders' consternation over the word "gay" in GSAs fought for by students at the Dufferin-Peel and Halton Catholic District School Boards in Ontario (see Chapter 2 and the Introduction to this book for details). This preoccupation with the word "gay" shows the powerful force of Catholic doctrine in directing policy and practice regarding sexual minorities in Catholic schools.

Mattingly's advice regarding the name of a support group for lgbtq students is aligned with the Alberta bishops' 2001 pastoral guideline, *A Resource for an Inclusive Community*, which states, "To refer to a person as 'gay' or 'lesbian' in our culture is not only to use politically charged language but to succumb to a reductionist way of speaking about someone else. Such labelling is not only inaccurate but tends to reinforce and, in some cases, legitimate an arrested psycho-sexual development" (as cited in CCSSA, 2007, sec. 3). Similarly, the Ontario bishops' PGASO also cautions that "attaching a label" such as homosexual, lesbian, or gay is "problematic" because it "implies that they are their orientation ... The orientation or act is homosexual or heterosexual but the person is not" (OCCB, 2004a, p. 26). I explore the way in which these two Catholic documents attempt to "produce" (in the Foucaultian sense) or portray lgbtq students and teachers as particular subjects in Chapter 5.

Despite Mattingly's warning to Catholic school administrators that "establishing a gay support group could be complicated," he nevertheless agrees they should exist because "research consistently shows [a GSA] is a major component for gay teens coming to self-acceptance" (as cited in CCSSA, 2007, sec. 4). Mattingly goes on to propose that gay support "groups could follow one of two models. A group could have lower visibility if it were run and known only in a school's counseling office. If a school desired a higher visibility, this group could be run as a club open to anyone with questions about sexual orientation issues" (as cited in CCSSA, 2007, sec. 4). In my upcoming discussion of Section 8 of *Towards an Inclusive Community*, I note that the Alberta bishops elected to avoid endorsing support groups for lgbtq students altogether, preferring the one-to-one counselling approach available through the counselling and chaplaincy offices.

The second article in the *Towards an Inclusive Community* workbook, "How Catholic Schools Are Creating a Safe Climate for Gay and Lesbian Students," by Sister Mary Ellen Gevelinger and Laurel Zimmerman, makes no apologies for Catholic doctrine that condemns, unlike Mattingly's article. Instead, they proceed as though such doctrine does not exist. Although Gevelinger and Zimmerman state they were part of their Archdiocese's Study Group on Pastoral Care and Sexual Identity for at least a year, involving a thorough examination of all Catholic Church documents on the topic of homosexuality, they concentrate solely on those aspects of Catholic doctrine that urge Catholics to "minister to all because all of us are God's creatures" (as cited in CCSSA, 2007, sec. 4).

Perhaps because of their refusal to address the existence of homophobic Catholic doctrine, the authors freely discuss their goals of offering general sensitivity training for Catholic school administrators, counsellors, and teachers, as well as specific training for "safe staff" provided by a local group called Family and Friends of Gay, Lesbian, Bisexual, Transgender Persons in Catholic Education (as cited in CCSSA, 2007, sec. 4). Remarkably, the authors also encourage Catholic schoolteachers to "incorporate discussions of homosexuality into the curriculum" (as cited in CCSSA, 2007, sec. 4), but the perspective and content of such discussions is left to the imagination. They stop short, though, of advocating for

GSAs in Catholic schools, suggesting instead that Catholic schools could agree to the establishment of "an off-site, interschool support group for students" (as cited in CCSSA, 2007, sec. 4). Aware that some traditional Catholic readers may accuse them of advocating for change in Catholic schools that goes against official Catholic doctrine on the topic of homosexuality, Gevelinger and Zimmerman are careful to point out that their "basic assumptions and guidelines are aimed at promoting chastity" (as cited in CCSSA, 2007, sec. 4).

The third article included in the *Towards an Inclusive Community* workbook manual, "Reflecting on Shattered Glass: Some Thoughts about Gay Youth in Schools" by Dr Kevin Alderson, is a review of existing literature on human sexuality, specifically homosexuality among young people. He concludes his essay with suggestions for school counsellors and recommendations on how schools can improve their treatment of sexual minority groups. Given that there are thousands of articles written by psychologists on this topic, the 2002 Alderson article was likely chosen for inclusion in the *Towards an Inclusive Community* teacher workshop manual for Catholic educators in Alberta because it is written by a local Albertan psychologist who identifies as gay, but, despite this fact, the essay nevertheless does not particularly challenge official Catholic belief on the topic of non-heterosexuality.

Presumably, adding Alderson's perspective enables the authors of *Towards an Inclusive Community* to claim they are presenting a balanced view on the topic. The overarching thesis of Alderson's article is "although teens are exploring same-sex behavior, it does not always lead to self-definition as gay. It is perhaps less well-known that some of those who identify themselves as homosexual will later change their self-definition to heterosexual" (as cited in CCSSA, 2007, sec. 4). Alderson therefore "encourage[s] young people to take their time self-identifying" (as cited in CCSSA, 2007, sec. 4) – a suggestion echoed by the ACB, whose 2001 pastoral guideline also cautions that "parents and educators should not assume that same-sex attractions during adolescence are necessarily indicative of a fundamental homosexual orientation" (as cited in CCSSA, 2007, sec. 3). Furthermore, Alderson writes that "youth should resist trying to self-identify for a few years, thereby avoiding a foreclosure on their identity" (as cited in CCSSA, 2007, sec. 4) – an outlook that would not be out of place among the opinions of the conservative Catholic educators who wrote *Towards an Inclusive Community* and the ACB, who provided guidance on this teacher in-service manual.

The authors of *Towards an Inclusive Community* close Section 4 with 12 pages of excerpts they selected from a 169-page Catholic study, *Being Gay and Lesbian in a Catholic High School: Beyond the Uniform* (Maher, 2001). The book's author is Michael Maher who holds a PhD in education from St Louis University, a Catholic Jesuit institution, and a master's in pastoral studies from Loyola University Chicago, a private Jesuit institution where he serves as campus chaplain (Maher, 2001).

Maher refers to all the relevant, contradictory teachings from the Catholic Church on the topic of homosexuality, including several of the same pivotal pieces of Catholic doctrine contained in the Alberta and Ontario bishops' pastoral guidelines discussed above. As a chaplain who studied in Catholic seminary college, Maher respects the Catholic Church's mandate that its teachings on homosexuality must be clearly presented in Catholic schools, but he stresses that "the Church's condemnations of homosexual activity must not prevent those working for the Church from providing pastoral care for homosexual persons" (Maher, 2001, p. 114).

In terms of a target audience for his book, Maher envisions Catholic educators who are working towards pastoral care for non-heterosexuals in Catholic schools and who need an acceptable rebuttal to conservative Catholic educators resistant to the idea of even discussing homosexuality in Catholic schools (Maher, 2001). Maher's book represents that rebuttal. To win over reluctant Catholic educators, Maher stresses the idea of "integration" – a recurring theme in Catholic educational philosophies that strives for education for the whole person. His thesis is that, rather than "integration," non-heterosexuals in Catholic schools experience a kind of "dis-integration," putting the Catholic goal of integration in education out of reach for them (Maher, 2001, p. 4). According to Maher, one way of reversing the "dis-integration" experienced by sexual minority groups in Catholic schools is to develop understanding and empathy for their plight by telling their stories. To illustrate his point, Maher interviewed 25 lesbian and gay adults who attended American Catholic high schools throughout the 1980s and 1990s and presented 16 of their stories in his book. The focus of Maher's study was to give a general impression of the experiences of some lesbian and gay students in some Catholic high schools.

In their brief introduction to the 12 pages of excerpts they chose to reproduce from Maher's book, the authors of *Towards an Inclusive Community* state, "Teachers and pastoral counselors can become better attuned to the life stories of homosexual students by examining a number of case studies" (CCSSA, 2007, sec. 4). Establishing empathy and developing sensitivity among Catholic educators towards non-heterosexuals in Catholic schools are the authors' stated reasons for excerpting selected portions of Maher's book. The authors of *Towards an Inclusive Community* excerpted three of the 16 stories presented in Maher's book: (1) Tom's Story, (2) Kevin's Story, and (3) Gina's Story. Tom's and Kevin's stories are about denying their homosexuality while in Catholic school because they did not feel safe there. Gina's story is about the sheltered homogeneity of her Catholic high school where the topic of homosexuality was generally avoided. Instead of providing any commentary or analysis of Maher's study, the authors of *Towards an Inclusive Community* reproduce a condensed version of Maher's own reflections on the stories of his participants. These reflections stress the students' shameful repression of their homosexual feelings while in Catholic school, the importance of teachers in influencing how safe or unsafe the students felt in their Catholic schools, and the lack of family support available to most lesbian and gay students who attend Catholic schools.

The fact that the authors of *Towards an Inclusive Community* have included these excerpts from Maher's book in their teacher in-service manual suggests they anticipated a need to develop sympathy and understanding towards sexual minorities among the teachers who would eventually lead and attend their workshop. I know when I attended a teacher in-service session called Sensitive Issues in Our Catholic Schools, which was the 2004 version of the 2007 *Towards an Inclusive Community* workshop, I witnessed other Catholic educators who were participating in the workshop with me actively resist learning about the topic of sexual minorities in Catholic schools. This resistance was expressed openly with questions such as, "Why do we have to learn about this?" as well as through less public homophobic grumblings, mutterings, and whispers among workshop participants. Empathy towards sexual minority groups can be challenging to establish among some educators in Catholic schools. Reading excerpts from Maher's book can be a way to reach out to a reluctant workshop participant. Including these brief excerpts from Maher's book is a step in the right direction, but the homophobic message underlying the Catholic doctrine at the centre of the *Towards an Inclusive Community* workbook is powerful enough to overshadow any empathy the excerpts from Maher's book may have generated.

Towards an Inclusive Community – *Section 7: Curriculum Support*

Section 7, Curriculum Support, is a collection of four one-page excerpted examples of existing curriculum materials Catholic educators can use to support curriculum and instruction on the topic of sexual minorities in

Catholic schools. The topic of sexual minorities is formally addressed in the human sexuality component of a class simply referred to as "religion" among Catholic educators, though its formal title found in teacher resource manuals and curriculum guides is Religious Studies. In Alberta, Religious Studies offered at the high school level is divided into three separate courses for each grade: grade 10 is Religious Studies 15, grade 11 is Religious Studies 25, and grade 12 is Religious Studies 35. The authors of *Towards an Inclusive Community* include reference information on the excerpted curriculum support pages so that Catholic educators teaching religion can consult the original text if they so desire.

The Alberta Ministry of Education does not develop the program for the Religious Studies classes taught in Catholic high schools throughout Alberta; instead, ACSTA develops it (Alberta Education, 2003). This concession is enabled through a special arrangement, called Policy 1.2.2: Locally Developed Religious Studies Courses, between the Alberta Ministry of Education and the ACSTA whereby Roman Catholic school districts in Alberta receive provincial education credits and financial support for instruction devoted to the study of the Roman Catholic faith (Alberta Education, 2003, 2011). The Alberta Ministry of Education approved Religious Studies 15-25-35 on the condition that ACSTA widen its focus from instruction solely in the Roman Catholic faith to have 20% of course content include comparative study of other world religions for each grade level (Alberta Education, 2003).

This 20% of comparative religious studies is normally taken care of in the first unit through an American textbook called *Exploring the Religions of the World* (Clemmons, 1999). This textbook follows the specific curriculum framework developed by the United States Conference of Catholic Bishops. It takes the Roman Catholic faith as a starting point for comparisons with other ancient religions and newer religious traditions that developed out of America's Protestant roots (Clemmons, 1999). The American textbook is widely used in the Catholic school districts of Alberta.

The one-page excerpt called "Religious Studies 15: Human Sexuality Unit" included in the Curriculum Support section of *Towards an Inclusive Community* does not contain any trace of an ecumenical dialogue between the Roman Catholic faith and any other religion on the topic of sexuality. Its "Materials and Resources" list includes the *Christ and Culture* grade 10 textbook developed by the CCCB in Ottawa; *The Catechism of the Catholic Church*; and the full text of the Alberta Bishops' document *A Resource for an Inclusive Community: A Teacher's Guide for and about Persons with Same Sex Attractions* (CCSSA, 2007). This list of teaching materials shows the substantial influence of the Vatican, the centralized association of Catholic bishops in Canada, and the Alberta bishops on the way the subject of human sexuality is taught in the Catholic schools of Alberta. It also shows the systematic school-level dissemination of Catholic doctrine that casts non-heterosexuals as "intrinsically disordered" (CCSSA, 2007, sec. 3) and sentenced to a life of celibacy if they are to be "good" Catholics. Despite the negative messages about non-heterosexuals contained in these curriculum materials, the stated overarching goal of this curriculum guide on human sexuality is to teach students the "Christian view of sexuality as a gift" (as cited in CCSSA, 2007, sec. 7).

Sexuality is only a gift for some, however, as the second example of curriculum support included in *Towards an Inclusive Community* makes clear. The one-page excerpt from a chapter called "Be Loving" in the CCCB's grade 9 Religious Education textbook *Be with Me* states, "The Church teaches that sexual intercourse belongs only in a lifelong, committed relationship that is open to new life" (CCCB, 1997a, p. 93). The excerpt also shows the dissemination of discriminatory Catholic doctrine in Canadian Catholic schools. The full grade 9 textbook comes from a centralized Catholic organization in Ottawa and is used in Catholic schools throughout Alberta and Ontario.

The misleading presentation of the "Christian view of sexuality as a gift" – for some – is further propagated in the third example of curriculum support contained in *Towards an Inclusive Community*. The one-page excerpt from a chapter called "Relating to the Other" in the CCCB's grade 10 textbook *Christ and Culture* contains an image of the famous scene known as the "Creation of Adam," a section of the fresco painted by Italian Renaissance artist Michelangelo on the ceiling of the Sistine Chapel in Rome. Beneath the image is a Catholic interpretation of the scene stating that it "suggests God's gift of sexuality to humanity" (as cited in CCSSA, 2007, sec.). The excerpt defines five acceptable kinds of love and describes "sexual love" as "instinctive" and restricted to "mutual attraction between a man and a woman" (as cited in CCSSA, 2007, sec. 7). This Catholic interpretation is deeply ironic given that innuendo and gossip throughout the centuries have invited some to read Michelangelo as gay. Although there may be no clear evidence of Michelangelo's homosexuality, the physical beauty of many of his monumental male nudes, including those depicted in the fresco *Creation of Adam* featured in this grade 10 textbook, suggests homoeroticism to some viewers. This understanding of Michelangelo as homosexual is further buttressed by historical accounts of the artist meeting and falling in love with a beautiful young Roman nobleman by the name of Tommaso dei Cavalieri (Stern, 2009). Alternative ways of seeing the image *Creation of Adam* suggest that God's gift of sexuality to humanity can also include same-sex attraction.

The excerpt concludes with the following warning: "There is no more powerful disorder in us than an unhealthy sexuality. Unhealthy sexuality hardens us in our selfishness. Nothing will make us more unhappy" (as cited in CCSSA, 2007, sec. 7). Although the CCCB, the authors of the text from which this excerpt is taken, does not define what they mean by an "unhealthy sexuality," it would not be a great leap for students in Catholic schools to imagine non-heterosexual forms of sexuality as "unhealthy sexuality" since the bishops make this clear in many ways in many other school materials. Catholic clergy members have written a great deal on the topic of non-heterosexuality in the form of Vatican encyclicals and local pastoral guidelines regarding "persons with same-sex attractions," and these writings are included in the curriculum materials lists of Religious Studies courses in Canadian Catholic schools.

The final one-page excerpt of curriculum support offered as an exemplar in *Towards an Inclusive Community* is a selection from the chapter "Marriage Matters" in the CCCB's grade 12 textbook *In Search of the Good: A Catholic Understanding of Moral Living*. This textbook was published in 2004 during the height of the same-sex marriage debates occurring across Canada – in 2005, Canada became the fourth country in the world to legalize same-sex marriage (Hull, 2006).

Under the heading "Secular Society and Homosexual Partners," this excerpt describes the fact that "people who are attracted to the same sex and cohabit have demanded the legal right of marriage" (as cited in CCSSA, 2007, sec. 7). The CCCB, the author of the excerpt, cites one of its own open letters called "Marriage in the Present Day," which it published on its website on 10 September 2003 (CCCB, 2003). The portion included in *Towards an Inclusive Community* is as follows:

> Marriage needs to be preserved as an institution uniting two members of the opposite sex. For the common good of society, it must be protected ... We reject the attempt of the State to reduce all intimate personal relationships to the same level, leading to the disappearance of the civil institution of marriage as understood in all human societies since time immemorial. Because of the recognized contributions that the institution of marriage brings to the stability of the family and to the future of society, legislators have the duty of

preserving the distinction between marriage and other forms of relationship involving two persons. (as cited in CCSSA, 2007, sec. 7)

This use of a student textbook to propagate a particular world view and influence the political leanings of students in Catholic schools is a clear example of the kind of indoctrination, rather than education, that the CCCB would like to see take place. The existence of uniform religion textbooks for grades 9 through 12 developed by the CCCB illustrates the influence of the Catholic Church and its discriminatory doctrine pertaining to homosexuality in the sexuality component of the religion curriculum being taught in Canadian Catholic schools.

Towards an Inclusive Community – Section 8: Media Questions

The final section of *Towards an Inclusive Community* that has some implications for this study is Section 8, labelled Media Questions. In this section is a single two-sided sheet dated 19 November 2004 that lists eight questions under the heading "Possible media questions to Catholic school districts on students and staff with same-sex attractions" (CCSSA, 2007, sec. 8). The authority of this one-page handout is clarified by a footnote at the end of the last question that states, "This document was prepared by a Committee of the Committee of the Council of Catholic School Superintendents of Alberta for implementing *A Resource for an Inclusive Community: A Teacher's Guide for and about Persons with Same Sex Attractions*" (CCSSA, 2007, sec. 8).

The need to develop stock answers to possible media questions is identified in a 17 September 2004 business report for the CCSSA from its Inclusive Communities subcommittee (CCSSA, 2004a). The second of two items under the heading in the business report labelled "Our Mandate" states, "To develop a mechanism whereby we can all 'speak with one voice' when the public, especially the media, requires us to say where we stand on the issue and on specific regulations" (CCSSA, 2004a, p. 1). This explicit mandate shows the CCSSA's desire to maintain control over what educators in Alberta Catholic schools may say publicly on the topic of non-heterosexual students and staff.

The most illuminating question, in terms of this study, is question 8: "Would your district support a pro-gay or lesbian alliance within a school? Why or why not? Response: *We offer support for our students to meet their personal and pastoral needs usually through our counseling and chaplaincy programs*" (italics in the original) (CCSSA, 2007, sec. 8). This question is particularly insightful for this study because the issue of being able to establish a GSA in a Catholic school rose to the forefront of discussion in the province of Ontario among educators, lgbtq activists, and conservative Catholics after *Xtra!* (Canada's foremost lgbtq news outlet) broke the story in January 2011 about the ban on GSAs by the Halton Catholic District School Board. For details on this story, refer to Chapter 3.

HCDSB held several meetings to gain approval for its trustees' policy recommendation that its schools should adopt broad equity clubs called By Your SIDE Spaces instead of GSAs – SIDE is a Catholic acronym that stands for Safety, Inclusivity, Diversity, and Equity (Brown, 2011). By Your SIDE Spaces is a gesture towards making schools more welcoming for everyone by attending to all forms of discrimination, such as racism and sexism, not just homophobia. A *Toronto Star* education reporter interviewed HCDSB trustee John Morrison, who commented, "If this policy passes, there won't be any GSAs in our schools because we've got something better" (as cited in Brown, 2011). From a Catholic perspective, this non-specific equity club would be "better" not only because it would be more inclusive but also because it would avoid the use of what the Ontario bishops call "problematic labels" (OCCB, 2004a, p. 26) and what the Alberta bishops call "politically charged language" (as cited in CCSSA, 2007, sec. 3) by not having the word *gay* anywhere in its name. Noa Mendelsohn Aviv, an equality program director with the CCLA, pointed out to the trustees of the HCDSB that "not allowing the word 'gay' is sending a message to students that there is something wrong with that identity" (as cited in Houston, 2011c, p. 1).

Until 2015, Catholic education leaders in Alberta had not been faced with this kind of public outcry for GSAs in Alberta Catholic schools,[1] but not because students have never attempted to start one. As I have described in a previous publication (Callaghan, 2007a), at a November 2004 University of Alberta education conference, a Catholic student spoke publicly about his success in setting up the first quasi-GSA – called a Diversity Club – in a Catholic high school in Alberta during the previous school year. His school would not allow a GSA but did eventually concede to a Diversity Club. Diversity Club is the most common name given to these Catholic versions of GSAs, though I have encountered

---

1 The Alberta Government introduced Bill 10, an *Act to Amend the Alberta Bill of Rights to Protect Our Children*, which requires all Alberta schools to allow GSAs if students request them; it received Royal Assent on 19 March 2015 (Callaghan & Mayr, 2015).

other names, such as Rainbow Alliance, Equity Group, and Social Justice Club, at school-based education conferences I have attended and where I have been spoken with lgbtq students from Catholic schools in Alberta, Ontario, and Saskatchewan.

In my discussions over the years with lgbtq youth (including those who participated in this study), I have discovered that Diversity Clubs vary considerably from school to school. Some Catholic schools allow students to form a Diversity Club, but the club may not meet on school property. Other Catholic schools that allow Diversity Clubs to meet on school property require the club's members to meet in the chaplaincy or guidance counselling offices with the chaplain or guidance counsellor as the adult moderator of the club meetings. Most Canadian Catholic schools that do allow Diversity Clubs to meet on school property place a number of restrictions on the way the students can advertise the club, such as limited or no use of the school's public address system, limited or no use of posters, and limits on use of the words *gay*, *straight*, and *queer*. Most Canadian Catholic schools that do allow Diversity Clubs to meet on school property require club members to make no public references, via posters or other announcements, to outside organizations, such as sexual health agencies where safe sex is promoted; lgbtq youth groups supported by a local lgbtq community association; or lgbtq community events, such as Pride Day. Likewise, students who have successfully formed a Diversity Club in their Catholic high school are usually not allowed to use lgbtq Pride symbols, such as inverted triangles or rainbow flags, on any posters advertising the club or the club's events.

Some Canadian Catholic schools that do allow Diversity Clubs to meet on school property allow club members to organize lgbtq events and celebrations, such as the National Day Against Homophobia or the National Day of Silence, but only if these actions can be contained under a broader focus, such as the No Name-Calling Week or the Anti-bullying Week. The National Day Against Homophobia occurs in Canada on 17 May, coinciding with the International Day Against Homophobia, also held on 17 May, the day the World Health Organization removed homosexuality from its list of mental disorders in 1990 (McCutcheon, 2011). Anti-bullying Week is a British action that takes place annually in November, and No Name-Calling Week is an American event that takes place in January each year – both the British and the American events use educational activities to build awareness of bullying in schools with the goal of eliminating bullying from schools (Actionwork, 2011; GLSEN, 2011c).

Other Canadian grassroots anti-bullying initiatives are also recognized in Canadian schools and involve wearing pink shirts as an act of solidarity with those who are bullied and to send a message that bullying in schools is not acceptable. They go by various names and take place at different times of the year, such as the International Day of Pink on 13 April (Canadian Teachers' Federation, 2016), Stand Up Against Bullying Day on the second Thursday of September (Nova Scotia Department of Education, 2007), and Pink Shirt Day on various dates in February (CKNewWestminter, 2009; Canadian Red Cross, 2011; British Columbia Ministry of Education, 2009).

The International Day of Pink is most closely connected with anti-homophobia education initiatives because it originates with Jeremy Dias, a young man who endured homophobic bullying, harassment, and assault while attending Sir James Dunn Collegiate high school in Sault St Marie, Ontario, from 1998 to 2001. When his attempts to start a GSA in his school were rebuffed by school administrators, he filed a complaint with the Ontario Human Rights Commission and eventually won a settlement of $5,000 three years later (Mohamed, 2012). Dias used the money from the settlement to start the Jeremy Dias Scholarship, a scholarship for youth working to stop bullying, homophobia, transphobia, and discrimination in their schools. Then, in 2005 when he was 22, Dias formed Jer's Vision: Canada's Youth Diversity Initiative, which became the Canadian Centre for Gender and Sexual Diversity in 2015 (Canadian Teachers' Federation, 2016). The organization seeks to encourage tolerance in the classroom by inviting youth to engage in dialogue about diversity, inclusion, and respect. It also attempts to raise awareness about homophobic bullying through the pink shirt campaign, the International Day of Pink on 13 April.

The other Canadian pink shirt days that take place in September and February also arose out of a homophobic incident. This one occurred in September 2007 at Central Kings Rural High School in Nova Scotia when a boy who was new to the school wore a pink shirt for the first day of grade 9 and was bullied for it. The bullies yelled gay slurs at the ninth grader and threatened to beat him up. When two grade 12 boys, Travis Price and David Shepherd, heard about the bullying, they went to a discount store that night and bought 50 pink T-shirts and tank tops and rallied their friends to wear them as a "sea of pink" show of support at the school the next day (CBC News, 2007). Although this initial student activism was a response to homophobic bullying, the pink shirt days that have sprung up across Canada since have become more about general anti-bullying campaigns and less about anti-homophobia education. In contemporary Western culture, pink is stereotypically associated with feminine characteristics and homosexuality (Koller, 2008), and there can be no mistaking the reason the grade 9 boy was bullied for wearing pink. It is therefore important to remember the origins of the pink shirt campaign. Nevertheless, because this campaign has broadened to be about bullying in general, it is more likely to be undertaken in Canadian Catholic schools, not known for tackling school-based homophobia. Students leading Diversity Clubs and other quasi-GSAs in Catholic schools may have more success convincing their school administrators to allow them to organize a pink shirt day in September or February because those campaigns are now associated with anti-bullying in general. What school administrator could be opposed to students wanting to rally around an anti-bullying campaign? Those in the know, however, are aware of the anti-homophobia origins of the campaign and the association between pink and femininity and being gay. This kind of a campaign in a Catholic school could be a stealthy act of resistance against institutionalized homophobia.

Back to the gay teenager who was able to establish a Diversity Club in his Edmonton Catholic school during the 2003–4 school year, before Catholic education leaders in the province banned GSAs from Alberta Catholic schools. Catholic bishops' and other Catholic education leaders' opposition to GSAs in Alberta Catholic schools is still strong despite the passing of Bill 10 that allows students in all Alberta schools, including Catholic schools, to start a GSA if they want. As Ben (not his real name) recounted to me, his achievement was hard fought. Ben and another gay teen, Kenan (not his real name), conceived the idea to start a GSA in their Catholic high school while Ben was in grade 11 and Kenan was in grade 10. It was just the two of them working together on this goal – no other students were a part of the initial groundwork for the club.

Ben and Kenan approached the chaplain of their school, who told them they would have better luck getting their club approved if they called it something other than a GSA and if it had a broader focus. Ben and Kenan went away to do some research and to develop a proposal to give to the school's administration. They came up with the name Diversity Club and wrote a brief proposal outlining the mission and focus of the club. Next came a lot of stalling by the administration involving requests to change the proposal for the club so that its focus was more clearly aligned with Church teachings on the topic of homosexuality. Then the two boys were required to accompany the chaplain of the school to a meeting with the head of Religious Studies for all Edmonton Catholic schools, as well as the Catholic

Archbishop for Edmonton. Both Catholic education leaders were support-ive of the Diversity Club, as long as the school chaplain and another teacher volunteer would serve as adult moderators of the club, the club respected Church teaching, did not discuss homosexual sex or promote safe sex, did not advertise an outside lgbtq youth group offered through the local lgbtq community association, and did not promote gay Pride. Ben recalls that the process of getting official approval for their Diversity Club took a year and a half, meaning that Ben was able to be part of the Diversity Club only during the last semester of his grade 12 year. Kenan was able to keep the club run-ning, though, after Ben graduated. Kenan told me in a Facebook message that the last he heard in 2007, the club was still running.

Given that the head of Religious Studies for all Edmonton Catholic schools and the Archbishop of Edmonton met with Ben and Kenan to determine if they would be granted their Diversity Club, it is conceivable that the head of Religious Studies and the Archbishop would have commu-nicated the news of the first Diversity Club in an Alberta Catholic school to other Catholic education leaders, especially the CCSSA who were develop-ing policy on this very issue. The CCSSA had formed its Inclusive Commu-nities subcommittee one year earlier, and its members were in the midst of developing a support plan for "students with same-sex attractions," as well as devising ways to ensure that Catholic school personnel are provided with clear direction on "this sensitive issue" (CCSSA, 2007, sec. 2).

The Inclusive Communities subcommittee took several years to develop its final version of the *Towards an Inclusive Community* workbook for Catholic educators, which was finally available in early 2005. A con-fidential draft version of the proposed stock answers to possible media questions, now available online, shows that the authors had a hard time developing an answer to question 8 about GSAs in the Media Questions section of their teacher in-service manual (CCSSA, 2004b). As quoted above, question 8 reads, "Would your district support a pro-gay or les-bian alliance within a school? Why or why not? Response: *We offer sup-port for our students to meet their personal and pastoral needs usually through our counseling and chaplaincy programs*" (italics in the original) (CCSSA, 2007, sec. 8). However, a 2004 draft version shows support for a Catholic adaptation of a GSA, commonly called a Diversity Club:

A group could be organized to:

- develop an understanding of homosexual orientation and Church teaching;
- provide support and enhance dignity and respect;

- devise strategies to counteract negative images;
- provide a safe space to dialogue and to give further guidance regarding chastity.

Allowing a support group for gay or lesbian students would be consistent with the [Council of Catholic School Superintendents of Alberta] document *Toward an Inclusive Community*. (CCSSA, 2004b, p. 2)

This draft version shows that, at least at one point, some authors of *Towards an Inclusive Community* supported Diversity Clubs in Alberta Catholic schools. It is not clear what changed their minds, but it is likely that the Alberta Catholic bishop the authors were consulting overruled the lay Catholic authors on this point. The fact that this supportive statement about Diversity Clubs was removed from the final 2007 version of the teacher in-service manual for Catholic educators means the official CCSSA policy is that GSAs are not permitted for queer and questioning youth in Alberta Catholic schools. As will become evident from the data I collected for this study, Diversity Clubs have been occasionally permitted in Alberta Catholic schools but only under certain constraints, and this will likely continue despite the passage of Bill 10 in the Alberta legislature (Callaghan & Mayr, 2015). Students, like Ben and Kenan above, who ask for permission to form a Diversity Club must first seek one-to-one counselling with either the Catholic school chaplain or counsellor. If students respond by stating that personal counselling is not what they were seeking and persist in their quest to form a Diversity Club, then stall tactics can be used until the students stop trying to establish a Diversity Club or graduate. If excuses and stalling tactics do not dampen lgbtq students' resolve, the students can be permitted to start a Diversity Club but only with several restrictions and close monitoring.

The existence of prescribed Catholic answers to possible media questions shows the level of control the Council of Catholic School Superintendents seek over any public remarks Catholic educators may be called upon to make regarding issues pertaining to sexual minority groups in the Catholic schools of Alberta. In fact, the entire document, *Towards an Inclusive Community*, is a testament to the Council of Catholic School Superintendents' desire to control the tenor of any discussions, school policy, or curriculum that may be introduced on the topic of sexual minorities in Alberta Catholic schools.

The main goal of the Alberta Catholic educators who wrote and selected the articles to be included in *Towards an Inclusive Community* is to ensure that the ACB's 2001 pastoral guideline is thoroughly circulated, absorbed and adhered to in all Catholic schools in Alberta. By writing an implementation guide for the ACB's 2001 pastoral guideline, the authors of *Towards an Inclusive Community* are attempting to ensure that the official Catholic Church "authority" on the topic of homosexuality is the only resource for information on how to manage sexual and gender minority groups in Alberta Catholic schools. As this chapter has shown, with the Council of Catholic School Superintendents at the helm, there is very little room for queer-affirming perspectives to be officially voiced in the Catholic schools of Alberta.

Concluding Remarks

This chapter analysed two primary texts: the first from Ontario Catholic bishops, the second from Alberta Catholic educators. The purpose of the text from Ontario is to clarify for educators in Ontario Catholic schools the official teaching of the Roman Catholic Church on the topic of homosexuality, to promote the "virtue of chastity" for "persons with same-sex attraction," and to advance the Catholic school as the "centerpiece of apostolic ministry to students experiencing same-sex attraction" (OCCB, 2004a, p. 11). The purpose of the Alberta text is to facilitate the circulation of the ACB's 2001 pastoral guideline *A Resource for an Inclusive Community: A Teacher's Guide for and about Persons with Same Sex Attractions* and to ensure that all Alberta Catholic educators "speak with one voice" when faced with media questions about how sexual minority issues are managed in Catholic schools (CCSSA, 2004a, p. 1).

In an attempt to strengthen their positions, both the Ontario and the Alberta texts cite, or in some cases entirely reproduce, other pastoral guidelines on the topic of homosexuality written by other groups of Catholic bishops, as well as the official Catholic doctrine on homosexuality from the Vatican. As we have seen, both texts circulate the most egregious elements of Catholic doctrine, such as excerpts from the *Catechism of the Catholic Church* that describe "homosexual acts" as "acts of grave depravity," which are "intrinsically disordered," and which count among the list of "sins gravely contrary to chastity" (as cited in OCCB, 2004a, p. 53). Both the Ontario and the Alberta texts stress the Catholic doctrinal directive that non-heterosexual lay Catholics must remain celibate for life. To assist non-clergy lgbtq Catholics in following through with this required celibacy, both texts recommend the corrective 12-step program Courage as a reputable method for arresting same-sex desire or even transforming non-heterosexual orientations into the more morally acceptable heterosexual orientation. This is in spite of documents included in these two same texts that insist non-heterosexuals do not need to be "fixed."

Despite the many examples of homophobic discrimination contained in both the Ontario and the Alberta texts, their authors maintain their texts are not homophobic. For example, the authors of the Ontario text state that they wrote their pastoral guidelines to "support school personnel in making Catholic school communities safe and nurturing for all students in their care" (OCCB, 2004a, p. 9). They also try to argue that "it should not be assumed ... that to guide others away from the practice of homosexual genital activity comes out of homophobia" (OCCB, 2004a, p. 25). Similarly, in their summary of the Alberta bishops' 2001 pastoral guideline, the authors of the Alberta text declare that "this is a document of HOPE!" (capital letters in the original) (CCSSA, 2007, sec. 3). This particular Catholic concept of "hope" and "care" for sexual minorities can be traced to official Catholic doctrine. The CCCB clarifies the kind of "care" it has in mind for non-heterosexuals in their 1997 summary of "The Catholic Church's Teaching on Homosexuality," as follows:

> The church recognizes and defends the human rights of each person. However, it cannot recognize as part of these rights the fulfillment of acts that are morally wrong. All persons have the basic human right to be treated by individuals and society with dignity, respect and justice regardless of their behaviour. For sure, the homosexual community is not an exception to this; it has a particular right to pastoral care from the Church. (as cited in OCCB, 2004a, p. 55)

The Catholic concept of "pastoral care" for non-heterosexuals derives from a Catholic doctrine that requires non-heterosexuals to commit to lifelong celibacy and advocates for conversion from a non-heterosexual to a heterosexual orientation via the Church-sanctioned corrective 12-step program Courage. This is not care that most professionals in the helping professions (education, medicine, nursing, psychotherapy, social work, etc.) would recognize.

So, how does power operate within and across Alberta and Ontario Catholic schools? The authors of the Alberta and Ontario texts would have readers believe that power resides solely with the authority of the Catholic Church, where it operates primarily by means of control, repression, and discipline. The goal of both documents is to control the message that circulates in these provinces' Catholic schools about lgbtq individuals.

How do Catholic documents portray teachers and students as subjects? The Alberta and Ontario Catholic documents frame lgbtq students and teachers solely as "persons with same-sex attraction" who suffer from "an arrested psycho-sexual development" and whose behaviour should be closely monitored and controlled.

What effects do Catholic documents have on the experiences of lgbtq individuals in Alberta and Ontario Catholic schools? The contradictions inherent in the Alberta and Ontario texts undermine their authors' attempts to persuade the reader of the pastoral and benevolent purpose of the two texts. The discrepancies that plague these two Catholic documents reveal the underlying message of Catholic doctrine at the core of both texts, a message that promotes the *opposite* of a "welcoming and safe environment" for sexual minority groups in the Catholic schools of Alberta and Ontario and attests to the dominating force of the Catholic Church when it comes to regulating the sexual conduct of sexual minority groups. But my research also reveals the good news that resistance to the church's doctrinal disciplining of non-heterosexuals *is* possible.

5
Theorizing the Data:
The Many Modes of Power

To uncover and explore the doctrinal disciplining of non-heterosexuals in Alberta and Ontario Catholic schools, I completed a study of participants' experiences, news media accounts of homophobia occurring in Catholic schools in Alberta and Ontario, and Catholic documents written to clarify for Catholic educators in those provinces the official Catholic doctrine about non-heterosexuality. I discovered that each part points to systemic and active school-board-approved and Church-sanctioned homophobia and transphobia occurring in these provinces' Catholic schools. This type of oppression represents one mode of power – the dominating control and authority that groups or institutions can hold over others. However, resistance to oppression is another mode of power – the personal potential inherent in the everyday relations between people and institutions – and I discovered, too, that resistance is thriving.

This study is grounded in empirical matters, but it is also informed by the epistemology of critical theory. Critical theories of education – such as those of well-known critical pedagogues Paulo Freire, Michael Apple, and Henry Giroux – trace injustices to their source by revealing the institutional structures and processes that perpetuate inequality in educational practice (Gibson, 1986). Drawing upon critical theories is helpful in constructing an account of homophobia in Alberta and Ontario Catholic schools that goes beyond participant experience and textual evidence. In particular, I have chosen to draw upon the following critical theories to help explain the phenomenon of homophobia in Alberta and Ontario Catholic schools: Antonio Gramsci's notion of hegemony (1971), Louis Althusser's concept of the ideological state apparatus (1970/2008), and Michel Foucault's theory of disciplinary surveillance (1975/1995).

All three theorists explore in different ways how institutional control operates in governmentally controlled organizations, such as schools, churches, and prisons. Perhaps because Althusser was once Foucault's professor at the École Normale Supérieure in Paris, Foucault, like Althusser, conceptualizes power as a major oppressive force in *Discipline and Punish*. However, unlike Althusser and other Marxist theorists more generally, Foucault also conceives of what he calls "a micro-physics of power" (1975/1995, p. 26) whose field of operation is more minute, such as at the level of the body, operating between and among individuals in an exchange that allows for possible resistance to power.

Major differences exist among these theorists. For example, Althusser is viewed as a Marxist structuralist whose work critiques the humanist aspects of Western Marxism, allowing no room for human agency (Macey, 2001). Gramsci, on the other hand, is regarded as one of the principal representatives of Western Marxism – a movement within Marxism that took shape after World War I and is generally characterized by a turn away from the economic theory of traditional Marxism and towards a more philosophically oriented critical examination of ideology, culture, and aesthetics (Macey, 2001). The chief contribution of Gramsci's wide-ranging *Prison Notebooks* (1971) is his notion of hegemony, or domination through consent, which adds a new element to Marxism's understanding of ideology (Macey, 2001). Foucault, meanwhile, breaks from both Althusser and Gramsci, especially in his attention to multiple forms of power and his rejection of the opposition between ideology and truth. Although I do not adopt these thinkers as my main theoretical influences, I do treat their works as resources providing useful concepts that shed light on the dynamics of power and authority operating in Catholic schools.

Ideology has many competing definitions. The Marxist conception of ideology posits that history is the product of class conflict whereby the ideas of the ruling class become the dominant ideology through an apparently seamless process of coercion (Macey, 2001). Gramsci's notion of hegemony makes an important contribution to later Marxist theories of ideology in that it offers an alternative to the base/superstructure model, the original theory of ideology outlined by Marx and Engels in *The German Ideology* (1845–6), which contends there is a relationship of determination between an economic base (i.e., the forces and relations of production) and a superstructure comprising the state and legal, political, and ideological forms (Macey, 2001). Gramsci's analysis of organic ideologies, or world views of various social classes, stresses the cultural factors associated with ideology, thereby avoiding the economic determinism of the classic base/superstructure model of ideology and the original Marxist theory that ideology is a skewed manifestation of an underlying economic reality (Macey, 2001).

The work of Althusser, on the other hand, suggests a critique of Western Marxism, especially its humanist elements – for Althusser, individual subjects are the supports not the agents of historical processes (Macey, 2001). Althusser locates ideology as a vital component in the reproduction of social relations in all societies. He theorizes ideology's mechanism of interpellation (a process of hailing a subject in such a way that the subject recognizes her own existence within the dominant ideology of her society, thereby demonstrating how subjects are products of ideology) constitutes individuals as subjects (Macey, 2001). Through his theory of interpellation, Althusser shows his interest lies in the way the state oppresses people and the way ideology produces people as individuals. In Althusser's schema, people are simply cogs in the ideology machine.

Unlike Althusser, Foucault conceives of a bottom-up model of power in his focus on how power relations permeate all aspects of society. This allows for an account *of la vie quotidienne*, or the daily, banal, and minute ways power is exerted and resisted, which showcases the individual as an active subject rather than a "passive dupe" succumbing to ideological pressures (Mills, 2003, p. 34). Where Marxist theorists use the term "ideology" to describe how the ideas of the ruling class dominate those of subordinate classes, Foucault employs the term "discourse" to describe relations of power. In *The History of Sexuality, Vol. I*, Foucault (1976/1990) argues:

> Discourses are not once and for all subservient to power or raised up against it, any more than silences are. We must make allowance for the complex and unstable process whereby discourse can be both an instrument and an effect of power, but also a hindrance, a stumbling-block, a point of resistance and a starting point for an opposing strategy. Discourse transmits and produces power; it reinforces it, but also undermines and exposes it, renders it fragile and makes it possible to thwart it. (pp. 100–1)

Here, we see that Foucault's analysis of power differs from the Marxist analysis of power. Foucault rejects the Marxist notion of ideology because it implies the existence of universal rationality and truth, concepts that Foucault strongly contests. Foucault breaks from Althusser in his attention to multiple forms of power and his rejection of the opposition between ideology and truth. Gramsci's non-reductionist theorizing of hegemony and power conceives of power as being exercised at all levels of society, which is far removed from the Althusserian notion of power being localized solely in repressive and ideological state apparatuses. In this way, Gramsci's theories on power have some resonance with the conception of power found in the work of Foucault. The upcoming discussion of Foucault's theory of Panopticism explores further how Foucault sees power as the constant surveillance of a population based upon visibility and silence, rather than as a matter solely of repression in the traditional Marxist sense.

The preceding discussion emphasizes how ideology, hegemony, and disciplinary surveillance are premised on different, and, in some ways, incompatible assumptions. Although Gramsci, Althusser, and Foucault belong to fundamentally different theoretical traditions, it is not impossible to imagine a basis for their convergence. Several scholars have made theoretically worthwhile links between Marxist thinkers and Foucault (Cocks, 1989; Kenway, 1990; Laclau & Mouffe, 1985; Mouffe, 1979; Olssen, 2006; Smart, 1986). Australian scholar Jane Kenway studies the sociology and politics of education. In one of her earlier essays, Kenway (1990) successfully draws upon Foucault and Gramsci to explore what she calls the "educational right's discursive politics" (p. 172). Although her argument may be unconvincing to those who emphasize the incompatibility and difference between Foucault and Marxism, she nevertheless manages to underscore the more pragmatic advantages of drawing upon different aspects of each theorist to offer an explanation of the social phenomenon under study. Similarly, British political theorist and education scholar Mark Olssen (2006) examines the utility of combining Foucault and Gramsci in a common frame of reference and concludes that the greatest advantage of such a combination is that each theorist moderates the weakness of the other. Olssen (2006) argues, "Foucault's focus on the molecular and on the microphysics of power supplements and enriches the Gramscian focus on structures in an analysis that enables a theorization of both the sources and structural basis of power in institutions as well as its consequences and capillary effects" (p. 96). Given their various and differing historical and national contexts and theoretical interests, Gramsci, Althusser, and Foucault each explain and explore power differently, but there is overlap between their theories that facilitates an unpacking of the ways in which power and control function in Alberta and Ontario Catholic schools. These theorists are helpful in illuminating various aspects of the empirical data of this study, and I draw upon their theories to better understand the dynamics of power and authority operating in Catholic schools, but I remain attentive to the limitations of those theories, particularly around the issue of resistance. On the topic of resistance, none of these theorists adequately conceptualizes the possibility of a social system with conflicting ideologies and competing power structures. This may be because resistance is easier to conceive of when there are conflicting ideologies and power structures, and part of the reason, perhaps, that none of these theorists effectively theorizes resistance is that they conceived of ideology and the state as unified systems. Of course, resistance may not be strictly a matter of resisting a dominant ideology. It may be just a matter of embracing a particular ideology and opposing a dominant one.

A critical theory of education has resistance as its central motif, and this chapter also draws upon the work of critical pedagogue Henry Giroux (2001), who has proposed an encompassing critical theory of education with resistance to all forms of domination as its central concept. Although Foucault makes room for resistance to power in some of his writings, how resistance might be realized is not often clearly articulated in his work. Giroux fills in this gap by specifying how resistance can be achieved in a variety of cultural institutions, including schools. Giroux's criticism of Althusser's theory of power for its failure to account for the forces of human agency and resistance is particularly illuminating and hopeful for this present study, as is Giroux's ability to see in Gramsci's work an active human subject capable of affecting real radical change. Just knowing that resistance is possible against such a seemingly indomitable force as the Catholic school system gives those enduring its repressive policies the courage to defy them.

This chapter on theorizing the empirical data sets is divided into two sections. The first section draws upon the above theories to illuminate the participants' experiences, and the second section draws upon the same theories to give further insight into the textual evidence of the media accounts and the Catholic documents.

Theorizing the Participants' Experiences

The experiences of the teachers and students whose stories are recounted in this study can be approached via Gramsci's (1971) notion of hegemony, Althusser's (1970/2008) concept of the ideological state apparatus, and Foucault's (1975/1995) theory of disciplinary surveillance. These theories reveal not only how the participants were dominated by the Vatican and its Catholic doctrine about non-heterosexuality but also how power relations between and among individuals in Catholic schools manage to circumvent the power of the Vatican. As mentioned earlier in this chapter, however, Althusser, Gramsci, and Foucault's conceptualizations of power have their limitations – especially when used to unearth the ways in which power operates in and around Alberta and Ontario Catholic schools.

Gramsci's notion of hegemony

Italian Marxist Antonio Gramsci is best known today for invigorating the conceptualization of ideology within Marxism and for his theory of hegemony (Macey, 2001). Derived from the Greek *hegemon* ("dominant state or leader"), hegemony can be summarized as domination through consent, or the apparently seamless acquiescence of a subordinate group to the ideas of the dominant group (Macey, 2001). For general hegemonic dominance to function, the dominant group must first secure its ideological hegemony over the subordinate group. Schools are an efficient vehicle for achieving this. In schools, ideological hegemony is established mainly through the formal curriculum but also secondarily through the routines and expectations of social relationships (Giroux, 2001). The way ideological hegemony functions through social relationships involving the regulation of sexuality in Catholic schools can be observed through some examples from the experiences of some of the participants in this study.

The two teachers in this study who continue to work in Catholic schools (Mark in Alberta, and Luke in Ontario) must closet or hide their non-heterosexual identity to keep their jobs. They strategically act out their consent to their own domination by pretending to live within the confines of Catholicity – namely the Catholic doctrine that requires non-heterosexuals remain celibate for the rest of their lives (see Chapter 4 for details on specific Catholic doctrine). They experience a form of doctrinal disciplining in the tremendous amount of emotional and psychological energy they feel obligated to expend to pretend they are conforming to the Catholic doctrine that requires them to live a life of chastity and celibacy (i.e., not living as they do in committed relationships with their same-sex partners).

This dissimulation not only consumes a great deal of personal energy but also robs the two teachers of one privilege taken for granted by most heterosexuals in contemporary North American society – sharing information about their romantic love and happiness with others. Nevertheless, these two teachers consent to their own domination in this regard to keep their jobs. This is not to imply that a teacher's decision to remain closeted at school equates with compliance, consent, non-resistance, or non-agency. As feminist scholar and critical pedagogue Didi Khayatt (1997, 1999) makes clear, it is not necessary for lgbtq teachers to come out at school for the heteronormativity of schooling to be disrupted – lgbtq teachers can be out at school in other ways besides openly declaring their sexual orientation. Gramsci's writings on hegemony do not necessarily assume individuals undergo complete psychological acceptance of dominant ideologies. The teachers and students in this study personally reject the dominant homophobic ideology of their Catholic schools (they recognize and act on their lgbtq identities), but some choose to hide their identity, beliefs, and behaviour for fear of the consequences. This choice to remain closeted can be regarded as a kind of strategic consent to the dominant ideology of their immediate environments that enables them to act as subversive agents of change from within. These participants' decisions to remain closeted appear to be conscious ones and in this way reflect their own personal agency. For example, the fact that the two closeted gay teachers (Mark and Luke) do not actually live "celibate lives," coupled with the fact that they chose to participate in this study, show that they have not consented entirely to Catholic heterosexist domination. Both of these teachers explained to me while we set up their interviews that they chose to share with me their experiences of working as closeted gay men in Catholic schools so that others would learn of their working conditions and hopefully be moved to begin the discussions that might reverse such workplace heterosexism and homophobia.

Similarly, the majority of the student participants in this study strategically consented to their own domination by remaining closeted about their sexual orientation or gender identity while attending Catholic school. For these students, the fear of what would befall them if they were to come out about their non-heterosexuality far outweighed the control of the closet. Like the closeted teachers, these closeted students told me they chose to take part in this study so that others would learn about what they face and possibly start taking measures to make Catholic schools safer for all students, including the non-heterosexual ones who are too afraid to make themselves known.

Althusser's concept of the ideological state apparatus

According to Gramsci (1971), consent is as crucial as coercion for hegemony to function. This idea overlaps with the theories of Louis Althusser, the French Marxist thinker who came to prominence a generation after Gramsci. Like Gramsci before him, Althusser (1970/2008) posits that ideology is essential for the subtle influencing of members of subordinate groups to accept and reproduce dominant social systems – repression alone is insufficient to the task. According to Althusser, "ideology" is "the system of the ideas and representations which dominate the mind of a man or a social group" (1970/2008, p. 32). As discussed above, the sociological concept of ideology originated with the work of Karl Marx and continues to figure prominently in the Marxist sociological tradition, as well as in the social sciences more generally (Marshall, 1998). In the Marxist tradition, the state is conceived as a "repressive apparatus" (Althusser, 1970/2008, p. 11), represented by "the Government, the Administration, the Army, the Police, the Courts, the Prisons, etc., which [Althusser calls] the Repressive State Apparatus" (1970/2008, pp. 16–17).

Recognizing that repression on its own is not sufficient to produce existing social relations, Althusser developed a category called the "ideological state apparatus" (Althusser, 1970/2008, p. 17) that includes religious organizations, the education system, the family, the legal system, trade unions, the political system, arts and culture, and the media. The function of the ideological state apparatus (ISA) is threefold: (1) to transmit the values of the dominant culture, (2) to ensure the majority of the populace consents to the dominant culture's values, and (3) to render individual members of society "subjects" of the dominant social order.

In Althusser's schema, the repressive state apparatus (RSA) differs from the ISA in the following ways: the RSA is a singular, unified entity; it belongs to the public domain; and it functions by force (Althusser, 1970/2008, pp. 18–19). Althusser's ISA, on the other hand, is a multiplicity of methods of inculcating consent; it operates in the private domain; and it functions by ideology (Althusser, 1970/2008, pp. 18–19). ISAs are powerful not through violence but by gaining the implicit consent of the populace through accepted and repeated practices. For example, individuals tacitly learn to obey authority at home, in religious centres of worship, and at school. Of these three examples, the school is the most dominant in Althusser's theory. Althusser (1970/2008) posits:

> Behind the scenes of its political ideological state apparatus, which occupies the front of the stage, what the bourgeoisie has installed as its number-one, i.e. as its dominant ideological State apparatus, is the educational apparatus, which has in fact replaced in its functions the previously dominant ideological State apparatus, the Church. (pp. 27–8)

In today's information age and its attendant hyper-credentialism, coupled with the increasingly secular culture of many knowledge societies that are able to transform the raw data of the information age into resources that help improve the human condition, it certainly appears as though education has replaced religion as the principal and most effective Althusserian ISA. We could suggest that, in certain more politically conservative situations, the media have operated as a tool of the government (an Althusserian RSA) – in effect leading to the conclusion that the media may have replaced education as the dominant ISA. But for resistance against the Vatican's influence inside Ontario Catholic schools, the media can function as an effective tool. Just as it is ironic that the Canadian government (an RSA in Althusser's schema) is in conflict with the Catholic Church, so are the individual members of the media (an ISA in Althusser's schema) ironically resisting the Catholic Church's disciplining of what it calls "intrinsically disordered" (as cited in OCCB, 2004a, p. 53) lgbtq students and teachers in Ontario Catholic schools.

In the Catholic schools of this study, we can see Althusser's theory of the ISA operating if one imagines Althusser's "State" to be a combination of (1) the provincial governments of Alberta and Ontario via their respective ministries of education and (2) the Vatican. In Canada, publicly funded schools are required to teach the provincial curriculum and follow provincial educational policies. However, as both Chapter 3 and Chapter 4 show, special concessions are made by provincial (and ultimately federal) governments that enable Catholic schools to teach provincial curricula with a Catholic slant and develop Catholic versions of particular provincial educational policies about accommodating sexual diversity. Despite the fact that in 2009 the Ontario Ministry of Education identified homophobia as a major problem in all Ontario schools and proposed ways to redress this problem, the Vatican's position on non-heterosexuality still seems to reign as the ultimate authoritative position in the Catholic schools of Ontario. In Alberta, the Ministry of Education under the Progressive Conservative provincial government was not as proactive about reducing homophobia in Alberta schools as the Liberal provincial Government of Ontario's Ministry of Education. In Alberta Catholic schools under the Conservative provincial government, the Vatican's role as the authority on matters pertaining to sexuality was not challenged by any Alberta Ministry of Education policy.[1]

When it comes to addressing homophobia in Catholic schools through curriculum and policy, it appears the Althusserian state apparatus that has the most force is not the provincial ministries of education but the Vatican. Althusser's theory of the ISA, then, is helpful but not sufficient for understanding how power operates in Catholic schools. Althusser's notion of the ISA is limited, for example, in theorizing how one part of the ISA – the Catholic Church – comes to dominate another – the educational system – and it does not explain the role of other ISAs, such as the media, in circumventing the dominant ISA of the Church. Althusser (1970/2008) contrasts his theory of the ISA with his theory of the RSA by stating, "While there is *one* (Repressive) State Apparatus, there is a *plurality* of ideological state apparatuses," (p. 18 italics and brackets in the original) yet his theory does not explain hierarchies that can exist among ISAs or how one ISA can come to dominate another. The empirical evidence of this study, however, does show that the ideology being circulated in Catholic schools is not Ontario's Equity and Inclusive Education Strategy, but the *Catechism of the Catholic Church* and other statements on the topic of homosexuality issued from the Vatican. This evidence suggests the ISA of the Church is in a position of dominance over the ISA of the educational system, but Althusser's theory of the ISA does not explain how hierarchies among ISAs happen. The dominant ideology in the Catholic schools of this study is not to respect and value sexual diversity but to correct and control sexual diversity and to ensure that it finds no physical expression. The manner in which this particular Althusserian ISA of the Church partially functions in the Catholic schools of this study is best illustrated with a few examples of some participants' experiences. Keep in mind, however, that Althusser's theories

---

1 This changed in May 2015 with the swearing in of Rachel Notley as the 17th premier of Alberta. Notley's New Democrats ended 44 years of Progressive Conservative rule in the province. In January 2016 the Alberta education minister set a new tone by introducing progressive guidelines for all Alberta schools to ensure they are safe spaces for lgbtq students. Alberta Catholic schools have resisted these guidelines, and it remains unclear if the guidelines are being implemented.

do not entirely fit the complexities of religiously inspired homophobia in Catholic schools.

Abigail, Hannah, and Jacob are three student participants who were able to be out about their non-heterosexuality to themselves and most of their friends. Although not out to their parents, these students' positive coming out experiences to their friends and certain teachers at school gave them the impression it was acceptable to be open about their sexuality at their Catholic schools. Abigail and Jacob opened up about their lesbianism to a trusted teacher (Jacob identified as a lesbian in school but now identifies as a transman). Hannah exclaimed in exasperation, "I'm gay and I don't know what to do!" when two school administrators were questioning her about wearing the boys' shirt and tie component of the school uniform and about her truancy. The teachers in whom Abigail and Jacob had confided informed their administrators about the students' disclosure, and the administrators then arranged for the students' parents to come into the school so the students' disclosure could be shared with them. The administrators in Hannah's case responded by promptly calling Hannah's mother into the school so she could be informed of what Hannah had revealed. Being outed to their parents by the school was devastating for the students. Both Hannah and Jacob were kicked out of their family homes and ended up renting their own apartments at the age of 16, and Abigail had a difficult time with her mother at home and was placed under a quasi-restraining order at school.

School administrators who respect and value sexual diversity should be aware that others may not be as accepting of difference. These administrators therefore may be reluctant to inform the parents of a student who had just come out as lgbtq at school out of concern for the student's safety in the home environment. They may also conclude on their own that a student's sexual orientation is not a matter worth calling parental attention to in the first place, as they would not view non-heterosexuality as a "problem." The Catholic school administrators who outed lgbtq students to their parents appear to be more concerned for their reputations in the Catholic system as good shepherds guiding lgbtq students than for the students' immediate safety. Catholic school administrators who espouse the Catholic ideology that sexual diversity must be controlled and corrected are compelled by Catholic doctrine and school policy to inform the parents of a student who has come out as lgbtq at school, making all the more evident the church's ISA dominance.

Here we see two competing ideologies in Canadian culture vis-à-vis sexual minority groups in schools: one represented by a provincial Ministry of Education and its policies that respect diversity and work towards protecting sexual minority groups from discrimination, the other represented by the Vatican and its Catholic doctrine that characterizes the physical expression of sexual diversity as "intrinsically disordered" and "contrary to the natural law" (as cited in OCCB, 2004a, p. 53). Given that the Catholic school administrators in this study adhere more strongly to Catholic doctrine than to provincial educational policy when it comes to managing sexual minority groups, it appears that the more persuasive force operating in Catholic schools is Catholic doctrine rather than provincial educational policy. According to Althusser, societies that are able to carry on into the future are those that are able to reproduce themselves ideologically and materially through the judicious use of various ideological apparatuses. Catholic societies or cultures reproduce themselves through the Catholic Church and its close cousin, the Catholic school. If Catholic schools made room for competing ideologies, such as those represented by provincial ministries of education, they might be in danger of dying out or at the very least being unrecognizably transformed. Therefore, Catholic cultures ensure reproduction by employing the ideological apparatus of the Catholic school to make Catholic subjects who adhere more strongly to Catholic doctrine than to secular law, represented in this case by provincial educational policy.

These Catholic school administrators' warnings to the parents of lgbtq students cement the supremacy of Catholic doctrine over provincial educational policy in Catholic schools. According to Althusser's ISA, the "State" that is operating in the Catholic schools of this study, in relation to sexual minority groups, is the Vatican, and the dominant ideology being circulated is Catholic doctrine. Because the lgbtq students are in danger of falling outside Catholic doctrine, their parents must be informed so they can be corrected. As Althusser (1970/2008, p. 19) explains:

> The ideological state apparatuses function massively and predominantly *by ideology*, but they also function secondarily by repression ... Thus Schools and Churches use suitable methods of punishment, expulsion, selection, etc., to "discipline" not only their shepherds, but also their flocks [italics in the original].

The Catholic Church's position on sexual diversity is circulated in Catholic schools primarily by ideology (i.e., via curriculum taught through a Catholic filter) but also secondarily by repressive policy (informed by Catholic doctrine) that would direct a school administrator to out to the parents their lgbtq child so that the parents can discipline their lgbtq child at home according to Catholic doctrine.

Other examples of Althusser's ISA functioning secondarily by repression can be seen in the stories of the four teacher participants who lost their jobs. Of the six teacher participants whose stories are recounted in this study, three said they were fired for not upholding Catholic doctrine related to non-heterosexuals: Job said he was fired for transitioning from female to male, Naarai said she was fired for attempting to get pregnant and raise a baby with her female partner, and Anna said she was fired for acting as a "straight ally" by offering her classroom as a "Positive Space" in which lgbtq students could meet. A fourth teacher, Naomi, said she was not fired but rather was harassed about her suspected lesbianism – to the point of almost being run out of the northern Ontario town where she had just moved to take up her first teaching job – until she was able to complete her temporary contract. Each of these teachers experienced the discipline of the repressive arm of Althusser's ISA in the form of the Catholic Church and its doctrine.

Job knew he would not be able to report for work in the fall as a man without explaining his transition from female to male to his employers. He chose to inform his employers of his medical condition and they responded by firing him.

Naarai thought she could be open about her lesbianism at her Catholic school and spoke freely with her work colleagues about her plans to raise a baby with her female partner. This caught the attention of the principal of the school, who then monitored her behaviour closely. When Naarai started taking time off of work to see a fertility specialist, the principal reminded her that he had warned her earlier about how the Catholic Church would not approve of her constructed family with her lesbian partner and initiated the process of terminating her employment on these grounds.

Anna's lunchtime refuge for lgbtq students might have gone unnoticed by the Catholic school administrators if it were not for Anna's placement of "Positive Space" and Pride flag stickers in the window of her classroom door. This brought the repressive force of Althusser's ISA in the form of school policy down on Anna. She said her temporary teaching contract was not renewed because she helped lgbtq students socialize with one another in a way that was forbidden by her school board.

Naomi was heavily monitored from the moment she moved into town to take up a temporary teaching assignment. Community members watched her to see if she was just sharing accommodation with her female friend or if they were sharing the same bedroom too. Colleagues found ways to let her know they suspected her friend was really her lover and that "homosexuality is a sin." Naomi responded by ignoring the subtext of her colleagues' and neighbours' close scrutiny of her life and by insisting on completing her temporary contract despite the difficulties.

It is hardly a coincidence that, historically, the Catholic Church has explicitly operated as an Althusserian RSA. As a government/state, it acted and ruled through its religiously sanctioned military campaigns, known as the Crusades, and through its *Inquisitio Haereticae Pravitatis* (Inquiry on Heretical Perversity), known as the Inquisition. The Catholic Church's historical RSA status can still be seen today in the repressive arm of its ISA, the Catholic school, which effectively punishes and otherwise disciplines teachers and students who do not conform to Catholic doctrine.

Althusser offers a structuralist account of ideology, which looms large in his view of power and domination. Critical pedagogue Henry Giroux (2001), one of the original theorists of resistance in education, criticizes Althusser's conceptual orientation for relying too heavily on a reductionist concept of power and for dismissing the notions of struggle and human agency. Giroux (2001) is particularly critical of what he calls Althusser's "undialectical" (p. 82) notion of ideology, which he says fails on two counts: (1) ideology is presented by Althusser as an abstract force able to diffuse all manner of resistance and (2) ideology appears in Althusser's schema as an institutionalized form of domination, functioning so seamlessly that the ISA becomes an "administrative fantasy" (p. 82). Yet according to Althusser's theoretical framework, when it comes to managing sexual minority groups, the Catholic schools in this study reveal Althusser's "administrative fantasy" is not fantastical. They effectively transmit the Catholic doctrine of the Vatican on the topic of non-heterosexuality, thereby ensuring that most students, teachers, staff, and other faculty consent to the Vatican's values regarding sexual minorities, all without any apparent opposition.

The apparent lack of opposition may certainly appear this way given that the three lgbtq student participants in this study described above, who were out to themselves (i.e., had acknowledged and admitted to themselves that they were gay or trans) and their friends at school, had the challenging experience of being outed to their parents by their Catholic school administrators. However, a closer examination shows that these lgbtq student participants were not docile actors in a straightforward hegemonic play but active agents in their own lives.

Jacob, for example, had the foresight to inform himself about other ways of living by getting up at 1 a.m. each week at the age of 11 to watch *Queer as Folk* on TV and by borrowing gay-related materials from the public library. Jacob's autodidactic drive enabled him to unlearn or, at the very least, rigorously question the Catholic ideology that permeated his school and informed the reparative therapy sessions his parents forced him to take after they found out about his sexuality from the school. Jacob's newfound knowledge gave him the confidence he needed to put an end to the Catholic counselling sessions, find his own apartment at the age of 16 after his parents kicked him out of the house, and to stand up to a homophobic religion teacher in his Catholic high school.

Like Jacob, Hannah had a difficult time at home once "all hell had broken loose" after the school informed her mother that Hannah had come out as a lesbian. Hannah's mother laid down restrictive house rules and, when Hannah did not follow them, her mother kicked her out. After bouncing between friends' houses and the psychiatric ward of the local hospital (Hannah was suicidal), Hannah dropped out of school, took on full-time hours at the local café where she had formerly worked part-time, and at the age of 16 acquired an apartment with some friends. Despite being emotionally and psychologically devastated, before she eventually quit school altogether, Hannah took on the homophobia of her Catholic high school by planning acts of resistance there. Together with another lesbian classmate, Hannah chose to do a class project about the local gay community and drew the school's attention to its homophobic "net nanny" that blocked all affirming websites about non-heterosexuals while allowing those that condemned non-heterosexuals through. Hannah and her friend did manage to convince the school to change its Internet filtering system. Hannah also attended a school board meeting to protest the banning of a book that presented homosexuality in a positive light, though the school board banned it despite her efforts. Hannah learned what she could about lesbianism online and was able to counter her Catholic family counsellor who told her to avoid gay people because they are promiscuous and disease-ridden. Online, Hannah also learned about the Day of Silence and observed it at school on her own, but teachers told her she could not participate in this kind of activism because it was not approved by the administration. Hannah never gave up. Overall, Hannah says there were some students, teachers, and administrators in her Catholic high school willing to tackle the systemic homophobia and she's "hoping that things are getting better and students are trying to get their voices out more because it needs to be done."

Like Jacob and Hannah, Abigail also filled in the gaps of her Catholic education by informing herself about non-heterosexuality through regular visits to her town's public library, where she read every lgbtq-themed young adult novel in the collection. Like most of the other lgbtq student participants in this study, Abigail was a frequent user of the Internet and learned about GSAs and the Day of Silence online. Through these outlets, Abigail gained access to a vastly different perspective about sexual diversity than she was learning in her Catholic school. This new outlook emboldened her to take action at her school. She established a quasi-GSA called Equality Awareness, managed to observe a toned down version of the Day of Silence, arranged for the school to host a benefit concert for the local AIDS group, and did a queer reading of Virginia Woolf's novel *Mrs Dalloway* for one of her grade 12 English presentations. Abigail is convinced that more people will start to combat homophobia in Ontario Catholic schools because, as she says, "The resistance is already starting to happen ... It'll change one day, but we have to change it."

These examples of lgbtq students' attempts to change the systemic homophobia of their Catholic schools show that Althusser's notion of the ISA does not allow for the occurrence of smaller, subversive acts of resistance against a seemingly static and monolithic force. The Vatican (Althusser's "State") is certainly a powerful presence in the Alberta and Ontario Catholic schools of this study, and its homophobic doctrine (Althusser's "Ideology") is thoroughly disseminated in these schools. However, as Giroux points out in his critique of Althusser's ideological state apparatus, the particular ISA of the Canadian Catholic school is not able to fend off all opposition to the way in which it institutionalizes homophobia, nor is it able to eliminate entirely the powerful, though often overlooked, force of human agency of which these students are prime examples. The inability of the Canadian Catholic school to be an absolute dominating force in the manner of Althusser's ISA has a lot to do with the fact that these schools are located in a country whose social policies are often out of step with those of the Vatican.

Foucault's theory of disciplinary surveillance

The two teacher participants in this study who remain in the closet about certain aspects of their homosexuality to continue being employed by the Catholic school boards are not only subject to the wiles of the Catholic Church ISA but also experience a kind of Foucaultian disciplinary surveillance known as the Panopticon. In his book *Discipline and Punish*

Foucault draws upon the work of eighteenth-century British utilitarian philosopher Jeremy Bentham (1748–1832) who describes the Panopticon as an architectural device that can be used in institutions such as prisons to observe all the prisoners without the observer being seen. Prisoners never know if they are being observed or not and therefore must act as though they are always being observed. The power of the Panopticon is its ability to cause those being observed to discipline themselves and to "induce [within them] a state of conscious and permanent visibility that assures the automatic functioning of power" (Foucault, 1975/1995, p. 201). The Panopticon is a useful metaphor for the doctrinal disciplining of non-heterosexuals in Alberta and Ontario Catholic schools.

Mark and Luke, the two teacher participants who keep their jobs by hiding the fact that they each live with a male partner, experience the disciplinary gaze of Foucault's metaphorical Panopticon while at work, and, in some instances, even at home. Foucault (1975/1995) describes the efficiency of the Panopticon's power as follows:

> He who is subjected to a field of visibility, and who knows it, assumes responsibility for the constraints of power; he makes them play spontaneously upon himself; he inscribes in himself the power relation in which he simultaneously plays both roles; he becomes the principle of his own subjection. (pp. 202–3)

Mark and Luke become the "principles of their own subjection" by monitoring and adjusting their behaviour to ensure that it outwardly appears to conform to Catholic doctrine. Luke, for example, stopped bringing his long-term partner to any school function because it had become too difficult to pretend they were not a couple. Because Mark is a principal, the disciplinary constraints around him are tighter than those around Luke. In Mark's case, Foucault's Panopticon has an even greater field of visibility, capable of subjecting Mark to its disciplinary gaze even in his own home. Part of Mark's role as a principal requires him to host staff barbecues and other colleague-bonding events at his home. To prepare for such hosting duties, Mark has to "de-gay the house ... do a major sweep" so that the evidence of his refusal to conform to the celibacy requirement of Catholic doctrine for non-heterosexuals will not be detected by any of his guests who may have the power to get him fired. Even though Luke is out with certain colleagues, he nevertheless harbours a similar "nightmare scenario" as Mark does of being turned in by someone at work. Both men worry that one day they will end up losing their livelihoods.

The disciplinary gaze of Foucault's metaphorical Panopticon also has a controlling effect on the student participants in this study. The four closeted students (Judith, Caleb, Shiloh, and Junia) do their best to hide their sexuality, gender identity, and gender expression from everyone in their Catholic schools lest they be subjected to some kind of ill treatment for being different. Shiloh, for example, learned from his closeted gay drama teacher that it would not be safe to let anyone in the school know that the principal refused the drama teacher's request to produce *The Laramie Project,* a play about the 1998 homophobic murder of a gay university student in Laramie, Wyoming. Shiloh wanted to protest the Catholic school administration's decision, but he knew that doing so would only invite questions about why he was so interested in taking part in a play about homophobic violence. He worried that other people would assume that only gay people would be interested in the subject matter of *The Laramie Project* and that his interest in it would mark him as gay. Shiloh felt that remaining silent on the matter was safer than being subjected to close scrutiny that might reveal his sexuality. This is an example of the Panopticon's continuous surveillance that enforces a regime of silent disciplining.

This example of Shiloh and his closeted gay drama teacher is not only about the doctrinal disciplining of homosexuals in Catholic schools but also about the way power operates between and among different people within these institutions. As Foucault points out in *The History of Sexuality, Vol. I,* "Where there is power, there is resistance" (1976/1978, p. 95). The closeted drama teacher's attempt to obtain permission from the school principal to produce *The Laramie Project* highlights the drama teacher as an active subject, as someone willing to resist the repressive heteronormativity of his Catholic school. According to Foucault, resistance is necessary for power to be effective. In an interview about truth and power, Foucault asks, "If power was never anything but repressive, if it never did anything but say no, do you really believe that we would manage to obey it?" (1972/1980, p. 119). Although the principal's ultimate answer was no, the drama teacher must have thought there was a possibility for a yes, otherwise he would not have tried to get permission to produce the play. At first glance, this exchange between the principal and the teacher seems to be an example of the repressive influence of power, but it also represents the productive force of power in that the overwhelming heteronormativity of the Catholic school actually invites new acts of resistance, such as the drama teacher's asking to produce the play.

Mark and Luke must be vigilant regarding the information they reveal about themselves to avoid getting fired. This form of disciplining surveillance is not entirely successful, however, as one of the gay men (Luke) is able to be open about his sexuality with select colleagues at work, and he is also able to express his commitment to social justice activism by regularly arguing with school administrators over their indoctrinating ways. Furthermore, Luke and Mark are not completely dominated by the doctrinal disciplining of their Catholic schools in that they both have long-term partners with whom they live, despite the fact that this is decidedly against Catholic doctrine. Through personal will, Mark and Luke have managed to not fully internalize the disciplining gaze of the Panopticon. I can only guess at the number of closeted teachers who have internalized the gaze, however, and so would never participate in a study such as this – they have been effectively silenced, and, sadly, continue to silence themselves.

One problem in drawing upon Foucault's *Discipline and Punish* to examine how homophobia is exercised in Alberta and Ontario Catholic schools is that the individual subject appears to be subjected to the point where resistance to disciplinary practices is futile. One way to begin to imagine the possibility of resisting an oppressive regime is to also draw upon another text from Foucault's genealogical period: *The History of Sexuality Vol. 1: An Introduction.* In this book, Foucault (1976/1990) explores how the Victorian period's characteristic repression of sexuality actually "speaks verbosely of its own silence" (p. 8) in the sense that it ushered in a new set of discourses on questions of sexual expression while under the guise of a forced silence on the topic. The oxymoron of articulated silence that Foucault points to has both repressive and productive elements – repressive in the sense that certain structural measures are put in place to try to control sexual expression, and productive in the sense that these very obstacles invite new forms of behaviour that effectively subvert attempts at disciplining control.

In this study, the Vatican appears to try to control the lived expression of non-heterosexuality by disseminating Catholic doctrine on the topic in Catholic schools. In its persistent refusal to recognize non-heterosexuality (and its various subcategories) as a legitimate sexual orientation, the Vatican and Catholic schools make themselves obligated to define and to "take great pains to relate in detail the things it does not say" (Foucault, 1976/1990, p. 8). The pastoral guidelines outlining what constitutes unacceptable same-sex behaviour, in effect, results in the Catholic Church declaiming at length on something it does not want its followers to endorse, condone, or even think about. Increasingly, the Catholic Church is obligated to defend and explain its position – thereby elaborating even more on a topic it does not want to address.

The Vatican also tries to control any objection to its homophobic message by limiting discussions about homophobia in Catholic schools to only those instances of homophobic bullying that occur among students and by circulating incomplete definitions of homophobia that do not implicate the Vatican itself as a major contributor to homophobic discrimination. Some students and teachers in Catholic schools respond to these silencing attempts by "speaking verbosely" of them by taking part in studies such as this one and by taking their stories to the media. In their raw and original forms, the interviews I conducted for the narrative research texts that appear in this book produced transcripts that were, on average, 20 pages long, single-spaced, in 10-point type. Many of the interviewees regularly ran overtime without any encouragement from me. Clearly, the participants in this study had a lot to say. The repressive silencing that arises from being a non-heterosexual student or teacher in an Alberta or Ontario Catholic school makes these interviewees quite literally "verbose" on their own institutional silencing. Because of this active silencing by the Vatican and its ISA, the Catholic school, some lgbtq students and teachers who have experienced institutionalized homophobia in their Catholic schools contact news media to bring their stories to public attention and to find room to assert their Charter rights. Examples from Chapter 3 are the stories of Joseph Stellpflug, Marc Hall, and Lisa Reimer. An example from Chapter 2 is Job's story. The Catholic school's act of silencing is paradoxically becoming quite well articulated in the media.

The experiences of the participants in this study appear to show that the repressive force of doctrinal disciplining is more powerful than its productive force. Nevertheless, I would suggest that the productive force of doctrinal disciplining is discernible in the pastoral guidelines that the Catholic bishops have had to write to regulate non-heterosexuality in Catholic schools. These have, in turn, invited various acts of subversion on the part of some of the participants in this study who resist the homophobic repression that pervades their Catholic schools.

Theorizing the Media Accounts and the Catholic Documents

Chapter 3 reviews and discusses a collection of Canadian media stories concerning homophobia in Catholic schools. The media reports range from court cases (involving the wrongful dismissals of lgbtq teachers and the discriminatory refusal of a same-sex date to the high school prom) to school policies (involving the censoring of a book about homophobia, the non-participation of any Canadian Catholic school district in a national survey about homophobia, and the banning of GSAs). The media accounts offer a rare glimpse into the supremacy of Catholic canonical law over Canadian common law on the topic of lgbtq individuals in Canadian Catholic schools.

The two primary texts from Alberta and Ontario written to make clear the official Catholic doctrine on non-heterosexuality, discussed in Chapter 4, reveal the powerful influence of Catholic bishops and education leaders in ensuring that Catholic doctrine regarding non-heterosexuality is the ideology that governs the management of non-heterosexuals in Alberta and Ontario Catholic schools.

Like the experiences of the participants in this study, selections from the media accounts and the Catholic documents data sets in this study can be examined through Gramsci's (1971) notion of ideological hegemony and contradictory consciousness, Althusser's (1970/2008) concept of ideology and interpellation, and Foucault's (1975/1995) theory of the disciplinary surveillance of the Panopticon.

Foucault's Panopticon

The manner in which Foucault's Panopticon disciplines the participants in this study is also observable in some of the media accounts describing teachers who had their jobs terminated because they contravened the Catholic doctrine that requires non-heterosexuals to remain celibate for the rest of their lives. Joseph Stellpflug, for example, took his story to the media after he said he was fired in 1997 from his job as a lay chaplain and religion teacher at a Catholic high school in Toronto after his school district learned about the commitment ceremony he had participated in with his male partner. Although Stellpflug's commitment ceremony was a private affair, an unknown person passed along one of the invitations to Stellpflug's Catholic board, which sparked the board's investigation that led eventually to Stellpflug's termination. The act of slipping the Catholic board an invitation is analogous to training the Panopticon's "full lighting and the eye of a supervisor" (Foucault, 1975/1995, p. 200) on a previously dark and obscured corner.

Part of the investigation of Stellpflug's sexual behaviour involved Stellpflug's employers, together with the local archbishop, privately questioning Stellpflug until he confessed that he did have a male partner and they did have a commitment ceremony. Foucault engages in a lengthy discussion of this kind of forced confession in his book *The History of Sexuality, Vol. 1* (1976/1978, pp. 58–68) and tells us that "from the Christian penance to the present day, sex was a privileged theme of confession.

A thing that was hidden" (p. 61), yet Foucault argues that "it is in the confession that truth and sex are joined, through the obligatory and exhaustive expression of an individual secret" (p. 61). Foucault describes the confession as follows:

> The confession is a ritual of discourse in which the speaking subject is also the subject of the statement; it is also a ritual that unfolds within a power relationship, for one does not confess without the presence (or virtual presence) of a partner who is not simply the interlocutor but the authority who requires the confession, prescribes and appreciates it, and intervenes in order to judge, punish, forgive, console, and reconcile; a ritual in which the truth is corroborated by the obstacles and resistances it has had to surmount in order to be formulated; and finally, a ritual in which the expression alone, independently of its external consequences, produces intrinsic modifications in the person who articulates it: it exonerates, redeems, and purifies him; it unburdens him of his wrongs, liberates him, and promises him salvation. (pp. 61–2)

In a collection of essays, Foucault (1980) describes knowledge as an intersection of power relations and information-gathering, a process he calls power/knowledge. According to Foucault, knowledge is a form of power – the search for knowledge is also an expression of a will to power over other people. When Stellpflug's employers and archbishop subjected him to this form of forced confession, they were establishing their "authority" and their "relationship" of power and control over him. Stellpflug was controlled in his Catholic school not only by the disciplinary gaze of the Panopticon, but also by the authoritative discourse of truth known as the confession. In a way, Stellpflug was "liberated" when he confessed and also "intrinsically modified," but the liberation was from his job and the modification was that he was now identified as gay rather than straight and therefore "punishable" as a gay man as far as his employers were concerned. Clearly, this liberation is not a positive condition for someone like Stellpflug. All the power of the confession in this case was plainly on the school's side as it turned its "full light" on Stellpflug, ignored the Charter, and doled out its judgment.

The authority that enables and facilitates the firing of lesbian and gay teachers in Catholic schools who violate Catholic doctrine about non-heterosexuality by living with their same-sex partners or by raising children is traceable to various pieces of Catholic doctrine developed by the Vatican. The goal of such Catholic doctrine is to "guide others away from the practice of homosexual genital activity" (OCCB, 2004a, p. 25). The Catholic doctrine on non-heterosexuality is itself a metaphorical Panopticon in the sense that those who fully believe in its message can use it as a guide when scanning the behaviour of others, or even themselves, to determine if their behaviour conforms to the expectations of Catholic doctrine. If an individual's behaviour is found lacking, such as Joseph Stellpflug's was, then the doctrine functions as a kind of law that can be enforced by terminating his employment. The Catholic doctrine also becomes a scanning device that individuals can use to detect behaviour in others that is contrary to Catholicity – then they can use that newly gathered information to justify taking disciplinary action against the offending individual. In this way, Catholic doctrine about non-heterosexuality functions like a metaphorical Panopticon to observe and correct any lgbtq behaviour that appears to be against the values of the Vatican.

Another example that illustrates this point is the Durham Catholic District School Board's attempt to stop Marc Hall from taking his boyfriend to his high school graduation dance. Before his raising of the issue of whether or not same-sex dates were welcome at the very public and school-sanctioned prom, Hall did not attract the disciplinary gaze of his school administrators. They may have known he was gay, but according to Catholic doctrine, being gay is not the problem – being gay only becomes a problem when gay people start behaving in ways that would lead to "homosexual genital activity" (OCCB, 2004a, p. 25). From my observations, students are relatively freer to be queer within Catholic school environments than are queer teachers and staff. That is to say, the majority of teachers in this study who are found to be lgbtq are ejected from the schools through intimidation or termination of their employment; students are rarely kicked out, although they are certainly policed by school administration in other ways. This is largely because students generally have more rights than employees under the law and can take greater risks because they are in the school for a limited time (between three and six years).

Once Hall asked for permission to take his boyfriend to the prom, his Catholic school administrators had to examine his request through the filter of Catholic doctrine. Here, again, the Catholic doctrine functioned as a Panopticon – a tool used to closely examine Hall's request to determine if what Hall was proposing would conform to Catholicity. Hall's Catholic school administrators concluded that a gay student who has a boyfriend and who proposes to dance with his boyfriend in a public way at a graduation dance sanctioned by the Catholic school is contrary to Catholicity and it was on these grounds that they refused Hall's request. However, Marc Hall managed to escape the disciplining gaze of Foucault's metaphorical Panopticon by appealing to another authority that, in a limited fashion, also governs Ontario Catholic schools – Canadian anti-discrimination law. Therefore, when Catholic doctrine is used as a kind of Panopticon scanning tool with Catholic school students (as opposed to teachers), it is limited in its ability to uncover, expose, and discipline its subjects precisely because of the Canadian government (an example of an Althusserian RSA), which, of course, is an interesting irony.

Althusser's ideology and interpellation

The above description of Catholic doctrine functioning as a Foucaultian Panopticon overlaps with the threefold function of Althusser's ISA. As discussed above, when examining the problem of sexual minority groups in Alberta and Ontario Catholic schools, Althusser's "State" is the Vatican, and his "Ideology" is Catholic doctrine. Also discussed above are the institutions Althusser lists as examples of his ISAs, namely: religious organizations, the education system, the family, the legal system, trade unions, the political system, arts and culture, and the media. This discussion is limited to the ISAs represented by religious organizations, specifically the Catholic Church, and the education system, specifically the Catholic school. Although Althusser's logic operates at a very high level of abstraction, his ideas are still at least partially applicable to the kinds of institutions he identifies as ISAs and the particular situations that can take place within those institutions involving individuals. Althusser's theory of the ISA is helpful in elucidating aspects of the data collected for this study, especially in understanding the dynamics of power and authority operating in Catholic schools, but it is important to remain attentive to the limitations of his theory as well. One obvious limitation is that Althusser's theory of the ISA does not help explain a system with competing ideologies and competing power structures, nor does Althusser explain how individuals might negotiate a social system with competing ideologies and conflicting ISAs. In the matter of how to manage sexual minorities in the Catholic school setting, Althusser's ISA, the Catholic school, has a threefold purpose: (1) to teach the Catholic doctrine of Vatican, (2) to ensure that most people in the Catholic school consent to that doctrine, and (3) to render teachers and students in the Catholic school "subjects" of the Vatican. When Catholic doctrine functions as a Foucaultian Panopticon, it is occupied with the Althusserian task of ensuring that the majority of those involved in Catholic schooling consent and conform to the Vatican's values regarding non-heterosexuality.

In Althusser's theory of the ISA, ideology "interpellates" individuals as subjects (1970/2008, p. 44). Althusser describes his vision of "interpellation" as a "precise operation" through which ideology "recruits" subjects and "transforms" them in such a way that they recognize their own existence in the values of the dominant culture and therefore acquiesce to them (1970/2008, pp. 48–9). Althusser interchanges the word "interpellate" with the word "hail," which he says "can be imagined along the lines of the most commonplace everyday police (or other) hailing: 'Hey, you there!'" (1970/2008, p. 48). In this example, the individual the police hail in the street then turns around and recognizes that she or he is being addressed. According to Althusser, in this simple act of recognition, the individual is rendered a subject. The manner in which ideology interpellates individuals as subjects is best illustrated with the following example from the Catholic doctrine pertaining to non-heterosexuals examined in this book.

Chapter 4 analyzes two primary texts from Alberta and Ontario that were meant to clarify for Catholic educators the official teaching of the Roman Catholic Church on the topic of homosexuality. Although the two texts are clearly about the existence of lgbtq individuals in Alberta and Ontario Catholic schools, neither text addresses these sexual minority groups by the acronym "lgbtq" nor as "non-heterosexuals." Instead, the authors of these two Catholic documents prefer to call lgbtq people "persons with same-sex attractions." The Alberta bishops who wrote the 2001 pastoral guideline called *A Resource for an Inclusive Community: A Teacher's Guide for and about Persons with Same Sex Attractions* attempt to justify their use of the moniker "persons with same sex attractions" by claiming that "to refer to a person as 'gay' or 'lesbian' in our culture is not only to use politically charged language but to succumb to a reductionist way of speaking about someone else. Such labelling is not only inaccurate but tends to reinforce and, in some cases, legitimate an arrested psycho-sexual development" (as cited in CCSSA, 2007, sec. 3). Similarly, in their 2004 *Pastoral Guideline to Assist Students of Same-Sex Orientation*, the Ontario bishops also warn that "attaching a label" such as homosexual, lesbian, or gay is "problematic" because it "implies that they are their orientation ... The orientation or act is homosexual or heterosexual but the person is not" (OCCB, 2004a, p. 26). When the Catholic bishops and other Catholic education leaders refer to lgbtq people as "persons with same-sex attraction" (or variations on this), they also subliminally associate this group of people with an illness – the phrase has a similar ring to it as "sickle cell anemia," for example, and the word "with" connects the group to an illness or a disorder that needs a cure. The cure in this case is pastoral care and reparative therapy.

According to Althusser's theory, in these examples of Catholic documents from Alberta and Ontario, the ideology of the Catholic Church is attempting to interpellate or hail lgbtq people as "persons with same-sex attractions" and thereby render them a particular kind of subject that conforms to Catholic doctrine about non-heterosexuality. However, for interpellation to function correctly, the subject being addressed must respond with some form of recognition, such as, "Yes, it really is me!" (Althusser, 1970/2008, p. 52), otherwise a form of misrecognition occurs. Given that none of the participants in this study referred to themselves as a "person with same-sex attraction" and often refer to themselves as lesbian or gay, it appears as though the Catholic ideology has not managed to interpellate these lgbtq individuals as the subjects it has determined for them.

Furthermore, some of the lgbtq students in this study attempted to form GSAs in their Catholic schools, not Persons with Same-Sex Attraction and Persons with Opposite-Sex Attraction Alliances. The use of the word *gay* by participants in this study suggests these lgbtq people have failed to recognize the Catholic ideology attempting to interpellate and thereby further prescribe and limit them as subjects. It appears as though these lgbtq participants were already successfully interpellated as subjects by another ideology – that of the lgbtq human rights movement, not the Vatican.

Gramsci's ideological hegemony

Like Althusser's theory of ideology, Gramsci's (1971) theory of ideological hegemony regards ideology as a necessary component in the continued reproduction of social relations in any given culture. For Gramsci, the ideas of the ruling class are reproduced and circulated as the dominant ideology through a process of ideological hegemony involving the strategic use of cultural institutions, such as churches and schools, to secure the necessary consent of the masses. In schools, ideological hegemony is achieved primarily through the formal curriculum, but it is also maintained through the various informal ways knowledge is produced and controlled (Giroux, 2001). The way ideological hegemony controls the production of knowledge about sexual minority groups in Catholic schools can be observed through some examples from Chapter 3 and Chapter 4.

An example of how ideological hegemony partially functions in the formal curriculum of Catholic schools is evident in the media account describing the development of a special Catholic version of Ontario's 2010 health and physical education curriculum. The architects of this Catholic version would have excised elements of the curriculum that actively discussed gender identity and sexual orientation as a way to redress homophobic discrimination in all Ontario schools. The excising of such information is clearly influenced by Catholic doctrine that regards lgbtq people as "persons with same-sex attractions" (i.e., an affliction), designates the physical expression of non-heterosexuality as "intrinsically disordered" (i.e., a sin), and generally disapproves of any promotion of non-heterosexuality as a viable way of living (as cited in OCCB, 2004a, p. 53).

As it turns out, there was eventually no need for the Catholic version of the province's new sexual education curriculum because the provincial government bowed to opposition from a non-Catholic conservative religious coalition to revamp the curriculum. Reacting to conservative religious opposition, Ontario's Ministry of Education ultimately chose to release a revised version of its 2010 health and physical education curriculum that omitted all the controversial components having to do with the topics of non-heterosexuality and gender identity.

Religious opposition to this curriculum highlighted for the Canadian public a little-known arrangement between the provincial Ministry of Education and the Catholic school system that allows Catholic education leaders to revamp and reconstruct provincial curricula on matters of morality and sexuality so that these topics can be taught in Catholic schools through a Catholic faith perspective. This media account exposes the previously obscured inner machinations of Gramsci's ideological hegemony operating in the formal curriculum of Catholic schools. It shows how the ideology of Catholic doctrine is more powerful than the ideology of the provincial curriculum when it comes to the topics of non-heterosexuality and gender identity in Catholic schools, despite (or perhaps especially because) of the fact that provincial curriculum and the RSA ideology it represents is the vehicle that allows for resistance. Seen through Althusser's theory of the ISA, this media account underscores how the Catholic Church (an example of an ISA in Althusser's theory) is actually functioning more like an Althusserian RSA (i.e., a government), or at the very least, is operating in collaboration with an RSA while simultaneously working against the RSA of the provincial government. This distinct arrangement, in fact, once again shows the limitations of Althusser's theories and seriously convolutes Gramsci's otherwise neat categorizations of ideology and hegemony.

Another example of how Gramsci's ideological hegemony partially functions in Catholic schools is the media account describing Waterloo Catholic District School Board's censoring of *Open Minds to Equality*, a curriculum resource that promotes diversity in schools by discussing various forms of discrimination, including homophobia. This censorship incident came about because a local Christian organization, Defend Traditional Marriage and Family, demanded the WCDSB remove the book from its schools and stop referring Catholic lgbtq students and their families to queer-positive therapists and support groups. A spokesperson for DTMF pointed out that the presence of a book about homophobia, along with WCDSB's practice of making queer-positive referrals, violated Catholic doctrine about non-heterosexuality.

As Chapter 4 makes clear, the Ontario Catholic bishops choose to present an incomplete understanding of homophobia: they choose to see homophobia as confined to acts of mistreatment students may inflict on one another in the form of homophobic bullying, but their definition of homophobia does not include the general condemnation of non-heterosexuality in which the bishops themselves are culpable. In absolving themselves of the charge of homophobia, the Ontario bishops declare that "it should not be assumed ... that to guide others away from the practice of homosexual genital activity comes out of homophobia" (OCCB, 2004a, p. 25). It poses a threat to the supremacy of the ideology of Catholic doctrine in Catholic schools that a book about homophobia as a form of discrimination that should be eliminated from all schools might exist in the teacher resource room. For this reason, *Open Minds to Equality* was removed from general circulation in Waterloo Catholic schools.

Although this media account is ostensibly about banning the book *Open Minds to Equality*, it also indirectly reveals the presence of vibrant resistance to the dominant ideology of homophobic Catholic doctrine in some Waterloo Catholic schools. The very existence of a book about homophobia in Waterloo Catholic schools is a form of resistance. A Catholic educator, or group of educators, would have had to make the conscious decision to purchase this book and make it available to teachers.

This act goes against the Catholic doctrine about non-heterosexuality that these Catholic educators would have previously absorbed.

Other acts of resistance are detectable in the following approvals undertaken by the WCDSB's Family Life Advisory Committee: (1) referring lgbtq students in Catholic schools throughout the district to a queer-positive Rainbow Therapist; (2) referring lgbtq students in Catholic schools throughout the district to a local lgbtq youth group called OK 2B Me; and (3) referring the parents of lgbtq students throughout the district to the support group PFLAG. The referrals are to organizations that do not present Catholic doctrine on non-heterosexuality. This shows that the Catholic educators who approved these referrals have not completely absorbed the ideology of homophobic Catholic doctrine they would have previously learned at home, at church, and at school.

Gramsci (1971) describes this incomplete absorption of the dominant ideology as a "contradictory consciousness," which he elucidates as follows:

> The active man-in-the-mass has a practical activity, but has no clear theoretical consciousness of his practical activity, which nonetheless involves an understanding of the world in so far as it transforms it. His theoretical consciousness can indeed be historically in opposition to his activity. One might almost say that he has two theoretical consciousnesses (or one contradictory consciousness): one which is implicit in his activity and which in reality unites him with all his fellow workers in the practical transformation of the real world; and one, superficially explicit or verbal, which he has inherited from the past and uncritically absorbed. (p. 333)

Here, Gramsci makes room for human agency in his theory of ideological hegemony by accounting for the actions of everyday people who have the power to enact the "practical transformation of the real world." As Giroux (2001) observes, Gramsci's general notion of ideology has emancipatory implications for critical pedagogy in that it does not "obliterate the mediating faculties of ordinary people"; furthermore, as Giroux goes on to underscore, Gramsci's concept of "contradictory consciousness," in particular, points to a "sphere of contradictions and tensions that is pregnant with possibilities for radical change" (p. 152). At first glance, the above media account about the banning of the book *Open Minds to Equality* appears to be about the ideological domination of Catholic doctrine in Catholic schools, but a closer look reveals the existence of ordinary Catholic educators performing relatively extraordinary acts of resistance and radical change.

Gramsci's theory of hegemony, Althusser's theory of the ISA, and Foucault's theory of disciplinary surveillance have been helpful in offering partial explanations of how homophobia is institutionalized and maintained in Catholic schools. Does the institutionalization of homophobia mean that non-heterosexuals will be forever subjected to a kind of doctrinal disciplining in Alberta and Ontario Catholic schools? Not necessarily. According to Gramsci, Foucault, and Giroux, resistance to repressive forces is possible. Although the majority of the participants' experiences in this study appears to show that the repressive force of doctrinal disciplining is more powerful than its productive force, various acts of subversion and resistance are discernible in some of the participants' stories and in the subtext of at least one media account. Just because most media accounts show the domination of non-heterosexuals in Canadian Catholic schools, it does not mean that resistance is not occurring. As lesbian student participant Abigail says, "The resistance is already starting to happen ... It'll change one day, but *we* have to change it."

Conclusion

Evidence of a particular kind of "holy homophobia" operating in some Catholic schools of Alberta and Ontario is discernible in the three different data sets of this book: the participants, the media accounts, and the Catholic documents. This section reviews the important aspects of each data set, summarizes the arguments of the data chapters, and underscores the findings of each data chapter. To explain the doctrinal disciplining of non-heterosexuals in Alberta and Ontario Catholic schools, this book theorizes the data through the lens of critical theories formulated by Gramsci, Althusser, Foucault, and Giroux that have to do with how power is both wielded and resisted in institutional settings, such as schools. This section summarizes these theoretical arguments, offers specific suggestions for further research, and discusses the particular implications for practice that this study points towards.

Participants

Little is known about the experiences of non-heterosexuals in Canadian Catholic schools. Accordingly, this study sought the participation of lgbtq individuals who have had some experience in Alberta or Ontario Catholic schools, either as a current or former teacher or as a former student. Twenty individuals took part in the study, all of whom self-identify as lgbtq, except for one female former Alberta Catholic schoolteacher who identifies as a "straight ally."

Because this is a comparative study of the Catholic school systems of Alberta and Ontario, an even representation from the two provinces is ideal. Consequently, 10 participants are from various regions of Alberta and 10 are from towns and cities throughout Ontario. Of the Alberta participants, four are teachers (one lesbian, one gay man, one transman, and one "straight ally" woman), and six are students (two lesbians, two gay men, one transwoman, and one transman). Of the Ontario participants, three are teachers (two lesbians, one gay man), and seven are students (three lesbians and four gay men). The most illustrative and potentially illuminating of the participants' experiences are retold through the qualitative method of narrative inquiry. The stories of 18 of the 20 participants are recounted in brief narrative vignettes; two are excluded because of insufficient detail and to avoid repetition.

Of the six teacher participants whose stories are recounted in this book, four are no longer teaching in Catholic schools. Of the Alberta teacher participants, three believe they lost their jobs for contravening Catholic doctrine about non-heterosexuality: one for transitioning from female to male, one for attempting to get pregnant to raise a child with her lesbian partner, and one for offering her classroom as a Positive Space where lgbtq students could meet at lunchtime. An Ontario teacher participant experienced such severe homophobic harassment in the northern Ontario town where she had moved to take a temporary teaching position at a Catholic elementary school that she barely completed her contract and is now pursuing graduate studies. Of the remaining teacher participants, two (one in Alberta and one in Ontario) continue to teach in a Catholic school but do so closeted about their homosexuality.

Five of the 12 student participants whose stories are recounted in this study also felt it was safer for them to stay in the closet about their sexuality and gender identity while studying in Catholic schools. Of the other student participants, four were outed at school: one lesbian student in northern Alberta was outed by bullies; two lesbian students (one in northern Ontario and the other in southern Ontario), and one female-to-male participant who identified as a lesbian while in his southern Alberta Catholic junior and senior high schools, were outed by school personnel who deemed it appropriate to call the students' parents into the school to inform them about their child's sexual orientation. The other three student participants (one gay male in southern Ontario, one gay male in northern Alberta, and one lesbian in southern Alberta) were able to be out to varying degrees about their non-heterosexuality while in Catholic school. All four of the student participants who were outed against their will in Catholic school responded with explicit acts of resistance to the systemic homophobia of their schools.

Resistance on the part of teacher participants is less pronounced than that of the students. This is largely because the majority of the teacher participants were apparently fired for behaving in ways that contravened Catholic doctrine about non-heterosexuality and no longer had an opportunity to resist the systemic homophobia of their Catholic schools. Overall, the teacher participants in this study experienced greater degrees of doctrinal disciplining regarding non-heterosexuality than the student participants. All the participants experienced some form of homophobia in their Catholic schools, and none described a Catholic school environment that was accepting and welcoming of sexual diversity. This does not mean that positive experiences with Catholic schools do not exist among lgbtq people and their allies. It means only that the 19 lgbtq people and 1 straight ally who participated in this study experienced a homophobic environment in their Alberta and Ontario Catholic schools. This is not a surprising finding considering this study is about homophobia in Alberta and Ontario Catholic schools, and it accordingly attracted participants with stories of homophobia to tell. The similarity of experiences among participants in terms of the heteronormative repression to which they were subjected in Alberta and Ontario, which are some distance apart, suggests that Catholic doctrine from the Vatican is directing school policy and practice regarding the management of sexual minority groups in both provinces. This contradictory Catholic doctrine, which casts lgbtq students and teachers solely as "persons with same-sex attraction" who suffer from "an arrested psycho-sexual development" (as cited in CCSSA, 2007, sec. 3) and are therefore in need of "pastoral care," showcases Alberta and Ontario Catholic schools as the opposite of a "welcoming and safe environment" (OCCB, 2004a, p. 23) for sexual minority groups and conversely positions Alberta and Ontario Catholic schools as potential sites of religiously inspired homophobia and genderism.

In keeping with the It Gets Better project (Savage, 2010) in the United States, which urges suicidal lgbtq youth to "hang on" until they can graduate and escape their homophobic school environments, life did "get better" for the student participants in this study once they graduated from their Catholic high schools. It could be argued that life also got better for the teacher participants who said they were fired and otherwise forced out for not upholding Catholic doctrine related to sexual minorities in the sense that they no longer had to contend with such an oppressive system. Nevertheless, it is important to note how difficult a task it is for lgbtq teachers who said they were fired by their Catholic boards to recover from such a devastating dismissal and find teaching positions in a saturated market, exacerbating the power of homophobia. Of the three Alberta teachers who believed they lost their jobs for behaving in ways deemed contrary to Catholicity, one eventually got a job in the secular public school system, one worked in a pet shop for a while until she could find a job teaching outside of Canada, and one enrolled in graduate studies in education. The one Ontario teacher who was harassed out of her temporary teaching job also enrolled in graduate studies in education. It does not get better, however, for those teacher participants who must remain strategically closeted to keep their jobs and who look mainly to retirement as a rescue from the institutionalized homophobia that rules their days.

Media Accounts

The Canadian media have been instrumental in shedding light on various clashes between Catholic canonical law and Canadian common law in relation to non-heterosexuals in Canadian Catholic schools. Chapter 3 provided snapshots of some higher profile Canadian media reports of homophobia in Canadian Catholic schools. The media reports are meant to provide a context for the stories shared by the participants in the study and to highlight the important role the media plays in animating discussion around this little-known aspect of Canadian schooling. The reports range from important court cases to incidents of homophobic school policies. The court cases show a progression of same-sex legal rights in Canada following the enactment of the *Canadian Charter of Rights and Freedoms* (1982), specifically the use of Section 15 – the equality rights provision – to challenge discrimination on the basis of sexual orientation in Canadian schools. The media accounts also show a concerted Catholic resistance to the advancement of same-sex legal rights. This Catholic backlash is discernible in the appearance of new pastoral guidelines on the topic of "persons with same-sex attractions" since the highly publicized advancements of same-sex legal rights in Canada.

This Catholic backlash is most clearly evident in the 2002 case of Marc Hall, an Ontario student who was granted an interlocutory injunction that allowed him to take his boyfriend to his Catholic high school graduation dance. The Ontario bishops responded to this court decision by developing a restrictive pastoral guideline about how to manage sexual minority groups in Catholic schools, which they claimed was necessitated by the *Hall* case. This 2003 pastoral guideline titled *To All Involved in Catholic Education* eventually developed into the much longer policy document released in 2004 by the Ontario bishops called *Pastoral Guidelines to Assist Students of Same-Sex Orientation*. Both pastoral guidelines are the official Catholic Church directives that Ontario Catholic school administrators use when deciding how to manage matters of sexual diversity in Ontario Catholic schools, resulting in a number of homophobic school policies that have caught the attention of the media.

Chapter 3 describes and discusses the following homophobic school policies taken in Catholic schools throughout Ontario: WCDSB's banning of the inclusive education book *Open Minds to Equality* because it mentions homophobia; the Institute for Catholic Education's circumvention of aspects of the Ontario Ministry of Education's proposed 2010 health and physical education curriculum that address gender identity and sexual orientation; the unwillingness of any Catholic school board in Canada to participate in a national survey on homophobia in schools; and the general disregard for aspects of the Ontario Ministry of Education's Equity and Inclusive Education Strategy that attend to homophobia, culminating in Halton Catholic District School Board's banning of GSAs from all its schools.

This brief review of the media reports of homophobic school policies covered in Chapter 3 may give the impression that homophobic discrimination dominates Canadian Catholic schools and that resistance to such oppression is scant or non-existent. From my experience collecting media reports of homophobic incidents occurring in Canadian Catholic schools since 2006, I found that this topic is rarely covered in the media. Of course, rare media coverage of homophobic discrimination in Canadian Catholic schools does not mean that such incidents are not occurring; it only suggests that such incidents may be underreported or that the media are slow to realize the significance of such stories. If negative stories about homophobia occurring in Canadian Catholic schools rarely appear in the media, then positive stories about resistance to homophobic school policies and curriculum are even rarer. An explanation for this may be found in the sayings that circulate among journalists, such as "bad news sells," and "good news is no news." These truisms find validity in a recent study that shows the topics that dominate the global news agenda tend to be crime, violence, politics, and government. Nevertheless, resistance to homophobic school policies and practices is discernible in the subtext of one media report's oblique reference to Waterloo Catholic school officials' referral of queer youth and their families to queer support services. Furthermore, Marc Hall's reversal of his Catholic school's homophobic policy that forbade same-sex dates at the high school prom is a major success story of resistance to religiously inspired homophobic discrimination. Other success stories of resisting homophobia in Alberta and Ontario

Catholic schools, found in Chapter 2, may not receive the same level of media coverage as incidents of homophobia in Canadian Catholic schools, but resistance to this kind of discrimination is certainly occurring.

The fact that most of the stories in Chapter 3 are about incidents of homophobia in the Catholic schools of Ontario does not mean that this is exclusively an Ontario problem. As the stories from Chapter 2 attest, homophobia is very much a part of Catholic schooling in Alberta. Stories of homophobic school policies in Alberta Catholic schools are rarely covered in the media for any number of reasons. One possibility is that Alberta's Ministry of Education during that time had been more conservative and less proactive about reducing homophobia in schools than Ontario's Ministry of Education. Unlike its Ontario counterpart, in the first decade of the twenty-first century, Alberta's Ministry of Education had not devised overarching Equity and Inclusive Education Strategy that attended to homophobia in schools (among other forms of discrimination), nor had it proposed a health and physical education curriculum that addressed gender identity and sexual orientation in the . sexuality unit. The absence of these measures suggests a more harmonious relationship between the Alberta Ministry of Education (and, by extension, the once long-standing provincial Conservative government) and Alberta Catholic school districts in terms of educational policy and curriculum related to sexual diversity.

The ideology that underlies the policies and curriculum proposed by the Ontario Ministry of Education clashes with the values and traditions of Ontario Catholic school districts, and these clashes invite controversy, which in turn invites media coverage. The media have been instrumental in heightening Canadians' awareness of conflicts between Catholic canonical law and Canadian common law regarding sexual minorities in Canadian Catholic schools. Without media coverage, initial discussions among ordinary Canadians about the problem of homophobia in Canadian Catholic schools – the necessary groundwork for initiating progressive change – may never take place.

Catholic Documents

The homophobic incidents in Canadian Catholic schools, described in both Chapter 2 and Chapter 3, show that Catholic doctrine on the topic of non-heterosexuality is the guiding principle behind curricular and policy decisions taken in Canadian Catholic schools related to sexual minority groups and sexual diversity. Non-Catholics may not be aware of specific Catholic doctrine about non-heterosexuality and how it is disseminated in Catholic schools. Accordingly, Chapter 4 examines two primary texts from Alberta and Ontario written by Catholic bishops and Catholic education leaders to make clear to Catholic educators the official Catholic doctrine on non-heterosexuality.

The Ontario text is known as a pastoral guideline, a sanctioned letter from a bishop, or group of bishops, outlining official policy on a topic involving the moral care of a congregation. Several Catholic education leaders from Ontario, along with members of the Education Commission of the OCCB, collaborated to write the 2004 Ontario text *Pastoral Guidelines to Assist Students of Same-Sex Orientation*. Catholic education leaders from Alberta met regularly over a period of years to produce the 2007 Alberta text, a guide for Catholic educators called *Towards an Inclusive Community*, designed with a twofold purpose: (1) to facilitate the circulation of the ACB's 2001 pastoral guideline *A Resource for an Inclusive Community: A Teacher's Guide for and about Persons with Same Sex Attractions*, and (2) to ensure that all Alberta educators respond in a similar manner when faced with media questions about how sexual diversity is managed in Alberta Catholic schools.

Both the 2004 Ontario text and the 2007 Alberta text liberally cite, or in some cases wholly reproduce, other groups of bishops' pastoral guidelines (such as the United States Conference of Catholic Bishops' *Always Our Children: A Pastoral Message to Parents of Homosexual Children and Suggestions for Pastoral Ministers*), including, of course, the all-powerful Vatican's Congregation for the Doctrine of the Faith's *Letter to the Bishops of the Catholic Church on the Pastoral Care of Homosexual Persons*, and relevant parts of the *Catechism of the Catholic Church* dealing with the topic. Both the Ontario and the Alberta texts circulate and endorse the most damning elements of Catholic doctrine that describe "homosexual acts" as "acts of grave depravity," which are "intrinsically disordered," and which count among the list of "sins gravely contrary to chastity" (as cited in OCCB, 2004a, p. 53). Both the Ontario and Alberta texts stress Catholic doctrine that calls non-heterosexuals to a lifetime of celibacy. Both texts recommend, in a subtle way, the corrective 12-Step program called Courage as a reputable resource to assist non-heterosexual Catholics in attaining the goal of lifelong celibacy. Sanctioned by the Roman Catholic Church, Courage is a prescriptive program designed to arrest same-sex desire and even possibly transform non-heterosexual orientations into the heterosexual orientation, which the Catholic Church considers to be a more morally acceptable way of life.

The chief finding of Chapter 4 is that the Catholic concept of "pastoral care" for non-heterosexuals, derived as it is from condemning Catholic doctrine, is not any kind of "care" for lgbtq people. The pastoral guidelines about how to manage non-heterosexuals in Alberta and Ontario Catholic schools are not about developing empathy towards vulnerable sexual minority groups but are instead guidelines on how to perpetuate the Catholic tradition of homophobia in Catholic schools.

Theorizing the Data

To help explain the phenomenon of homophobia in Alberta and Ontario Catholic schools, the aforementioned data sets (participants, media accounts, and Catholic documents) are theorized using the following critical theories: Gramsci's (1971) notion of hegemony, Althusser's (1970/2008) concept of the ISA, Foucault's (1975/1995) theory of disciplinary surveillance, and Giroux's (2001) theory of resistance to all forms of domination.

Gramsci theorized that consent is as vital as coercion if ideological hegemony is going to function. Examples from Chapters 2, 3, and 4 show that many lgbtq teachers and students strategically consent to their own domination by remaining closeted about their sexual orientation or gender identity in Catholic schools, and that hegemony controls the production of knowledge about sexual diversity in Catholic schools. Gramsci's theories account for the ideological domination of Catholic doctrine about non-heterosexuality in Catholic schools, but they also allow for acts of resistance to Church-sanctioned homophobia.

Like Gramsci, Althusser posits that repression on its own cannot reproduce the existing social relations of production in any given culture and that ideology plays a vital role in the reproduction of the status quo. Drawing upon Althusser's theory of the ISA to illuminate the problem of homophobia in Alberta and Ontario Catholic schools reveals that the state apparatus that has the most power in these schools is not the provincial ministries of education but the Vatican. In Althusser's framework, resistance to ideological domination appears to be impossible.

Giroux criticizes Althusser's theory of the ISA for relying too heavily on a reductionist concept of power and for overlooking the role of human agency in effecting change. Several examples of students in this study who resist the apparently seamless transmission of the Vatican's values in their Catholic schools show that Althusser's notion of the ISA is incomplete because of its inability to account for the power of human resistance to transform the status quo.

Foucault's theory of disciplinary surveillance in the form of the Panopticon helps to explain how homophobia is institutionalized in Alberta and Ontario Catholic schools. The Panopticon reveals how the repressive force of Catholic doctrine causes students and teachers in Catholic schools to conform to the disciplinary regime required of them. Unlike Althusser, Foucault does not overlook the possibility of resistance. Foucault also theorizes the productive force of power, which can explain how the heteronormativity of the Catholic school unexpectedly invites new acts of resistance.

The chief finding of Chapter 5 is that by analysing the data collected for this study through the lens of critical theories, it is clear that the Vatican is able to assert a dominant and hegemonic power within Catholic schools. In terms of disciplining the sexual conduct of members of sexual minority groups, the Vatican's power prevails over other governments, such as provincial ministries of education and, by extension, the Canadian government in the publicly funded institution of the Alberta and Ontario Catholic school. The Vatican's power is "panoptic" (Foucault, 1975/1995, p. 201) and operates by means of discipline, surveillance, and self-regulation. Although the Vatican's power is clearly a leading force, it is not entirely successful in achieving total domination over sexual minority groups. This is evident in the instances of resistance that this study also documents. Institutions are certainly influential in forming individuals, but various critical theories show that the relations between institutions and individuals are not only those of repression and constraint. Analysing the data of this study through the lens of critical theory shows that resistance is also possible within power relations. Some vestiges of the influence of Canadian anti-discrimination law and equality rights legislation are discernible in acts of resistance undertaken by some participants in this study against the hegemonic homophobia of their Catholic schools.

Further Research

Homophobia in the Hallways is the only study of its kind in Canada, and further research is needed to test its findings. Are other Canadian Catholic schools as homophobic as the ones in this study? Are other lgbtq teachers and straight ally teachers in other Canadian Catholic schools at a similar risk as the teachers in this study for unfair dismissal because of a perceived violation of Catholic doctrine about non-heterosexuality? Are most lgbtq students in other Canadian Catholic schools choosing to remain closeted about their sexual orientation or gender identity while still in Catholic school? Is resistance to homophobia in Canadian Catholic schools starting to gain momentum among students, as lesbian student participant Abigail predicted?

This book examines homophobia in publicly funded Catholic schools of Alberta and Ontario, but how homophobic are private Canadian Catholic schools? Has progressive legislation that respects gender and sexual diversity recently enacted by provincial governments and school boards made any difference for lgbtq students and teachers in public and private Catholic schools? Has Ontario's Bill 13 (2012), the *Accepting Schools Act* (described in the Introduction to this book – the legislation that attempts to reduce school-based homophobic bullying by mandating that *all* Ontario schools allow students to establish GSA support groups) made any difference? Have changes in Church leadership, from the pope onwards, made any improvements for the conditions faced by lgbtq students and teachers in Catholic schools?

In Canada, publicly funded separate Catholic schools have constitutional status in Alberta, Saskatchewan, and Ontario; in the Northwest Territories, Yukon, and Nunavut, they have federal statutory status. This means that civil authorities direct separate Catholic schools through the use of a school board, which, in the cases of the three provinces, is mandated by the Canadian Constitution and, in the cases of the three territories, by federal statutes. What are the experiences of lgbtq students and teachers in the Catholic schools of Saskatchewan, the Northwest Territories, Yukon, and Nunavut? Are other Canadian faith-based schools as unwilling to respect Canadian anti-discrimination law and human rights legislation regarding sexual minorities as the Catholic schools in this study?

The scholarly studies highlighted in the literature review of this book show that proponents of anti-homophobia education have been relatively successful (to varying degrees) in introducing anti-homophobia education concepts in secular schools but not in faith-based schools. The resistance with which anti-homophobia education is met in Canadian Catholic schools points to a new challenge for this field of research. Anti-oppression educators must turn their attention to the monumental challenge to equity and inclusivity in public schooling posed by Catholic schools, which operate under homophobic Catholic doctrine, and so regularly disregard anti-discrimination law and human rights legislation pertaining to sexual minorities. This study's revelations of the effects homophobic Catholic doctrine has had on students' and teachers' lives belies an apathetic attitude currently prominent in Canada that suggests it is normal for Catholic schools to perpetuate homophobic discrimination as simply a part of the Catholic faith. This type of silent, passive complicity is so normalized in Canada that attempting to point out the injustice of it may make this study stand out as bold and unusual to some. The plight of sexual minority groups in Canadian faith-based schools is a neglected research topic because of Canadians' deep respect for the fundamental freedom of religion and a corresponding prevailing belief that religiously inspired homophobic practices occurring in publicly funded institutions, such as schools, are a normal part of religious freedom that should continue to go unchallenged. Of course religious beliefs should be respected, but when the expression of certain religious beliefs calls for the suppression of a particular group's equality rights, an untenable situation develops. Religious beliefs that fly in the face of the laws of the land or otherwise disregard human rights legislation cannot be respected and should not continue to prevail in publicly funded institutions. Anti-homophobia education researchers must overcome their reluctance to include religious schools in their research.

Implications for Practice

The practice of anti-homophobia education often begins in teacher education programs throughout Canada. Although this study does not specifically examine teacher education programs, schools of education are nevertheless an obvious place to begin the difficult work of redressing homophobia in public schooling. Teacher preparation courses about Canadian multiculturalism, diversity, equity, and inclusion issues in education often feature a unit about gender and sexual minority groups and the oppression these groups can face in schools. The problem is, these courses are not always mandatory for teachers in training. Those pre-service teachers who do take some kind of a diversity course as part of their training often learn about their legal obligation to uphold various elements of Canadian law that protect against discrimination on the basis of sexual orientation and gender identity in public schools. Anti-homophobia education for teacher candidates encourages beginning teachers to redress school-based homophobic discrimination by drawing upon age-appropriate, government-approved, and school district-approved curricular resources that offer information about non-heterosexual family configurations, lgbtq role models in history, the advancement of same-sex legal rights in Canada, and ways to reduce homophobic bullying in schools.

Another problem is that much of this anti-homophobia education neglects to address ideological clashes between anti-homophobia education and religious education. Just because attempts to introduce anti-homophobia education in Canadian Catholic schools are met with strong resistance from Catholic education leaders does not mean that this problem should be ignored in Canadian postsecondary schools of education. On the contrary, this particular clash between Canadian common law and Catholic canon law, articulated in the arena of Canadian public schooling, should be openly addressed in Canadian teacher training programs. Beginning teachers who are interested in redressing homophobic discrimination and who intend to teach in a Canadian Catholic school should be adequately prepared to navigate their way through these inevitable ideological clashes.

Developers of anti-homophobia education materials, such as sensitivity training workshops, guides for creating safe and caring schools, and films about homophobia in schools, should consider including specific sections about combating homophobia in faith-based schools. Religious freedom should not mean the freedom to ignore progressive educational policy and curricula designed to redress homophobia in Canadian schools in accordance with Canadian law. Developers of anti-homophobia education materials who may choose to design a specific set of materials for Canadian Catholic schools should not reference Catholic pastoral guidelines for managing "persons with same-sex attractions" in Canadian Catholic schools as these guidelines are fundamentally homophobic, counterproductive, and at cross purposes to the mandate of anti-homophobia education. Anti-homophobia education materials developed for use in Canadian Catholic schools may be more successful in reaching their intended audience if they convey a Catholic ethos and tone that reflects the language of the Catholic social justice tradition. However, the guiding ideology of any anti-homophobia education materials intended for Canadian Catholic schools should be the ideology of Canadian anti-discrimination law not Catholic canonical law.

Canadian provincial ministries of education have an important leadership role to play in promoting the practice of anti-homophobia education. The Government of Ontario attempted to move beyond basic coexistence and tolerance of difference through its innovative Equity and Inclusive Education Strategy. The most progressive policy framework of its kind in Canada at the time, Ontario's Ministry of Education 2009 equity strategy identifies homophobia as a serious problem in Ontario schools and proposes the development of GSAs as a way to mitigate this problem. Ontario has set the gold standard in promoting the promise of diversity to which other Canadian ministries of education should aspire. Other Canadian provinces and territories that continue to publicly fund Catholic schools, and where Catholic schools are subsequently well represented (Alberta, Saskatchewan, and the territories), should take proactive measures to reduce homophobia in all their public schools, especially the religiously inspired homophobia that this study shows particularly plagues Catholic schools.

These implications for the practice of anti-homophobia education at the levels of Canadian ministries of education and pre-service teacher education programs in Canadian schools of education may not assuage the frustration of members of the general public who are disappointed with the ongoing inability of education leaders to ensure schools are safe places for sexual minorities. An example of this frustration is the It Gets Better campaign that started in the US, which bypasses education leaders altogether and instead addresses school-aged suicidal lgbtq youth, urging them to persevere until they can graduate from their homophobic schools. Changes at the levels of ministries and schools of education can take years to envision, create, and implement – years that suicidal lgbtq youth simply cannot afford.

One way to implement anti-homophobia education more immediately is through the strategic use of grassroots organizations, such as Pride centres, lgbtq youth groups, and camps for queer youth. The University of Alberta's Camp fYrefly already trains lgbtq youth to lead anti-homophobia education initiatives in their schools, but this excellent leadership training could be broadened to include strategies for lgbtq youth in faith-based schools, especially Catholic schools. One of the chief findings of this study is that students are freer to resist the doctrinal disciplining of their Catholic schools than teachers because they have more rights than employees under the law and they can graduate from the school in a few years. Students are therefore more likely to lead the revolution against homophobic oppression in Canadian Catholic schools than are teachers. Anti-homophobia education efforts should therefore concentrate on reaching student leaders, keeping in mind that student leaders should not be the only ones working towards change nor should this project be the province of lgbtq people solely. Everyone involved in the education enterprise should be working towards the critical social justice cause of ensuring that all schools are safe spaces for everyone.

Each of the key resistance leaders in this study (Jacob, Abigail, and Hannah) tried to unlearn the homophobia of their Catholic schools by visiting their local public libraries and by searching for queer-positive information online. Leaders of lgbtq Pride centres across Canada could fulfil this pressing need on the part of lgbtq youth in Canadian Catholic schools by devoting a section of their Pride centre websites to information about undertaking anti-homophobia education initiatives in Canadian schools, including specific strategies for Catholic schools. Adult volunteers who work with lgbtq youth in Pride centres could also be specially trained to assist lgbtq youth in planning anti-homophobia initiatives in their schools, with particular attention paid to the hurdles faced by youth in faith-based schools, such as Catholic schools. Similarly, Egale Canada (formerly Equality for Gays and Lesbians Everywhere) could pay particular attention to the problems posed by Canadian Catholic schools in their latest campaign for anti-homophobia education in Canadian schools.

Although the non-publicized stories of Jacob, Abigail, and Hannah will not be familiar to lgbtq youth in Canada hoping to undertake anti-homophobia initiatives in their Catholic schools, it is likely that many will be familiar with Leanne Iskander, whose story opened this book. Iskander made national and international headlines for attempting to start a bona fide GSA at St Joseph Secondary School in Mississauga, Ontario. Iskander's story could be transformed into a teaching tool for future lgbtq students in Canadian Catholic schools who would like to follow her lead. With its new focus on assisting with anti-homophobia education in Canadian schools, Egale Canada could take the lead on this project and local Pride centres throughout the country could post a link to Egale Canada's profile on the steps Leanne Iskander took to resist the homophobia of her Catholic high school. These steps are important, even though Iskander was not successful in establishing a bona fide GSA in her school and had to settle for the weaker version known as By Your SIDE Spaces (an acronym for Safety, Inclusivity, Diversity, and Equity), which some Catholic education leaders reluctantly agreed to after much pressure and debate from Catholic students, Canadian human rights and civil liberties groups, the media, and members of the general public (Brown, 2011). Some Catholic education leaders accept By Your SIDE Spaces and other general equity clubs in Catholic schools on the condition that they do not have the word *gay* anywhere in their title and that they focus solely on homophobic bullying among students, rather than the anti-homophobia activism and lgbtq Pride that typify a bona fide GSA.

Coverage of the details and facts surrounding Iskander's case by *Xtra! Canada's Gay and Lesbian News*, *The Globe and Mail*, the CBC News, and the Canadian Television News Network have the potential to ignite a spark that may encourage Canada-wide discussion and activism in Canada's lgbtq communities. Catholic teachers, staff, and parents who do not agree with Catholic school policies regarding sexual minorities are increasingly stepping forward to express their opposition to homophobic discrimination in Canadian Catholic schools. The media accounts and interviews with participants reported in this study reveal a problematic disregard for the human rights frameworks of Canada, whether taken at the systemic or individual level. These stories demonstrate the need to address these specific instances of human rights violations, egregious in their disregard for constitutional protections, but made particularly more so by their existence in publicly funded institutions.

Some human rights activists, guardians of civil liberties, scholars, educators, politicians, and concerned members of the general public in both Alberta and Ontario have been openly questioning the continued public funding of Catholic schools that do not comply with provincial and federal human rights legislation vis-à-vis gender and sexual minorities. There is certainly some validity in that line of reasoning. However, there is also the possibility that Catholic education leaders may return to the tradition of Catholic social teaching involving justice for the weakest for guidance in how to embrace and even celebrate gender and sexual diversity they encounter in Catholic schools. The outlook has been grim for many years, but these small pockets of discussion and youth-based activism provide hope that publicly funded Canadian Catholic schools, should they continue to exist, will become safe learning environments and places of freedom of expression for all, rather than sites of homophobic and transphobic oppression.

Appendix:
Interview Guide

1. In what capacity are [or were] you involved in a Catholic school?
2. How do you self-identify as a sexual person or in terms of your gender?
3. What is your understanding of the Catholic Church's teachings regarding homosexuality?
4. How did you come to learn about these teachings?
5. Are you aware of any lessons on the topic of homosexuality, sexual orientation, or gender identity occurring in any classrooms at your Catholic school? If not, how, if at all, do you think these topics should be addressed?
6. If there is no discussion of homosexuality, sexual orientation, or gender identity in formal classroom settings in your Catholic school, are there any other ways a person can learn about these topics in a Catholic school?
7. Has anyone attempted to bring guest speakers into your school to talk about their experiences as a lesbian, gay, bisexual, transgender or queer (LGBTQ) individual in a faith-based, Christian, or Catholic environment? If not, why do you suppose that is?
8. Has anyone attempted to set up in your school a support group for students such as a Gay/Straight Alliance or a Diversity Club? If not, why not?
9. What is your understanding of how the subject of human sexuality or family life is taught in your Catholic school?
10. Are you aware of any students from lesbian-led or gay-led families in your Catholic school? If so, what have their experiences been?
11. Are you aware of any school policies regarding LGBTQ students taking a same-sex date to the high school prom or a male-to-female

transsexual participating in athletic competitions, for example? If not, what are your thoughts on these issues?

12. Are [or were] you aware of any other LGBTQ individuals in your Catholic school? Did you make any attempt to make yourself known to them? If so, how did this come about? If not, why not?

13. Are [or were] you able to be "out" about your sexuality or gender identity in your Catholic school? If so, to what degree? How important is this to you?

14. Have you had to be silent and secretive about your sexuality or gender identity while at your Catholic school? If so, how has this affected you? If not, what was your experience as an "out" individual like?

15. Have you experienced homophobia or transphobia during your time in your Catholic school? If so, how did you respond? If not, did you witness others experience this?

16. What supports or barriers affect your ability to be your true, authentic self in terms of your sexuality or gender identity in a Catholic school?

References

Actionwork. (2011). Anti-bullying week. Retrieved from http://www.actionwork.com/bullying.html

Alberta Catholic Bishops. (2001). *A resource for an inclusive community: A teacher's guide for and about persons with same sex attractions.* Edmonton, AB: Author.

Alberta Catholic School Trustees Association. (2004, September 17). *Alberta Catholic school trustees association executive director's report.* Edmonton, AB: Author.

Alberta Education. (2003, January). *Policy 1.2.2. – Locally developed religious studies courses.* Retrieved from https://education.alberta.ca/department/ipr/ldcr/policy-122.aspx

Alberta Education. (2011). *2011–2012 funding manual.* Retrieved from https://education.alberta.ca/admin/funding/manual.aspx

Althusser, L. (2008). *Ideology and ideological state apparatuses (notes toward an investigation).* London, England: Verso. (Original work published 1970)

Apple, M. W., & Jungck, S. (1993). Whose curriculum is this anyway?. In M. W. Apple (Ed.), *Official knowledge: Democratic education in a conservative age* (pp. 118–42). NY: Routledge.

Artuso, A. (2010, April 21). Catholic bishops question sex education curriculum. *Toronto Sun.* Retrieved from http://www.torontosun.com/news/canada/2010/04/21/13670261.html

Australian Human Rights Commission. (2007). *A guide to Australia's anti-discrimination laws.* Retrieved from http://www.humanrights.gov.au/employers/good-practice-good-business-factsheets/quick-guide-australian-discrimination-laws

Babbage, M. (2010, April 21). Catholic schools must follow new sex ed curriculum: McGuinty. *The Globe and Mail.* Retrieved from https://www.theglobeandmail.com/news/national/catholic-schools-must-follow-new-sex-ed-curriculum-mcguinty/article1542267/

Baird, V. (2007). *The no-nonsense guide to sexual diversity* (updated ed.). Toronto, ON: New Internationalist.

Baluja, T., & Hammer, K. (2011, March 18). Mississauga high school bans gay-straight alliance. *The Globe and Mail*, p. A13.

Bayly, M. J. (Ed.). (2007). *Creating safe environments for LGBT students: A Catholic schools perspective.* New York: Harrington Park Press.

Bickmore, K. (1999). Why discuss sexuality in elementary school? In W. J. Letts, IV, & J. T. Sears (Eds.), *Queering elementary education: Advancing the dialogue about sexualities and schooling* (pp. 15–26). Lanham, MD: Rowman & Littlefield.

Bickmore, K. (2002). How might social education resist heterosexism? Facing the impact of gender and sexual identity ideology on citizenship. *Theory and Research in Social Education, 30*(2), 198–216. https://doi.org/10.1080/00933104.2002.10473191

Bill 13: Accepting Schools Act. (2012). 1st session, 40th Legislature, Ontario, 61 Elizabeth II. Retrieved from the Legislative Assembly of Ontario website: http://www.ontla.on.ca/bills/bills-files/40_Parliament/Session1/b013ra.pdf

Bill 10: An Act to Amend the Alberta Bill of Rights to Protect Our Children. (2014). 3rd session, 28th Legislature, Alberta, 63 Elizabeth II. Retrieved from the Legislative Assembly of Alberta website: http://www.assembly.ab.ca/ISYS/LADDAR_files/docs/bills/bill/legislature_28/session_3/20141117_bill-010.pdf

Blumenfeld, W. J. (1995). Gay/Straight alliances: Transforming pain into pride. In G. Unks (Ed.), *The gay teen: Educational practice and theory for lesbian, gay, and bisexual adolescents* (pp. 211–24). New York: Routledge.

Boal, A. (1979). *Theatre of the oppressed* (C. McBride, & M. McBride, Trans.). London, England: Pluto Press. (Original work published 1974)

Borst, J. (2003). Education and the civil rights of gays. *Education Today, 15*(3), 20–3.

British Columbia Ministry of Education. (2009). *Province declares anti-bullying day.* Retrieved from https://archive.news.gov.bc.ca/releases/news_releases_2005-2009/2009OTP0037-000229.htm

Britzman, D. P. (1991). *Practice makes practice: A critical study of learning to teach.* Albany, NY: SUNY Press.

Britzman, D. P. (1995). Is there a queer pedagogy? Or, stop reading straight. *Educational Theory, 45*(2), 151–65. https://doi.org/10.1111/j.1741-5446.1995.00151.x

Brodkey, L. (1987). Writing critical ethnographic narratives. *Anthropology & Education Quarterly, 18*(2), 67–76. https://doi.org/10.1525/aeq.1987.18.2.04x0666p

Brown, L. (2011, March 23). Halton Catholic board committee rejects gay-straight alliances: By your SIDE spaces promoted as better option. *Toronto*

Star. Retrieved from https://www.insidehalton.com/community/education/article/970392–the-halton-catholic-board-is-on-your-side

Brown, L., & Strega, S. (Eds.). (2005). *Research as resistance: Critical, indigenous, & anti-oppressive approaches.* Toronto, ON: Canadian Scholars' Press / Women's Press.

Buechler, S. M. (2008). *Critical sociology.* Boulder, CO: Paradigm.

Burgess, A. H. F. (2005). *Disrupting heterosexual space? The implementation of a campus positive space campaign.* Unpublished master's thesis, Brock University, St. Catharines, Ontario.

Butler, J. (1999). *Gender trouble: Feminism and the subversion of identity.* New York: Routledge.

CKNewWestminster [CKNW] Radio News Talk AM 980 Orphans' Fund. (2009). *Pink shirt day.* Retrieved from http://pinkshirtday.ca/about-us/

Callaghan, T. (2007a, December 31). Contra/Diction: How Catholic doublespeak in Canadian Catholic secondary schools furthers homophobia. *Canadian Online Journal of Queer Studies in Education, 3*(1). Retrieved from http://jqstudies.library.utoronto.ca/index.php/jqstudies/article/view/3281/1411

Callaghan, T. (2007b). *That's so gay: Homophobia in Canadian Catholic schools.* Saarbrücken, Germany: VDM Verlag Dr. Müller.

Callaghan, T. (2007c). Acting OUT: Using Augusto Boal's theatre of the oppressed techniques to dramatize homophobic incidents in Catholic schools. In I. Killoran & K. Pendleton Jimenez (Eds.), *Unleashing the unpopular: Talking about sexual orientation and gender diversity in education* (pp. 129–39). Olney, MD: Association for Childhood Education International.

Callaghan, T. (2009). The historical, philosophical and sociological foundations that contribute to the institutionalization of homophobia in Canadian Catholic schools. In J. Nahachewsky & I. Johnston (Eds.), *Beyond presentism: Re-imagining the historical, personal, and social places of curriculum* (pp. 61–72). Rotterdam, The Netherlands: Sense.

Callaghan, T. (2010). David versus Goliath: Addressing contradictory Catholic doctrine head on [Review of the book *Creating safe environments for LGBT students: A Catholic schools perspective*]. *Journal of Lesbian, Gay, Bisexual, and Transgender Youth, 7*(1), 85–90.

Callaghan, T., & Mayr, S. (2015, September). A matter of acceptance: Why gay-straight alliances are essential. *Alberta Views Magazine: New Perspectives for Engaged Citizens,* 38–41. Retrieved from https://albertaviews .ab.ca/2015/08/18/a-matter-of-acceptance/

CBC News. (2002, May 10). *Gay teen wins fight over Catholic prom.* Retrieved from http://www.cbc.ca/news/canada/gay-teen-wins-fight-over-catholic-prom-1.348831

CBC News. (2007, September 18). *Bullied student tickled pink by schoolmates' T-shirt campaign*. Retrieved from http://www.cbc.ca/news/canada/bullied-student-tickled-pink-by-schoolmates-t-shirt-campaign-1.682221

Canadian Charter of Rights and Freedoms. (1982). Part I of the *Constitution Act, 1982*, RSC 1985, app. II, no. 44. Retrieved from http://laws-lois.justice.gc.ca/eng/Const/index.html

Canadian Civil Liberties Association. (2011, January 19). *Gay-Straight alliances not singled out any more*. Retrieved from https://ccla.org/2011/01/19/gay-straight-alliances-not-singled-out-anymore/

Canadian Conference of Catholic Bishops. (1997a). *Be with me*. Ottawa, ON: Author.

Canadian Conference of Catholic Bishops. (1997b). *The catechism of the Catholic church*. Ottawa, ON: Author.

Canadian Conference of Catholic Bishops. (2003, September 10). *Marriage in the present day*. Ottawa, ON: Author.

Canadian Medical Association. (1999). No to gay "reparative" therapies. *Canadian Medical Association Journal, 160*(6), 771.

Canadian Red Cross. (2011). *Pink day Saskatchewan history*. Retrieved from https://campaigns.redcross.ca/PinkDaySK-History

Canadian Teachers' Federation. (2002). *Seeing the rainbow: Teachers talk about bisexual, gay, lesbian, transgender and two-spirited realities* (2nd ed.). Ottawa, ON: Author.

Canadian Teachers' Federation. (2016). *Speak truth to power Canada: Jeremy Dias gender and sexual diversity biography*. Retrieved from http://sttpcanada.ctf-fce.ca/lessons/jeremy-dias/bio/

Carter, D. (2004). *Stonewall: The riots that sparked the gay revolution*. New York: St. Martin's Press.

Chase, S. E. (2005). Narrative inquiry: Multiple lenses, approaches, voices. In K. Denzin & Y. Lincoln (Eds.), *The Sage handbook of qualitative research* (3rd ed., pp. 651–79). Thousand Oaks, CA: Sage.

Chesir-Teran, D., & Hughes, D. (2009). Heterosexism in high school and victimization among lesbian, gay, bisexual, and questioning students. *Journal of Youth and Adolescence, 38*(7), 963–75. https://doi.org/10.1007/s10964-008-9364-x

Christopher, N. (2011, January 10). SK court upholds same-sex couples' rights. *Xtra! Canada's Gay and Lesbian News*. Retrieved from http://dailyxtra.com/vancouver/news/update-sk-court-upholds-sex-couples-rights

Civil Rights in Public Education. (2005). *Canada's defiance of UN human rights committee's decision prompts another submission*. Retrieved from http://www.cripeweb.org/actions-taken/submission-to-the-u-n-2005/

Clandinin, D. J., & Connelly, F. M. (1994). Personal experience methods. In N. K. Denzin & Y. S. Lincoln (Eds.), *Handbook of qualitative research* (pp. 413–17). Thousand Oaks, CA: Sage.

Clandinin, D. J., & Connelly, F. M. (2000). *Narrative inquiry: Experience and story in qualitative research*. San Francisco: Jossey-Bass.

Claussen, D. S. (Ed.). (2002). *Sex, religion, media*. Lanham, MD: Rowman & Littlefield.

Clemmons, N. (1999). *Exploring the religions of the world*. Notre Dame, IN: Ave Maria Press.

Cocks, J. (1989). *The oppositional imagination: Feminism, critique and political theory*. London, England: Routledge.

Collins, T. (2011, January 14). *Statement from the assembly of Catholic bishops of Ontario* [Via link: Ontario Catholic Bishops' Response to Equity and Inclusivity Strategy Issues]. Retrieved from http://www.acbo.on.ca/englishdocs/ACBO%20Statement%20-%20Equity%20and%20Inclusivity%20Jan%2014%202011.pdf

Conrad, D. (2005). Rethinking "at-risk" in drama education: Beyond prescribed roles. *Research in Drama Education, 10*(1), 27–41. https://doi.org/10.1080/13569780500053114

Council of Catholic School Superintendents of Alberta. (2004a, September 17). *Inclusive communities subcommittee report to CCSSA* [business report]. Edmonton, AB: Author.

Council of Catholic School Superintendents of Alberta. (2004b, November 19). *Possible media questions to Catholic school districts on students and staff with same-sex attractions* [confidential draft]. Edmonton, AB: Author.

Council of Catholic School Superintendents of Alberta. (2005, June 17). Pastoral care ministry and same-sex attraction [memorandum]. In CCSSA (Eds.), *Toward an inclusive community* [workbook] (section 3). Calgary, AB: Author.

Council of Catholic School Superintendents of Alberta. (2007, March). *Toward an inclusive community* [workbook]. Calgary, AB: Author.

Council of Catholic School Superintendents of Alberta. (2007b, March 7). *Instructions for changes to the "toward an inclusive community" binder (originally issued October 2005)* [memorandum]. Edmonton, AB: Author.

Council of Catholic School Superintendents of Alberta. (2011a). *Council of Catholic School Superintendents of Alberta members*. Edmonton, AB: Author.

Council of Catholic School Superintendents of Alberta. (2011b). *Mission statement*. Retrieved from http://www.ccssa.ab.ca/about/mission.htm

Council of Catholic School Superintendents of Alberta. (2011c). *Religious education network*. Edmonton, AB: Author.

Council of Catholic School Superintendents of Alberta. (2011d). *Constitution*. Edmonton, AB: Author.

Courage Apostolate. (2011). *Courage: A Roman Catholic apostolate*. Retrieved from http://couragerc.org/Courage_Apostolate.html

Covell, K. (2007). Children's rights education: Canada's best-kept secret. In R. B. Howe & K. Covell (Eds.), *A question of commitment: Children's rights in Canada* (pp. 241–63). Waterloo, ON: Wilfrid Laurier University Press.

Covert, J. R. (1993). Creating a professional standard of moral conduct for Canadian teachers: A work in progress. *Canadian Journal of Education, 18*(4), 429–45. https://doi.org/10.2307/1494942

Cowen, R., & Lipman, D. (Writers). Wellington, D. (Director). (2002, June 17). Out with a whimper [Television series episode 20, season 2]. In T. Jonas (Producer), *Queer as folk*. Toronto, ON: Showcase.

Craine, P. B. (2010). *Mandatory curriculum for Ontario schools promotes homosexuality, masturbation.* Retrieved from https://www.lifesitenews.com /ldn/2010/mar/10030216

Darder, A., Baltodano, M., & Torres, R. D. (2003). Critical pedagogy: An introduction. In A. Darder, M. Baltodano, & R. D. Torres (Eds.), *The critical pedagogy reader* (pp. 1–27). New York: Routledge Falmer.

Denzin, N. K., & Lincoln, Y. S. (2005). The discipline and practice of qualitative research. In N. K. Denzin & Y. S. Lincoln (Eds.), *The Sage handbook of qualitative research* (3rd ed., pp. 1–32). Thousand Oaks, CA: Sage.

Denzin, N. K., Lincoln, Y. S., & Tuhiwai Smith, L. (2008). *Handbook of critical and indigenous methodologies.* Thousand Oaks, CA: Sage. https://doi.org/10.4135 /9781483385686

DiManno, R. (1997, October 6). Gay teacher's "wedding" costs him job. *Toronto Star*, p. B1.

Dufferin-Peel Catholic District School Board. (n.d.). *Building safe, nurturing, inclusive communities: Teacher in-service on pastoral guidelines to assist students of same-sex orientation* [Brochure]. Mississauga, ON: Author.

Duncan-Andrade, J. M.R., & Morrell, E. (2008). *The art of critical pedagogy: Possibilities for moving from theory to practice in urban schools.* New York: Peter Lang.

Durocher, P. A. (2007, September). *Dear families* [Letter from Bishop Paul-André Durocher]. Retrieved from http://iceont.ca/wp-content/uploads/2015/07 /Durocher20letter_PDF.pdf

Durocher, P. A. (2010). Ministry of education policy/program memorandum no. 145. *Xtra! Canada's Gay and Lesbian News.* Retrieved from http://dailyxtra .com/catholic-bishops-vs-anti-discrimination-policies-wins

Egale Canada. (2005, April 18). *About Egale Canada.* Retrieved from https:// www.egale.ca/index.asp?lang=E&menu=2&item=1152

Egale Canada. (2009, March). *Youth speak up about homophobia and transphobia.* Retrieved from https://egale.ca/phase1/

Eisner, E. W. (1991). *The enlightened eye: Qualitative inquiry and the enhancement of educational practice.* New York: Macmillan.

Elementary Teachers' Federation of Ontario. (2010, December 1). *Toronto board's positive space campaign a model for others: ETFO*. Retrieved from https://web.archive.org/web/20101230060436/http://www.etfo.ca/MediaRoom/MediaReleases/Pages/Toronto%20Board%E2%80%99s%20Positive%20Space%20Campaign%20a%20Model%20for%20Others.aspx

Ellis, C., & Bochner, A. (Eds.). (1996). *Composing ethnography: Alternative forms of qualitative writing*. Walnut Creek, CA: AltaMira Press.

Ferfolja, T. (2005). Institutional silence: Experiences of Australian lesbian teachers working in Catholic high schools. *Journal of Gay & Lesbian Issues in Education, 2*(3), 51–66. https://doi.org/10.1300/J367v02n03_05

First public gay high school to open in NYC. (2003, July 29). Associated Press. Retrieved from http://web.archive.org/web/20050912190441/http://edition.cnn.com/2003/EDUCATION/07/28/gay.school.ap/

Flinders, D. J., Noddings, N., & Thornton, S. J. (1986). The null curriculum: Its theoretical basis and practical implications. *Curriculum Inquiry, 16*(1), 33–42. https://doi.org/10.1080/03626784.1986.11075989

Focus on the Family. (2010, November 6). *New focus on day of truth: Now day of dialogue*. Retrieved from http://www.focusonthefamily.com/about/newsroom/news-releases/20101111-new-focus-on-day-of-truth-now-day-of-dialogue

Fondation Émergence. (2011). *International day against homophobia*. Retrieved from http://www.homophobiaday.org/default.aspx?scheme=1204

Foucault, M. (1979). Truth and power [interview with Fontano and Pasquino]. In M. Morris & P. Patton (Eds.), *Michel Foucault: Power / truth / strategy* (pp. 29–48). Sydney: Feral.

Foucault, M. (1980). Two lectures. In C. Gordon (Ed.), *Power / Knowledge: Selected interviews and other writings 1972–1977* (pp. 78–108). London, England: Harvester Press. (Original work published 1972)

Foucault, M. (1981). The order of discourse. In R. Young (Ed.), *Untying the text: A post-structuralist reader* (pp. 48–79). London, England: Routledge, Kegan and Paul.

Foucault, M. (1982). The subject and power. [an afterword] In H. Dreyfus & P. Rabinow (Eds.), *Michel Foucault: Beyond structuralism and hermeneutics* (pp. 208–26). Chicago, IL: University of Chicago Press.

Foucault, M. (1990). *The history of sexuality, volume 1: An introduction* (R. Hurley, Trans. 1978). New York: Vintage Books. (Original work published 1976)

Foucault, M. (1995). *Discipline and punish: The birth of the prison* (A. M. Sheridan Smith, Trans.). New York: Vintage Books. (Original work published 1975)

Francis, P. (2016, March 19). *Amoris laetitia* [the joy of love]: Post-synodal apostolic exhortation on love in the family. Retrieved from https://w2.vatican.va/content/francesco/en/apost_exhortations/documents/papa-francesco_esortazione-ap_20160319_amoris-laetitia.html

Freire, P. (1970). *Pedagogy of the oppressed* (M. Bergman Ramos, Trans.). New York: Continuum. (Original work published 1967)

Garcia, M. (2011, June 10). *Catholic school bans rainbows.* Retrieved from https://www.advocate.com/News/Daily_News/2011/06/08/Catholic_School_Bans_Rainbows/

Gay, Lesbian and Straight Education Network. (2011a). *GLSEN mission and history.* Retrieved from https://www.glsen.org/cgi-bin/iowa/all/about/history/index.html

Gay, Lesbian and Straight Education Network. (2011b). *Day of silence.* Retrieved from http://www.dayofsilence.org/

Gay, Lesbian and Straight Education Network. (2011c). *No name calling week.* Retrieved from http://www.nonamecallingweek.org/cgi-bin/iowa/all/about/index.html

Geen, J. (2011, June 10). *Canadian Catholic school bans rainbows.* Retrieved from http://www.pinknews.co.uk/2011/06/10/canadian-catholic-school-bans-rainbows/

Gibson, R. (1986). *Critical theory and education.* London, England: Hodder and Stoughton.

Giroux, H. A. (1983). *Critical theory and educational practice.* Victoria, Australia: Deakin University Press.

Giroux, H. A. (2001). *Theory and resistance in education: Towards a pedagogy for the opposition.* Westport, CT: Bergin & Garvey.

Goldstein, T. (2006). Toward a future of equitable pedagogy and schooling. *Pedagogies, 1*(3), 151–69. https://doi.org/10.1207/s15544818ped0103_1

Goldstein, T., Collins, A., & Halder, M. (2008). Anti-homophobia education in public schooling: A Canadian case study of policy implementation. *Journal of Gay & Lesbian Social Services, 19*(3 & 4), 47–66.

Grace, A. P. (2004, November). *Lesbian, gay, bisexual, and trans-identified (LGBT) teachers and students and the post-Charter quest for ethical and just treatment in Canadian schools.* Featured speaker's paper presented at the Canadian Teachers' Federation conference entitled Building Inclusive Schools: A Search for Solutions, Ottawa, ON.

Grace, A. P. (2005). Reparative therapies: A contemporary clear and present danger across minority sex, sexual, and gender differences. *Canadian Woman Studies, 24*(2/3), 145–51.

Grace, A. P., & Wells, K. (2005). The Marc Hall prom predicament: Queer individual rights v. institutional church rights in Canadian public education. *Canadian Journal of Education, 28*(3), 237–70. https://doi.org/10.2307/4126470

Graham, J. (2011, January 10). Saskatchewan unlikely to appeal court ruling on gay marriage refusal law. *Winnipeg Free Press.* Retrieved from https://www

.winnipegfreepress.com/canada/breakingnews/court-rules-saskatchewan
-gay-marriage-refusal-law-unconstitutional–113205849.html

Gramsci, A. (1971). *Selections from the prison notebooks.* New York: International.

Greenberg, L. (2010a, April 22). Catholic leaders criticize new sex-ed curriculum. *The Ottawa Citizen.* Retrieved from http://globalnews.ca/toronto/Catholic +leaders+criticize+curriculum/2939271/story.html

Greenberg, L. (2010b, April 23). Ontario puts controversial sex-ed proposal on hold. *The Ottawa Citizen.* Retrieved from http://globalnews.ca/toronto/story .html?id=2939293

Griffin, P. (1992). From hiding out to coming out: Empowering lesbian and gay educators. *Journal of Homosexuality, 22*(3–4), 167–96. https://doi.org/10.1300 /J082v22n03_07

Habermas, J. (1971). *Knowledge and human interests* (J. J. Shapiro, Trans.). Boston: Beacon Press.

Haldeman, D. C. (2002). Gay rights, patient rights: The implications of sexual orientation conversion therapy. *Professional Psychology, Research and Practice, 33*(3), 260–4. https://doi.org/10.1037/0735-7028.33.3.260

Halton Catholic District School Board. (2010). *About our board.* Retrieved from https://www.hcdsb.org/Board/Pages/default.aspx

Hammer, K. (2011, March 16). Catholic schools feeling strain of doctrinal divide. *The Globe and Mail,* p. A4.

Hammer, K., & Howlett, K. (2010, April 21). Ontario plans more explicit sex education: Religious group threatens boycott over teaching of gender identity and sexual orientation, use of clear terminology. *The Globe and Mail,* p. A7.

Hammersley, M. (2007). *Educational research and evidence-based practice.* Los Angeles, CA: Sage.

Hammersley, M., & Atkinson, P. (1995). *Ethnography: Principles in practice* (2nd ed.). London, England: Routledge.

Harbeck, K. (Ed.). (1992). *Coming out of the classroom closet: Gay and lesbian students, teachers, and curricula.* New York: The Haworth Press.

Held, D. (1980). *Introduction to critical theory: Horkheimer to Habermas.* London, England: Hutchinson.

Herek, G. M. (2000). The psychology of sexual prejudice. *Current Directions in Psychological Science, 9*(1), 19–22. https://doi.org/10.1111/1467-8721.00051

Herek, G. M. (2004). Beyond homophobia: Thinking about sexual prejudice and stigma in the twenty-first century. *Sexuality Research & Social Policy, 1*(2), 6–24. https://doi.org/10.1525/srsp.2004.1.2.6

Hicks, K. A. (2000). "Reparative" therapy: Whether parental attempts to change a child's sexual orientation can legally constitute child abuse. *American University Law Review, 49,* 505–47.

Hiebert, J. L. (2003, October). From equality rights to same-sex marriage – parliament and the courts in the age of the charter. *Policy Options Politiques, 24*(9), 10–16.

Houston, A. (2011a, January 6). Halton Catholic schools ban gay-straight alliance groups. *Xtra! Canada's Gay and Lesbian News.* Retrieved from http:// dailyxtra.com/toronto/news/halton-catholic-schools-ban-gay-straight -alliance-groups

Houston, A. (2011b, January 12). Halton Catholic students may launch human rights challenge. *Xtra! Canada's Gay and Lesbian News.* Retrieved from http:// dailyxtra.com/toronto/news/halton-catholic-students-may-launch-human -rights-challenge

Houston, A. (2011c, April 7). Halton Catholic school board imposes silent ban on GSAs. *Xtra! Canada's Gay and Lesbian News.* Retrieved from http://dailyxtra.com /toronto/news/halton-catholic-school-board-imposes-silent-ban-gsas

How, A. (2003). *Critical theory.* New York: Palgrave MacMillan. https://doi .org/10.1007/978-0-230-80237-7

Howlett, K. (2010a, April 27). Ontario offered funding to help Catholic schools develop own sex-ed course. *The Globe and Mail,* p. A5.

Howlett, K. (2010b, April 29). Catholic groups say they'll work with Ontario on sex-ed. *The Globe and Mail,* p. A5.

Howlett, K., & Hammer, K. (2010, April 28). Ontario salvages reworked curriculum, minus the sex part: Non-controversial portions of lessons to begin in fall. *The Globe and Mail,* p. A6.

Huber, J. (2002, May 10). Gay teen wins fight over Catholic prom. *Canadian Broadcasting Corporation News.* Retrieved from http://www.cbc.ca/news/canada /gay-teen-wins-fight-over-catholic-prom-1.348831

Hull, K. E. (2006). *Same-sex marriage: The cultural politics of love and law.* Cambridge, England: Cambridge University Press. https://doi.org/10.1017 /CBO9780511616266

Hurley, M. C. (2005, September 26). Sexual orientation and legal rights: A chronological overview. *Parliamentary Information and Research Service of the Canadian Library of Parliament.* Retrieved from https://lop.parl.ca/content /lop/researchpublications/prb0413-e.htm

Jay, M. (1996). *The dialectical imagination: A history of the Frankfurt school and the institute of social research, 1923–1950.* Berkeley, CA: University of California Press.

Just the Facts Coalition. (2008). *Just the facts about sexual orientation and youth: A primer for principals, educators, and school personnel.* Washington, DC: American Psychological Association. Retrieved from http://www.apa.org/pi/lgbt /resources/just-the-facts.pdf

Kanpol, B. (1994). *Critical pedagogy: An introduction.* Westport, CT: Bergin & Garvey.

Kawawada, K. (2007, September 26). Defend marriage calls for board to pull book. *The Record.* Retrieved from http://www.therecord.com/News/Local /article/247150

Kawawada, K. (2008, January 31). Catholic board in no hurry to do homophobia survey. *The Record.* Retrieved from http://www.therecord .com/article/302615

Kawawada, K., & Mercer, G. (2007, November 27). Book yanked from school shelves. *The Record.* Retrieved from http://www.therecord.com/News/Local /article274865

Kenway, J. (1990). Education and the right's discursive politics: Private vs. state schooling. In S. J. Ball (Ed.), *Foucault and education: Discipline and knowledge* (pp. 167–206). London, England: Routledge.

Khayatt, D. (1997). Sex and the teacher: Should we come out in class? *Harvard Educational Review, 67*(1), 126–44. https://doi.org/10.17763/haer.67.1 .27643568766g767m

Khayatt, D. (1998). Paradoxes of the closet: Beyond the classroom assignment of in or out. In J. Ristock & C. Taylor (Eds.), *Inside the academy and out: Lesbian/gay/queer studies and social action* (pp. 31–48). Toronto, ON: University of Toronto Press.

Khayatt, D. (1999). Sex and pedagogy: Performing sexualities in the classroom. *GLQ: A Journal of Lesbian and Gay Studies, 5*(1), 107–13.

Kincheloe, J. L. (2007). Critical pedagogy in the twenty-first century: Evolution for survival. In J. L. Kincheloe & P. McLaren (Eds.), *Critical pedagogy: Where are we now?* (pp. 9–42). New York: Peter Lang.

Kincheloe, J. L. (Ed.). (2008). *Critical pedagogy primer* (2nd ed.). New York: Peter Lang. https://doi.org/10.1007/978-1-4020-8224-5

Kincheloe, J. L., & McLaren, P. L. (1998). Rethinking critical qualitative research. In N. Denzin & Y. Lincoln (Eds.), *Handbook of qualitative research* (pp. 260–99). Thousand Oaks, CA: Sage.

Kissen, R. (1996). *The last closet: The real lives of lesbian and gay teachers.* Portsmouth, NH: Heinemann.

Koller, V. (2008). "Not just a colour": Pink as a gender and sexuality marker in visual communication. *Visual Communication, 7*(4), 395–423. https://doi .org/10.1177/1470357208096209

Krathwohl, D. R., & Smith, N. L. (2005). *How to prepare a dissertation proposal: Suggestions for students in education & the social and behavioral sciences.* Syracuse, NY: Syracuse University Press.

Kumashiro, K. (2000). Toward a theory of anti-oppressive education. *Review of Educational Research, 70*(1), 25–53. https://doi.org/10.3102/00346543070001025

Kumashiro, K., & Ngo, B. (2007). *Six lenses for anti-oppressive education: Partial stories, improbable conversations.* New York: Peter Lang. https://doi.org/10.3726 /978-1-4539-1298-0

Kvale, S., & Brinkmann, S. (2009). *Interviews: Learning the craft of qualitative research interviewing* (2nd ed.). London, England: Sage.

L'Ecuyer, J. (Director), MacLennan, M., & Staines, K. (Writers), Haldane, H., & Young-Leckie, M. (Producers). (2004). *Prom queen: The Marc Hall story* [Motion picture]. (Available from Screen Door Productions, 2100 Bloor Street West, Suite 6124, Toronto, ON M6S 5A5).

Laclau, E., & Mouffe, C. (1985). *Hegemony and socialist strategy: Towards a radical democratic politics* (W. Moore, & P. Cammack, Trans.). London, England: Verso.

Lahey, K. A. (1999). *Are we persons yet? Law and sexuality in Canada.* Toronto, ON: University of Toronto Press. https://doi.org/10.3138/9781442670952

Lather, P. (1986). Research as praxis. *Harvard Educational Review, 56*(3), 257–78. https://doi.org/10.17763/haer.56.3.bj2h231877069482

Lather, P. (1991). *Getting smart: Feminist research and pedagogy with/in the postmodern.* New York: Routledge.

Lather, P. (1993). Fertile obsession: Validity after poststructuralism. *Sociological Quarterly, 34*(4), 673–93. https://doi.org/10.1111/j.1533-8525.1993.tb00112.x

Lather, P. (2007). *Getting lost.* Albany, NY: SUNY Press.

Laumann, E. O., Gagnon, H. H., Michael, R. T., & Michaels, S. (1994). *The social organization of sexuality: Sexual practices in the United States.* Chicago: University of Chicago Press.

Lawr, D. A., & Gidney, R. D. (Eds.). (1973). *Educating Canadians: A documentary history of public education.* Toronto, ON: Van Nostrand Reinhold.

Levy, Y. (2007). The right to fight: A conceptual framework for the analysis of recruitment policy towards gays and lesbians. *Armed Forces and Society, 33*(2), 186–202. https://doi.org/10.1177/0095327X06287616

Lienemann, W. (1998). Churches and homosexuality: An overview of recent official church statements on sexual orientation. *Ecumenical Review, 50*(1), 7–21. https://doi.org/10.1111/j.1758-6623.1998.tb00320.x

Litton, E. F. (2001). Voices of courage and hope: Gay and lesbian Catholic elementary schoolteachers. *International Journal of Sexuality and Gender Studies, 6*(3), 193–205. https://doi.org/10.1023/A:1011538501347

Love, P. G. (1997). Contradiction and paradox: Attempting to change the culture of sexual orientation at a small Catholic college. *The Review of Higher Education, 20*(4), 381–98. https://doi.org/10.1353/rhe.1997.0009

Macey, D. (2001). *Dictionary of critical theory.* London, England: Penguin.

MacKinnon, Justice R. (2002, May 10). *Smitherman v. Powers and the Durham Catholic District School Board* [Court File No. 12-CV-227705CM3]. Whitby, ON: Ontario Superior Court of Justice.

Maher, M. J. (2001). *Being gay and lesbian in a Catholic high school: Beyond the uniform.* New York: Harrington Park Press.

Maher, M. J. (2003). Review of research: Some background on addressing the topic of homosexuality in Catholic education. *Catholic Education: A Journal of Inquiry and Practice, 6*(4), 498–515.

Maher, M., & Sever, L. (2007). What educators in Catholic schools might expect when addressing gay and lesbian issues: A study of needs and barriers. *Journal of Gay & Lesbian Issues in Education, 4*(3), 79–111. https://doi.org/10.1300/J367v04n03_06

Marshall, G. (Ed.). (1998). *The Oxford dictionary of sociology.* Oxford: Oxford University Press.

Martin, J. I., & Meezan, W. (2009). Applying ethical standards to research and evaluations involving lesbian, gay, bisexual, and transgender populations. In W. Meezan & J. I. Martin (Eds.), *Handbook of research with lesbian, gay, bisexual, and transgender populations* (pp. 19–39). New York: Routledge.

Matas, R. (2010, April 28). Catholic school denies firing lesbian teacher. *The Globe and Mail.* Retrieved from https://www.theglobeandmail.com/news/british-columbia/catholic-school-denies-firing-lesbian-teacher/article4318315/

Maxwell, J. A. (2005). *Qualitative research design: An interactive approach* (2nd ed.). Thousand Oaks, CA: Sage.

McBrien, R. P. (Ed.). (1995). *The Harper Collins encyclopedia of Catholicism.* San Francisco: HarperSanFrancisco.

McCutcheon, L. (2011). *The international day against homophobia organized by Fondation Émergence.* Retrieved from http://www.homophobiaday.org/default.aspx?scheme=1204

McGowan, M. (2013). *A short history of Catholic schools in Ontario.* Retrieved from http://www.ocsta.on.ca/ocsta/wp-content/uploads/2013/04/A-Short-History-of-Catholic-Schools-in-Ontario-Mark-McGowan.pdf

McLaren, P. L., & Giarelli, J. M. (Eds.). (1995). *Critical theory and educational research.* Albany, NY: State University of New York Press.

Merriam, S. B. (1998). *Qualitative research and case study applications in education.* San Francisco: Jossey-Bass.

Meyer, E. J., & Stader, D. (2009). Queer youth and the culture wars: From classroom to courtroom in Australia, Canada and the United States. *Journal of LGBT Youth, 6*(2–3), 135–54. https://doi.org/10.1080/19361650902905624

Mills, S. (2003). *Michel Foucault.* London, England: Routledge. https://doi.org/10.4324/9780203380437

Mohamed, F. (2012). I used to think I won the lottery for losers. *The Globe and Mail.* Retrieved from https://www.theglobeandmail.com/life/giving/i-used-to-think-i-won-the-lottery-for-losers/article4202092

Mouffe, C. (1979). Hegemony and ideology in Gramsci. In C. Mouffe (Ed.), *Gramsci and Marxist theory* (pp. 168–204). London, England: Routledge & Kegan Paul.

Mulholland, J., & Wallace, J. (2003). Strength, sharing and service: Restorying and the legitimation of research texts. *British Educational Research Journal, 29*(1), 5–23. https://doi.org/10.1080/0141192032000057348

Nova Scotia Department of Education. (2007). *Stand up against bullying day proclaimed.* Retrieved from https://novascotia.ca/news/release/?id=20070925006

O'Brien, E., & Westen, J.-H. (2007, August 9). *Ontario Catholic school board approves referrals to gay-activist therapist.* Retrieved from https://www.lifesite news.com/ldn/2007/aug/07080907.html

O'Donohue, W., & Caselles, C. E. (1993). Homophobia: Conceptual, definitional, and value issues. *Journal of Psychopathology and Behavioral Assessment, 15*(3), 177–95. https://doi.org/10.1007/BF01371377

Olssen, M. (2006). *Michel Foucault: Materialism and education.* Boulder, CO: Paradigm.

Ontario Conference of Catholic Bishops. (2003, March 31). *To all involved in Catholic education* [Pastoral guideline]. Toronto, ON: Author.

Ontario Conference of Catholic Bishops. (2004a, August 3). *Pastoral guidelines to assist students of same-sex orientation.* Toronto, ON: Author.

Ontario Conference of Catholic Bishops. (2004b, September 15). *Pastoral guidelines to assist students of same-sex orientation: A parent's guide.* Toronto, ON: Author.

Ontario Conference of Catholic Bishops. (2006). *Ontario Catholic Secondary Curriculum Policy Document for Religious Education* [ISBN # 0-9699178-9-9]. Retrieved from http://www.carfleo.org/

Ontario Education Services Corporation. (2010a, March 24). *Equity and inclusive education initiative.* Retrieved from http://equity.oesc-cseo.org/Category.aspx?cid=239

Ontario Education Services Corporation. (2010b). *Equity and inclusive education policy English Catholic version* [via link: Template Education Policy – Catholic]. Toronto, ON: Author.

Ontario Ministry of Education. (2015). *Sex education in Ontario.* Retrieved from https://www.ontario.ca/page/sex-education-ontario

Ontario Ministry of Education. (2009a). *Ontario's* Equity and Inclusive Education Strategy*: Realizing the promise of diversity.* Toronto, ON: Author.

Ontario Ministry of Education. (2009b, June 24). *Developing and implementing equity and inclusive education policies in Ontario schools* [Policy/Program memorandum no. 119]. Retrieved from http://www.edu.gov.on.ca/extra /eng/ppm/119.html

Ontario Ministry of Education. (2009c, October 19). *Progressive discipline and promoting positive student behaviour* [Policy/Program memorandum no. 145]. Retrieved from http://www.edu.gov.on.ca/extra/eng/ppm/145.html

Oziewicz, E. (2002, May 11). Supreme court challenge looms: Catholic school board to take case to trial after judge overturns ban on gay prom date. *The Globe and Mail,* p. A4.

Parks, C. A., Hughes, T. L., & Werkmeister-Rozas, L. (2009). Defining sexual identity and sexual orientation in research with lesbians, gay men, and bisexuals. In W. Meezan & J. I. Martin (Eds.), *Handbook of research with lesbian, gay, bisexual, and transgender populations* (pp. 71–99). New York: Routledge.

Patton, M. Q. (2002). *Qualitative research & evaluation methods* (3rd ed.). Thousand Oaks, CA: Sage.

Peloso, L. (Writer/Director), & Tapestry Pictures & Canadian Television Network (Producers). (2002). *Prom fight: The Marc Hall story* [Motion picture]. (Available from the Canadian Television Network, P.O. Box 9, Station 'O,' Scarborough, ON M4A 2M9).

Pinar, W. F. (Ed.). (1998). *Queer theory in education.* Mahwah, NJ: Lawrence Erlbaum Associates.

Polkinghorne, D. E. (1995). Narrative configuration in qualitative analysis. In J. A. Hatch & R. Wisnieski (Eds.), *Life history and narrative* (pp. 5–23). London, England: Falmer Press. https://doi.org/10.1080/0951839950080103

Pratt, S. (2008, March 30). Reluctant gay rights hero seeks serenity abroad. *Edmonton Journal,* p. A1.

Rasmussen, D. M. (1996). Critical theory and philosophy. In D. M. Rasmussen (Ed.), *The handbook of critical theory* (pp. 11–38). Oxford: Blackwell.

Rayside, D. (2008). *Queer inclusions, continental divisions: Public recognition of sexual diversity in Canada and the United States.* Toronto, ON: University of Toronto Press. https://doi.org/10.3138/9781442688896

Rich, A. (1986). *Blood, bread, and poetry: Selected prose, 1979–1985.* New York: Norton.

Ricoeur, P. (1991). *From text to action: Essays in hermeneutics, II* (K. Blamey, & J. B. Thompson, Trans.). Evanston, IL: Northwestern University Press. (Original work published 1986)

Rivers, I. (2011). *Homophobic bullying: Research and theoretical perspectives.* London, England: Oxford University Press. https://doi.org/10.1093/acprof:oso /9780195160536.001.0001

Rodriguez Rust, P. C. (2009). No more lip service: How to really include bisexuals in research on sexuality. In W. Meezan & J. I. Martin (Eds.),

Handbook of research with lesbian, gay, bisexual, and transgender populations (pp. 100–30). New York: Routledge.

Ruypers, J., & Ryall, J. (2005). *Canadian civics.* Toronto, ON: Edmond Montgomery.

Saskatchewan Court of Appeal. (2011, January 10). In the matter of marriage commissioners [Citation: 2011 SKCA 3; Docket: 1800]. *Xtra! Canada's Gay and Lesbian News.* Retrieved from https://www.scribd.com/doc/46604133 /Full-Saskatchewan%E2%80%99s-Court-of-Appeal-Reference

Saunders, P. (2002, April). The charter at 20. *Canadian Broadcasting Corporation archives.* Retrieved from http://www.cbc.ca/news/canada/charter-of-rights -and-freedoms-marks-20th-anniversary-1.349295

Savage, D. (2010, September 21). *Welcome to the It Gets Better project.* Retrieved from https://web.archive.org/web/20101011092256/http://www.itgetsbetterproject .com/blog/entry/welcome-to-the-it-gets-better-project

Schniedewind, N., & Davidson, E. (2006). *Open minds to equality* (3rd ed.). Milwaukee, WI: Rethinking Schools.

Schwandt, T. A. (2007). *The Sage dictionary of qualitative inquiry* (3rd ed.). Thousand Oaks, CA: Sage. https://doi.org/10.4135/9781412986281

Segal, D. R., Gade, P. A., & Johnson, E. M. (1993). Homosexuals in western armed forces. *Society, 31*(1), 37–42. https://doi.org/10.1007/BF02693383

Simons, J. (Ed.). (2004). *Contemporary critical theorists from Lacan to Said.* Edinburgh, Scotland: Edinburgh University Press.

Smart, B. (1986). The politics of truth and the problem of hegemony. In D. Couzens Hoy (Ed.), *Foucault: A critical reader* (pp. 157–73). Oxford: Basil Blackwell.

Smith, J. (1994). Out and outcome. In K. Jennings (Ed.), *One teacher in 10: Gay and lesbian educators tell their stories* (pp. 212–18). Los Angeles, CA: Alyson.

Stake, R. E. (1995). *The art of case research.* Thousand Oaks, CA: Sage.

Stayshyn, J., & Houston, A. (2011, February 11). Catholic bishops prohibit gay-straight alliances in Ontario schools: Gay label to be "avoided," educators told. *Xtra! Canada's Gay and Lesbian News.* Retrieved from http://www.xtra .ca/public/National/Catholic_bishops_prohibit_gaystraight_alliances_in _Ontario_schools-4-9760-viewstory4.aspx - sidebar

Stern, K. (2009). *Queers in history: The comprehensive encyclopedia of historical gays, lesbians, bisexuals, and transgenders.* Dallas, TX: BenBella Books.

Strapagiel, L. (2015, June 4). This Canadian province just banned LGBT conversion therapy. *BuzzFeed News.* Retrieved from https://www.buzzfeed .com/laurenstrapagiel/ontario-just-banned-conversion-therapy-for-lgbt -kids?utm_term=.am0Q9MLG#.xkJ2QAMX

Tate, J., & Ross, L. E. (2003). Addressing the needs of lesbian, gay, bisexual, transgendered, queer and questioning clients within university psychiatric services: Reflections and recommendations. *Canadian Journal of Community Mental Health, 22*(2), 59–68. https://doi.org/10.7870/cjcmh-2003-0014

Torres, C. A. (1995). Participatory action research and popular education in Latin America. In P. L. McLaren & J. M. Giarelli (Eds.), *Critical theory and educational research* (pp. 237–55). Albany, NY: State University of New York Press.

Torres, C. A. (1998). *Education, power, and personal biography: Dialogues with critical educators.* New York: Routledge.

UK Legislation. (2007). *The equality act (sexual orientation) regulations 2007* [no. 1263]. Retrieved from http://www.legislation.gov.uk/uksi/2007/1263/contents/made

United States Conference of Catholic Bishops. (1997, September 10). *Always our children: A pastoral message to parents of homosexual children and suggestions for pastoral ministers.* Washington, DC: Author.

University of Winnipeg. (2009). *The first national climate survey of homophobia in Canadian schools.* Retrieved from http://www.uwinnipeg.ca/index/research-2009-taylor-c

Uribe, V. (1995). Project 10: A school-based outreach to gay and lesbian youth. In G. Unks (Ed.), *The gay teen: Educational practice and theory for lesbian, gay, and bisexual adolescents* (pp. 203–10). New York: Routledge.

Valpy, M., & Friesen, J. (2010, December 11). A twist of faith. *The Globe and Mail,* pp. A12 – A13.

van Dijk, L., & van Driel, B. (Eds.). (2007). *Challenging homophobia: Teaching about sexual diversity* [Foreword by Desmond Tutu]. Stoke on Trent, England: Trentham Books.

Van Maanen, J. (1988). *Tales of the field: On writing ethnography.* Chicago, IL: University of Chicago Press.

Vatican Congregation for the Doctrine of the Faith. (1986). *Letter to the bishops of the Catholic Church on the pastoral care of homosexual persons.* Rome: Author.

Vatican. (2011). *Congregation for the doctrine of the faith.* Retrieved from http://www.vatican.va/roman_curia/congregations/cfaith/documents/rc_con_cfaith_pro_14071997_en.html

Wallace, J., & Louden, W. (2000). *Teachers' learning: Stories of science education.* Dordrecht, The Netherlands: Kluwer.

Werner, W. (1991). Curriculum and uncertainty. In R. Ghosh & D. Ray (Eds.), *Social change and education in Canada* (2nd ed., pp. 105–15). Toronto, ON: Harcourt Brace Jovanovich.

Wheeler, D. P. (2009). Methodological issues in conducting community-based health and social services research among urban Black and African American LGBT populations. In W. Meezan & J. I. Martin (Eds.), *Handbook of research with lesbian, gay, bisexual, and transgender populations* (pp. 300–14). New York: Routledge.

Wilson, J. D., Stamp, R. M., & Audet, L.-P. (Eds.). (1970). *Canadian education: A history.* Scarborough, ON: Prentice-Hall.

Woog, D. (1995). *School's out: The impact of gay and lesbian issues on America's schools.* Boston, MA: Alyson.

Yin, R. K. (2009). *Case study research: Design and methods* (4th ed.). Thousand Oaks, CA: Sage.

Young, E., & Ryan, T. G. (2014). Canadian courts, constitution, charter, and Catholic schools: Intersecting powers. *Journal of Research on Christian Education, 23*(3), 237–54. https://doi.org/10.1080/10656219.2014.901933

Index